MW01274159

Balboa Press books may be ordered through booksellers or by contacting:

Balboa Press
A Division of Hay House
1663 Liberty Drive
Bloomington, IN 47403
www.balboapress.com
AU TFN: 1 800 844 925 (Toll Free inside Australia)
AU Local: 0283 107 086 (+61 2 8310 7086 from outside Australia)

Print information available on the last page.

ISBN: 978-1-5043-2178-5 (sc)
ISBN: 978-1-5043-2177-8 (e)

Balboa Press rev. date: 01/07/2021

DEDICATION

I dedicate this book MY MEMOIRS, MY LIFE to my wonderful wife Frances.
She spent countless hours helping to edit the 108 chapters that I wrote.
I am forever grateful to her unending support.

Ian David Fong

FOREWORD

By Anne King

Master in Health Science (Developmental Delay), University of Sydney

Work history is broadly Community Services with a focus on child protection.

Many Australians have a rich and fascinating history. Ian David Fong is one such person. Ian started writing his memoirs on Facebook and I was captivated by the stories and his vivid memories of his childhood and life as a young adult.

I anticipated with enthusiasm and genuine interest what the next chapter of Ian's life would present.

Ian shares his deep knowledge of culture through stories that are fascinating and entertaining at the same time.

Living across a number of countries, Ian's appreciation and respect for all cultures is evident. It is very clear that Ian has taken his learnings with him throughout life, he is wise, insightful and generous in sharing with us not only his success but also some of his lessons learnt.

Ian's family and the world have the benefit of first person accounts vividly recalled and shared of life from China to Australia and in-between. There is so much to learn and enjoy on this journey.

Ian David Fong, your stories are incredible. They represent historical accounts that only someone who was present can share. Thank you. Your memories are incredible and valuable. Your first person accounts will surely help future historians understand the joys and struggles of immigration and immigration policy and its application in the past.

I heard similar stories from my father-in-law, as Ian mentioned his name as I know it is David King.

I understood so much more about my father and mother-in-law from Ian's stories, the history, the shared challenges of immigration and the hope that life in Australia might offer their children.

So much resonates with me as the wife of a second generation Australian. I'm lucky to have people like Ian in my life to help me understand and respect the different cultural influences for our children and their children in the future.

Ian, you cover so much of Chinese history and philosophy, so much to learn from.

Enjoy the read everyone and thank you Ian for being so proactive in sharing your life and learning with us.

Anne is the daughter-in-law of my long-time friend and Marist Brothers' High School classmate in Suva, Fiji, David King, to whom I had included chapter 106 in my book. I am grateful to her for writing the foreword of my book.

Ian David Fong

CONTENTS

INTRODUCTION

For some years till now, my beloved wife Frances has been urging me to write my memoirs, so that my children and their descendants will know their origin.

I recollected late in June 2017, I complimented Norman Yee's book ("Catching the Wind") on Facebook. I have read most of its contents and have found them very entertaining. He hinted that I should write a book.

I gave him the same answer as I had given to my wife, that I am no writer, and I wouldn't know where to start, and what to write.

A week later, I suddenly remembered there would be lots of things to write.

On 1 July 2017, I started writing my memoirs on my 12 years in China, 33 years in Fiji, 3 years in New Zealand, 33+ years in Australia.

I chose to post my episodes on my Facebook timeline, so that some of my classmates/school mates of the Marist Brothers' High School, Suva, Fiji, who are in Facebook, will view and like/comment on them.

Also mentioned are the former President and Prime Minister of Fiji, Ratu Sir Kamisese Mara, the former Governor General of New Zealand, Sir Anand Satyanand (son of Fiji migrants) and Sean Fitzpatrick, former All Black and Captain. These three and I were old boys of Sacred Heart College, Auckland, New Zealand. Ratu Mara and the present Prime Minister of Fiji Frank Bainimarama, and I were old boys of the Marist Brothers' High School, Suva, Fiji.

At Sacred Heart College, Auckland, New Zealand, I represented the college in Athletics and Rugby Union.

In the 1956 Auckland Inter-Secondary School Athletic Championship, I ran in the Relay Team against Peter Snell of Mt Albert Grammar School, who later became the world record holder (for some time) of the 800 metres and 1,500 metres.

In Rugby, our first fifteen played against Tony Davies of Kings College, Mack Herewini and Waka Nathan of Otahuhu College. These three became famous All Blacks.

I have now finished writing 108 chapters of stories.

The title of my book will be "My Memoirs, My Life".

I hope that you will enjoy it.

Ian David Fong

CHAPTER 1
My date and place of birth

On 3 June 1938 (Chinese Calendar), I was born on 3 June 1938 (Chinese calendar) in my father's house. It was a three-bedroom made of bricks, situated in the Duntou Village, now grouped as part of Sha Kai district, Zhongshan, Guangdong, China. The house had a natural well from which we drew water for washing purposes. Drinking water was drawn from the public well about 500 metres away from my home.

At that time, my father Willie Fong War Sut was in Fiji, thus the male responsibility fell upon my grandfather's hands.

Before I came out to this world, grandpa was very excited. While waiting for my arrival, I was told he paced nervously around our house compound until the village midwife delivered me safely.

Zhongshan, Wade-Giles romanisation Chungshan, formerly Xiangshan, or Shiqi, a city in southern Guangdong sheng (province), southern China. Located in the south-central part of the Pearl (Zhu) River Delta, Zhongshan has a network of waterways connecting it with all parts of the delta and is on an express highway running north to Guangzhou (Canton) and south to Macau. Zhongshan is the marketing and commercial centre of one of the most prosperous and densely peopled areas in China. Great quantities of agricultural produce are collected for shipment to Guangzhou, and it is the main distribution point for manufactured goods, also mostly from the Guangzhou area.

Zhongshan was founded as a market town in the 11th century. It became the seat of a county (under the name Xiangshan), subordinate to Guangzhou, in 1162. The area was one of the first to become subject to influence from Western contacts, and many of its inhabitants were prominent in overseas trade and in the first modernising ventures in China during the 19th century. The county is famous for having been the birthplace of Sun Yat-sen (Sun Zhongshan), the leading figure in the Chinese Revolution of 1911–12; after his death in 1925 it was renamed in his honour.

With its close proximity to Hong Kong and Macau and because it is one of the main sources of overseas Chinese, Zhongshan has developed rapidly since 1980. Its industries include a sugar refinery, as well as plants manufacturing machinery and electrical appliances. Zhongshan is also a popular tourist destination and one of the key foreign-trade ports of Guangdong, and it has convenient water connections with Hong Kong. Pop. (2002 est.) 581,571.

Outside my house, Duntou Village, Zhongshan, Guangdong, China, 2000.

CHAPTER 2

My paternal grandfather

My mother told me that my father was in Fiji when I was born. My grandfather was extremely anxious of my pending birth. His name was Fong Charn Houn also known as Fong You Dai as I had learned. Apart from that, I knew nothing of my grandfather who passed away while I was an infant.

I was told he was addicted to gambling and so were his friends.

He earned money by selling pork in a village stall. After each sale, he gambled and lost all his money.

When he went home grandma was always furious.

When he needed money, he approached my mother who always obliged. My father was his favourite son.

The time came when my eighth Uncle Fong War Kit was about to get engaged so he arranged for eldest Uncle Fong War Jue in New Zealand to send money to buy gifts for the future bride's family.

He thought to himself the money received was not enough to buy what he wanted so he went gambling hoping to win some extra money. Unfortunately, he lost everything.

He asked my mother for help, but the sum was beyond her budget.

Grandfather wrote to eldest uncle to send money again, but uncle refused to help him.

In the end, his favourite 6th son my father in Fiji sent the same amount of money that my eldest uncle had previously sent.

Grandfather learned his lesson and bought presents for eighth uncle's future bride's family.

Soon after his marriage eighth Uncle Fong War Kit went to work in Fiji and stayed for many years until he retired to Hong Kong.

CHAPTER 3
My paternal grandmother

This very sad story happened in my village, Dun Tou, Zhongshan, Guangdong, China, when I was about 6 years old.

My grandmother in her late 80s was living alone at the family house next to my father's home. One early morning, she told my mother that the previous night some noises were heard under her bed, and so she was very frightened.

Mum got hold of me and two older cousins (teenage boys Fong Siu Yuen and Fong Wailee), to check what was underneath the bed. Nothing was found.

We then checked the rest of the house and found a young man in his early thirties hiding in the toilet. He happened to be a neighbour living behind our house.

We asked him why he was in the house and he replied that he was hungry and was looking for food.

We took him to the village constabulary, and he was to be punished for his crime. In those days, penalty for stealing food from a house, market garden or rice paddy was death by drowning.

As customary this thief was tied up to the tree in front of the village school, beaten up, fed with 3 large pork buns and Chinese tea, put into a pig basket, and taken to be drowned in the river outside the village.

CHAPTER 4
My father Willie Fong War Sut

He was no. 6 in the family of 9 siblings, an eldest sister and 8 brothers.

At the age of 12, I went to Fiji and met my father for the first time. He lived in the bachelors' quarters of Kwong Tiy & Co. Ltd, Suva, Fiji, where he worked as a clerk for many years.

My father arranged for me to board with his friends. We seldom saw each other mainly because of circumstances.

Of my dad I had very little knowledge of him. Why or when he came to Fiji, I had no idea. I was told he was in a fancy goods partnership with two distant Gock relatives in Cumming Street, Suva, the busiest street of the town. The business was going well, but a fire broke out and destroyed all the wooden buildings in the same street. He lost everything even the suitcase he brought from China.

Due to ill health, my father resigned from his job at Kwong Tiy in 1961. He retired to Hong Kong where he was reunited with my mother. He passed away on 10 March 1968, aged 69. He was buried in Hong Kong. According to regulations, after six years, his bones had to be transferred to another grave in Sandy Ridge in the New Territories, China.

In 1974, my mother and son Gerard aged 4, went to Hong Kong to arrange the transfer.

The following accounts were told to me:

1. The second time he went back from Fiji to the village in China he bought a gun (pistol). He and his good friend Man Ho Fong were the only civilians who owned guns. Then, one night, a robber pursued by a village constable, fled past our roof. My father climbed up to the attic, opened the window and with his gun fired into the sky. Big laughs. He realised that by shooting the robber, there could be consequences.
2. On a visit to his friend's shop one day he came across a Fijian man harassing the shop keeper. My father intervened and told him to go away. The troublesome man suddenly punched my father on the head, and he was hospitalised for some time. That punch often caused him headaches and pain. My father knew some kung fu tricks, but he was unexpectedly hit.
3. When my father was working in the Kwong Tiy branch store in Labasa, the store benzine lamp caught fire. Without thinking, he grabbed the burning lamp and ran out of the store. The lamp exploded and wounded him. He was rushed to hospital and remained as a patient for some time. In view of his brave action for saving the store, the managing director Mr Yee Kam Chee of Kwong Tiy, gave him an annual bonus of 100 Fijian pounds for some years.
4. My father had been a long-time friend of his Kwong Tiy bosses Yee Kam Chee and Yee Hoy Shang. Whenever they went to Hong Kong, they would visit him, although his home (flat) was up on the eighth floor of the building, which had no lifts. My father appreciated their visits especially they had to climb up to the 8th floor.

My mother and father.

Zhongshan (Chung Shan) Section Cemetery, Sandy Ridge, New Territories, China, 2010.

My father's grave at the Zhongshan Section Cemetery,
Sandy Ridge, New Territories, China, 2010.

At the Zhongshan Section Cemetery, Sandy Ridge, New Territories, China, 2010.
My Cousin Fong Wing's wife and her son Johnny Fong, preparing items for worship.
From left Johnny Fong, Cousin Fong Wing's wife, Grandson Jonathan Yee, Granddaughter Tiana Yee, Eldest daughter Geralyne Fong Yee, Frances Fong, Ian Fong.

CHAPTER 5
My mother Fong Lum Oy Wan

Mum was the youngest of three siblings, an eldest sister, an older brother and her. They lived in the Sha Pang Ha Village, about three kilometres parallel to my father's village, Dun Tow, Zhongshan, Guangdong, China.

My maternal grandfather was in America, but he came back to China just before the second world war two broke out. He feared that he might be drafted into the army, so he took off from America. I had a glimpse of him and that was all I knew.

My maternal grandmother was the caretaker of the village temple. She was a very kind lady, well-liked by the villagers and worshippers. I lived with her for a year when I went to her village school. In that year there was no school operating in my village.

There was no village school in those early days, but mum was fortunate to have received private tuition. She had learned a lot and was capable of writing the traditional Chinese beautifully.

At the age of 18 mum married my father who was 28. Not long after dad left her in the village and went back to work in Fiji. Mum had not conceived. Ten years later, dad came back from Fiji to the village for a little while, and left for Fiji again leaving a pregnant wife behind.

Mum insisted that she should go to Fiji and be with him, but my dad told her she was not robust enough to brave the hardships in Fiji. Besides dad had no intention to run a shop, due to the fact he was once hit by a Fijian man in a shop.

At the age of 12 in 1950 I went to Fiji and met my father for the first time.

Mum was very loving but very strict with me. When I was young, I often nagged her for pocket money. If she refused, I shook the bottom of the front door until it was broken. She would not give in to my demand, and right away she got hold of an inch diameter clothesline stick and hit me on my thigh. Soon, she would send for the village carpenter to come and repair the door. The irony part of it, although he was paid for the job, he always complained about why I damaged the same part of the door all the time.

There were times when my father couldn't send money through because the World War II was on, mum mortgaged our 5 acre rice paddies for a loan plus interest so that we could be out of hunger for a while.

Not long after, I left the village for Fiji in September 1950, mum was called to be trialled by the authorities in the village, for her being a landlord. She owned half an acre market garden and 5 acres of rice paddies. Her older brother was planting on the rice paddies, and harvests were shared by mum and him. Since the new regime took over China, landlords of all types were put on trial. Big landlords had to kneel on broken glass during trials, and if found guilty, they were prosecuted and shot dead. Luckily, my mother was spared.

Since then she had no confidence in the new government and the villagers who took advantage of her, so she left and lived in Hong Kong.

In July 1961, due to ill health, my father resigned from his job in Kwong Tiy in Suva, Fiji, and went to be reunited with my mother in Hong Kong. He passed away in Hong Kong on 10 March 1969, aged 69.

My mother came to Fiji, to be reunited with me and my family in January 1970. She had an excellent relationship with my wife Frances. Our house in Tanoa Street, Suva, Fiji, was just a few minutes' walk to the Yat Sen Primary and Secondary School, and that was convenient. Monday to Friday, my mother cooked lunches for Frances and our children, and our house girl delivered them to the school for them. Mum was a very good cook. She was capable of cooking dishes for a banquet table.

When the family migrated to Sydney, Australia, mum was included in the family group. She had had very happy times with the family in Fiji and in Sydney.

Sadly, she passed away on 2 January 1989, 29 days short of her 80th birthday.

The family organised a requiem Mass at the Holy Spirit Catholic Church in Cox's Road, North Ryde. She was buried in the Chinese Section Cemetery, Rookwood, NSW, Australia. My cousins Bill and Janice Fong came over from Auckland to attend her funeral. Frances' siblings and their families, and many relatives and friends paid their respects to mum. It was a big funeral.

Frances, my children and I have missed her ever since.

RIP mum, and grandma.

My mother and son Gerard (4 years old), Hong Kong, 1974.

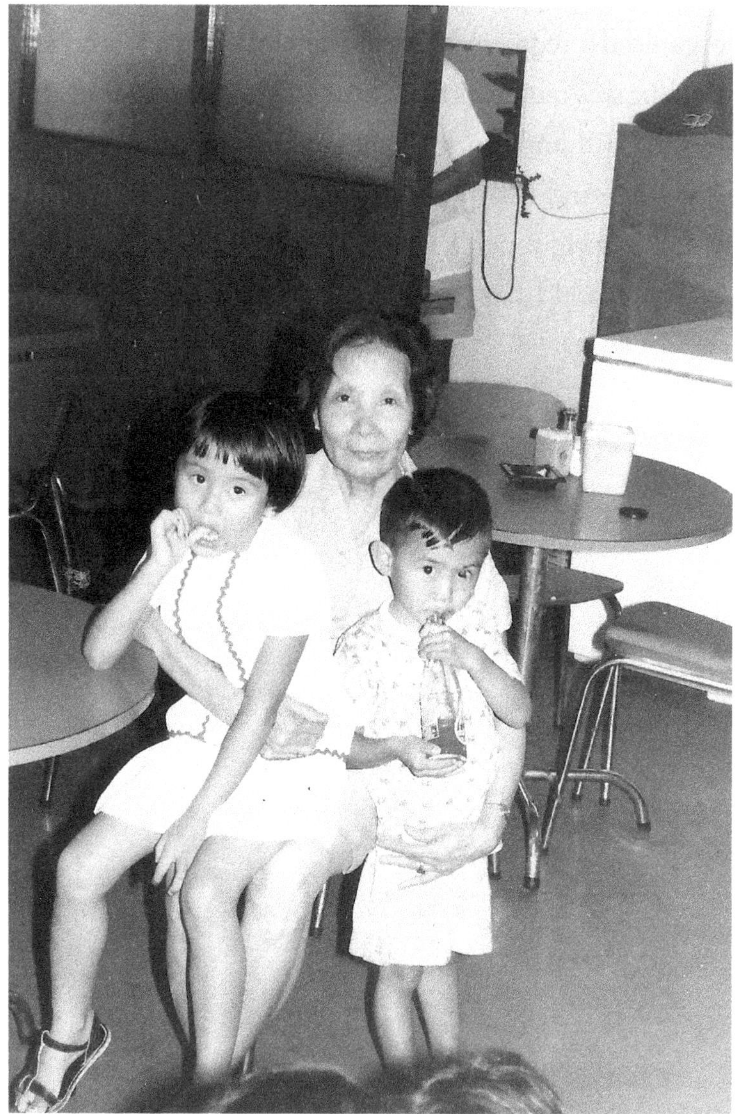

From left Geralyne Fong, my mother, Gerard Fong.
Geralyne is our eldest child, Gerard is our middle child, Magdalene is our youngest child. Magdalene was born a number of years later, so is missing from this photo.

Mum's birthday in 1988.

CHAPTER 6

My cousin Fong Wing and me

During the Japanese occupation of Guangzhou, the capital city of Guangdong Province, Wing's father passed away in Qujiang, a district in Shaoguan.

After that, he joined the Kuomintang army to protect our country.

Wing returned to our village in 1946 after the war.

On his return he visited my mother and me. He was 22 years of age and I was 8 years old. He had a long conversation with my mother, mainly about the Japanese occupation of Guangzhou.

After spending a few days in the village, he left for Hong Kong for a better horizon. He found a job and met the love of his life. Together they raised a family of 3 children who studied well and went on to have successful careers.

When my father passed away on 10 March 1969, Wing represented me in my father's funeral. At that time my wife Frances had given birth to our eldest daughter Geralyne on 6 March 1969, and she was still in the hospital. Also, I wasn't used to travelling, and lacked finance, so I couldn't attend my father's funeral. That was an extremely sad occasion for me. Wing and I met up again in May 2000. In a conversation, he said he went back to Qujiang to look for his father's grave, but he couldn't locate it.

In May 2000, I visited my village for the first time since I left in September 1950. My wife Frances and youngest daughter Magdalene accompanied me. Wing was a great help by escorting us to our village, to meet up with our cousins born after I left in 1950. They were 4 boys, sons of my 7th Uncle Fong War Mook. The eldest brother Fong Siu Gong was the head of the village.

I requested cousins Wing and Siu Gong to organise a get together with our relatives and neighbours in our village, and I would pay for all the expenses. About 50 people attended the dinner at the village restaurant. The dinner was delicious, and we were very happy to meet our relatives and neighbours.

On separate days, Wing took us to visit relatives in different villages. We went on a day tour to Guangzhou on an eight-seater van with a tour guide.

We had lunch at an up-market restaurant and did some sightseeing.

Back in Hong Kong, Wing and his family entertained us for lunch in his home, and Yum Cha at a restaurant.

He and his wife took us to visit my father's grave in the Zhongshan Section Cemetery, Sandy Ridge, New Territories, China. His wife was a big help by providing the essentials for worship. We took roast pork, chicken, rice, whisky, tea and fruits. We burnt incense sticks, paper money, clothes and shoes.

I always addressed Wing's wife as Dai So, meaning elder brother/cousin's wife. Out of respect I had never asked for her name as she was older than me.

In December 2010, my eldest daughter Geralyne and her family and us (Frances and me), visited China and came to Hong Kong afterwards.

Wing had problems walking, so he asked his wife and his son Johnny, to take us to visit my father's grave at the Zhongshan Section Cemetery Section, Sandy Ridge, New Territories, China. His wife provided the essentials for worship.

In 2013, on our way to a boat Diamond Princess cruise Bangkok Thailand to Tienjin China, Frances and I met up with Wing in Hong Kong, and took him to Yum Cha at a Tsim Sha Tsui restaurant.

In October 2016, my youngest daughter Magdalene was on a work assignment to Hong Kong. She met up with Wing and his family.

It was a very sad time in November 2016, when news came to tell me that Wing had passed away at the ripe age of 92.

My wife Frances and I attended his funeral.

A good man called to rest by God. Rest in peace Cousin Wing.

The wedding of Fong Wing in Hong Kong.
Sitting from left is Wing's brother-in-law, my father Willie Fong War Sut, my mother Fong Lum Oy Wan.
Standing from left is Dai So and Cousin Wing.

Wing's family entertained Frances and me on a fabulous steamboat dinner, Tsim Sha Tsui, Kowloon, Hong Kong, November 2016.

Wing's family entertained youngest daughter Magdalene for lunch, October 2016. She was on a work trip to Hong Kong.

CHAPTER 7
My cousin Bill Fong and me

It was a time when I went to study in New Zealand. Early in January 1956, a bus from the Whenuapai airport took us to the Auckland City office of TEAL, where my cousin Bill Fong and his mother's worker Sue Hing, were waiting to meet me. It was so wonderful for me to meet my younger cousin Bill for the first time.

From there I was taken to Aunty Fong Low Shee's home, where she and my older cousins Jean and Nancy greeted me cordially.

I lived with my Aunty and family until the beginning of the third school term in 1957. She and my cousins Jean, Nancy, and Bill treated me very well, just like one of them. Whenever Aunty and family were invited to parties, I was always included.

Billy was born in New Zealand on 19 March 1941. He has 3 older sisters Lois, Jean and Nancy. He is the son of my eldest uncle Fong War Jue. Uncle was the eldest of 8 brothers and an older sister, and my father Willie Fong War Sut was the sixth sibling in the family.

As Bill was the only boy in his family, he and I became very good friends, like brothers. We both played in a table tennis team in the weekly competition, represented the Auckland Chinese Youth Club in indoor basketball in the competition. Our weekends were socially busy which included going to the movies on Saturdays, at the famous Civic

Theatre and playing friendly basketball games with friends on Sunday afternoons, at the Victoria Park in the city. Bill and I had been connected in many ways.

He and his wife Janice, together with his mother, my eldest uncle's wife Aunty Fong Low Shee, attended my wedding in Suva, Fiji, in 1968.

In between years while passing through Fiji, he and Janice visited my family in Suva, Fiji.

After my family migrated to Australia on 19 December 1985, Bill and I met regularly:

1. When my mother passed away in 1989, he and Janice came for the funeral.
2. When my eldest daughter Geralyne celebrated her 21st birthday in 1990, Bill and Janice came for the occasion. He was MC at the party.
3. When Geralyne got married in 1991, Bill together with his wife Janice, son Anthony and daughter Michelle, attended her wedding.
4. Our children organised a surprise party to celebrate our 25th wedding anniversary in 1993. Bill and Janice came to join our celebrations.
5. My son Gerard got married in 2001. Bill together with his wife Janice and son Anthony, came over from New Zealand for the wedding.
6. My 70th birthday party on 5 July 2008, was an occasion Bill said he wouldn't want to miss. He and Janice and daughter Michelle (living in Sydney then), attended my party.

Over the years, Frances and I visited Auckland. We attended Bill's 50th, 60th, and 70th birthday parties.

In his younger days Billy was a very successful businessman, a talented television presenter on fruit and vegetable produce, a long-time respectable member of the Lion's club, the Zhongshan Chinese Association and several community associations. He devoted much of his time in helping others.

The words humbleness, generosity, thoughtfulness and kindness best describe Billy's attributes.

Sadly, Billy passed away on 14 September 2012.

Cousin Bill Fong and me, Panmure, Auckland, 1956.

CHAPTER 8

My fortune teller in China

When I was thirteen years old and living in Fiji, my mother sent me a large piece of paper containing black and red writings written by a fortune-teller.

For information to him my mother supplied my age, time and date of birth. With this little information the fortune teller wrote about my life.

The paper which I am still keeping has so many complicated technical words, some in a circle.

However, I can understand the passage on my character, favourable careers either military or business, marriage and so on.

The fortune-teller wrote that he could see me live till 63 years of age, if longer it would be due to my good luck. Three children will be farewelling me at my funeral, any additional child/children would bring about tears of grief.

Some people believe in fortune-telling while many don't but criticise this practice as well as feng shui.

Well as for me I do believe in fortune-telling but not feng shui which has many silly interpretations.

Why I believe in fortune-telling:

- My fortune-teller told me I would live till 63 years of age if longer it would be due to my good luck.

- In my 64th year, I had 2 heart by-passes meaning two arteries were repaired, and my life was saved.
- Three children will be farewelling me at my funeral. True, at present I have 3 children, any more would bring sorrow to the family.

He also told one day I would marry a maiden from the south seas.

In China I only knew my father was working in Fiji, but I didn't know where Fiji was.

In class 3 in China in a geography lesson I learned where South America was, about the Portuguese explorer Ferdinand Magellan who discovered Brazil. I couldn't have the possibility of going to South America.

You know what happened, I married Frances Wong, born in Levuka, Fiji.

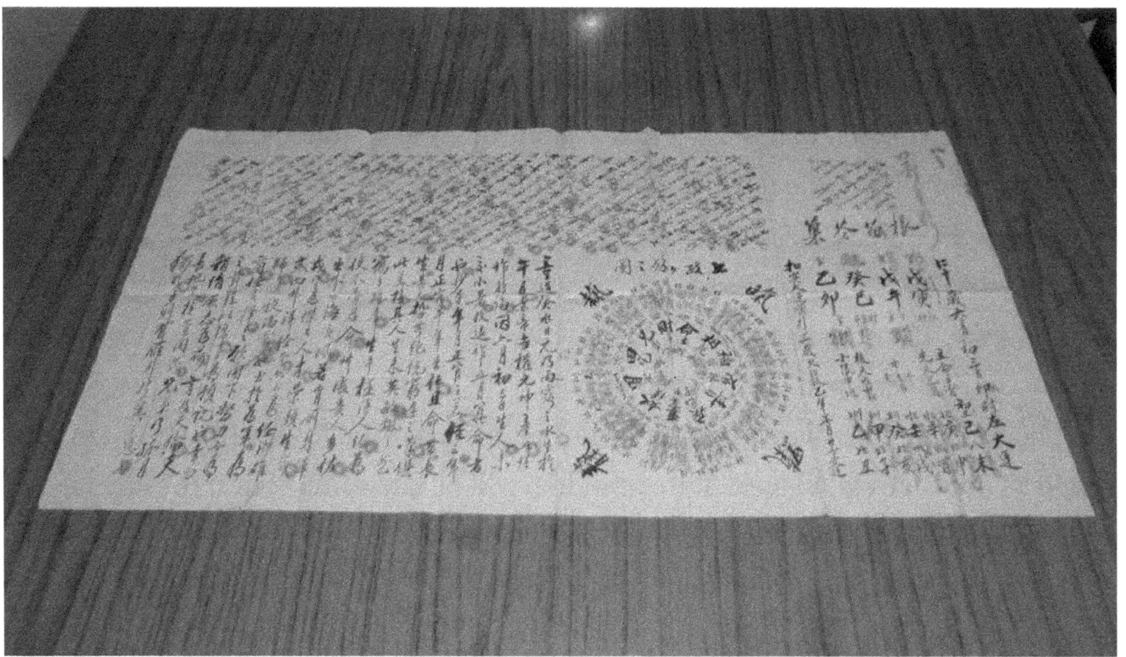

The paper containing black and red writings written by the fortune teller.

CHAPTER 9
Escape to Hong Kong and back to the village

My mother told me that when I was about 3 years old in early 1941, we escaped to Hong Kong and back to China just before Hong Kong surrendered to the Japanese Army.

It was early in the year 1941 when rumours of the Japanese soldiers marching to the south, so my mother and I, aided by Fong Bing Kin and his older physician brother Fong Bing Fatt, boarded a small ferry boat to Macau. When in Macau, Kin's older brother somehow found an old grenade and used it as a hammer to put nails into his wooden flip flop shoes. As soon as the first strike was done, the grenade exploded and wounded his eye and one hand. His eye was blinded, and his wounded hand had to be amputated. As a result, he and his younger brother Kin returned to the village.

My mother and I continued our journey by boarding a ferry from Macau to Hong Kong. We rented a room in a flat owned by Philip Wong's grandma, his mother was also in Hong Kong at that time. Philip was best man at my wedding. His mother and oldest sister were preparing to travel to Fiji.

Although I was so small, only 3 years old, I could remember going to the circus, it was fun seeing the animals and the clowns.

Soon my mother learned of the Japanese forces that were going to attack Hong Kong. She then decided the village might be a safer place. So, mum and I returned to our village in China. Not long after, the Japanese soldiers made their way to the villages. When I was 6 years old, I could remember a Chinese traitor (might be forced to work as a guide for the soldiers), took the soldiers around the village. I saw a chicken (not unusual to see) running around, and a Japanese soldier with a whip he carried, killed it and placed inside his large trouser pocket. I was terrified when I saw what the soldier did to the chicken.

Since that incident no further bad reports. The soldiers might have been warned by the top brass not to carry on destructive actions.

CHAPTER 10
Japanese soldiers came to our market garden

It happened on an afternoon in 1944 while my mother (34 years old) and me (about 6 years old) were doing some work in our 1/4-acre market garden in our village, Duntou, Zhongshan, Guangdong, China.

More than 100 Japanese soldiers appeared suddenly. We were so scared and wondered what they would do to us.

My mother and I moved away quietly to a crowd where some villagers were pelting rice.

Luckily the soldiers didn't pursue us. May be discipline had been installed after the lesson the Rape of Nanjing.

CHAPTER 11
My class 1 teacher

Jeung Shee Ling was introduced to Mr Fong Lee, by either David Cheefoo Fong or his sister Jane Fong, children of Mr Fong Lee. They were senior pupils in the village school, and they came from Fiji to study. They lived with their grandparents in our village.

Not long after, Mr Fong Lee married Jeung.

I was 7 years old in class 1 in the village school. Jeung had a big number of pupils in class 1, over 30 in number.

One girl was 16 when her parents could afford to send her for a little education. She left after that year.

The school roll had decreased to about 20 in class 2, 10 in class 3, 6 in class 4 and 5 in class 5. No class 6 as there were insufficient pupils.

Mr Fong Lee was a great man, a famous merchant around the western coast of Viti Levu, Fiji. After the 2nd world war, he bought an aeroplane and travelled with it and presented it as a gift to the President Chiang Kai Shek of China.

When Jeung met my father for the first time in Fiji she made a complaint to him. She said I was the naughtiest boy in the village. I suppose so because I was one of the naughty boys who had teased her for marrying an old man.

When I came to Fiji for the first time my father gave me a big growling. He also wrote to my mother telling her that she didn't control me properly. It was disgraceful.

CHAPTER 12
A cyclist ran over my legs

This story occurred on summer school holiday when I was about 7 years old. Some school mates and I were passing our time just outside the village, by the busy highway.

A challenge was created by us to run past any cyclist with a load in the back.

When it came to my turn, I ran but missed the timing before the cyclist with a heavy load of salted fish hit and ran over my legs. Both my legs were broken and as I lay in pain my mother was called.

Poor Mum who was 35 years old then and was of small build, carried me to the doctor in the next Fong village 2 or more kilometres away. She was very courageous.

The herbalist specialist doctor applied dried crushed pills mixed with Chinese whisky and wrapped both my injured legs with the special paste.

Miraculously the pain went away but I was unable to walk for a while.

Every three days Mum had to carry me to the doctor to change the bandages. After three weeks I managed to walk.

What a relief. What a stupid challenge that was.

CHAPTER 13

3 short stories in my village

In the village in China I was about 7 years old, often bullied by the bigger boys in the neighbourhood. Eventually I got smart and befriended a big boy of 15, gang leader Ernie Foo Kum Fong, living in the north of our village. Since then I lived in peace.

In the village, there lived a barber, the only barber in the village, who chose to have a holiday in a different manner.

On the last day of each month he would close his shop, get drunk, throw the furniture around and lay down on the floor sleeping. When he woke up in the night, he quickly put back the furniture in order. The next morning when he opened the shop, customers asked him what happened the day before and he replied: "Ï can't remember".

There lived a young widow about 45 years old further north to my house in the village. She was always whinging, and fowl mouthed the cheeky boys in the village. One morning when she opened her front door a bucket full of shit fell from the top on to her face and body. She shouted, "Ni gor hum gar charn". "Hum gar charn" is an extreme curse meaning the whole family perish. Since that incident, she controlled her tongue.

CHAPTER 14
Python in the temple

When I was turning 8 years old and preparing to go into class 2, there was a rumour that the village school won't be opened due to a lack of teachers teaching the local Zhongshan idiom.

My mother panicked and registered me at the school at her mother's village.

My maternal grandmother was the caretaker of Sha Pang Ha village temple. She provided accommodation. My two older cousins (girls) and I lived with my maternal grandma Lum.

Prior to the school's opening for the year, one afternoon, a large python with a diameter about 6 inches, curled itself around the beams in our living quarter.

The village constable was called, and he brought a one bullet refill rifle with him.

Soon many people gathered around not knowing what to do. Then, an elderly man persuaded the crowd not to do anything, because the python could be a snake god.

The python had come from a little forest behind the temple.

About 2 hours later the python slowly went away.

It was a big relief for us but the same night grandma, my 2 cousins and I were still very frightened and stayed awake the whole night.

Pythons are found in sub-Saharan Africa, Nepal, India, Sri Lanka, Burma, southern China, Southeast Asia, and from the Philippines southeast through Indonesia to New Guinea and Australia.

In the United States, an introduced population of Burmese pythons, Python molurus bivittatus, has existed as an invasive species in the Everglades National Park since the late 1990's.

Most members of this family are ambush predators, in that they typically remain motionless in a camouflaged position, and then strike suddenly at passing prey. They will generally not attack humans unless startled or provoked, although females protecting their eggs can be aggressive. Reports of attacks on human beings were once more common in South and Southeast Asia but are now quite rare.

Light Phase Asian Rock Python (Python molurus) at San Diego Zoo, USA sourced from Wikipedia Commons, a free media repository. The python I saw was coiled up like the one in this image. Photographer: Nathanael Maury

CHAPTER 15
My favourite music – Cantonese operas

In 1946, after the Second world war, the people of China celebrated the victories over their enemies.

In my cousin's village some old villagers, retired, returned from overseas to the village. These oldies donated money for the purpose of celebrations, hired a Cantonese Opera Troupe from Hong Kong, to perform at the temporarily erected bamboo theatre. It consisted of the changing room and toilet facilities in the back, then the performing stage in the front of it. In the front under the stage lay bamboo chairs. All the walls around the theatre were blocked leaving little gaps people outside could only peep through. Famous opera stars Law Kar Kin and Fong Yim Fun were in the troupe. The troupe lived in the village school compounds. Just wondering how they coped with the conditions.

My cousin, (my mother's eldest sister's son Wong Sai Ting), his gang and I, like many who couldn't afford tickets, often peeped through the gaps to get a glimpse of the performances inside the theatre. To do that we had to take along little benches to stand on and peeped through.

Since then, I became interested in Cantonese opera, the beautiful costumes, music loud and low (soothing), martial arts style, performances on happy and sad stories, all played a part. I watch at least an hour of Cantonese opera every day on YouTube. If any of you are interested, go to YouTube and search for "Cantonese opera", you will get free shows.

It is during the summer school holidays that year that I got involved with my cousin (2 years older than me) and his gang. We went swimming in a little natural pool full of grass and mud, playing games and smoking cigarettes. At the tender age of 8, I learned to smoke cigarettes. I had been smoking for 55 years from 1946 to June to 2001. I had to stop because in June 2001 I had surgery done on my heart, 2 bypasses done at the same time (2 arteries repaired). Recently I had an X-ray on my lungs and they were found to be free from cancer. Lucky me. I don't want to smoke cigarettes anymore.

CHAPTER 16

At a school roll call, Fong Wing Cum to Fong Wing Yum

At a school roll call in my village in China, the newly appointed headteacher was from Guangzhou (Canton City), called out Fong Wing Yum.

Nobody answered.

He repeated and still nobody answered.

I told him we have my classmate here called Fong Wing Cum; could he be the one?

He said he was calling Fong Wing Yum. After a while the headteacher looked at Wing Cum and asked him why he didn't answer.

Wing Cum said his father gave him the name of Wing Cum not Wing Yum.

The headteacher told the assembly that in Proper Cantonese the name should be Wing Yum (forever admirable).

In the Zhongshan City dialect it is Wing Cum (forever durable).

方永欽

Wing Cum written in simplified Chinese.

CHAPTER 17
This is my book

这本书是我的
Zhè běn shū shì wǒ de
When two persons of different races fight, we say racist.
When two or more persons of the same race fight, we say …?

My father's name is Fong War Sut.

During a class 3 Mandarin lesson in my village in China we followed the teacher to say "Zhe běn shū shi wǒ de", but instead the class except me said "Zhe běn shū shi war sut".

This made me cry because they teased and made fun of my father's name.

The teacher found out but didn't do anything to reprimand the class.

I had to swallow the teasing.

In Fiji, a Marist Brothers' High School form 3 classmate now RIP, teased me by saying "See that monkay is yuming" instead of "Monkey is coming". Hahaha.

He didn't live long enough for me to tease him back.

CHAPTER 18
Wrong pupil punished

School corporal punishment refers to causing deliberate pain or discomfort in response to undesired behaviour by students in schools. It often involves striking the student either across the buttocks or on the hands, with an implement such as a rattan cane.

Fong Lup Wai was my village primary school's master of discipline; he was of robust built and feared by all the pupils in the school. He lived in a house with the kitchen in front of my house. He wanted his kitchen to be moved further back to give him more space in his house, so he approached my mother; and sought permission to buy a portion of the land in the front of the 3 houses owned by my ancestors.

My mother refused his request, and he was furious and hated her from then on. Somehow, he found a way to induce my grandmother to sell the piece of land space to him.

I was about nine years old.

In one instance at my village primary school in China, the master of discipline with a rattan cane, cruelly beat my both legs, causing severe bleeding. He didn't investigate who had committed the offence. I was wrongly pulled up.

In the presence of the school teachers and pupils, my mother caused a big stir at the school, cursing him for such cruelty. My father was working in Fiji then. Lucky for the cane beater; if my father was in the village, he would have gunned him down. Father and his friend Fong Marn Ho, were the only two apart from the village constables, who owned pistols.

Fong Lup Wai's niece had a load of two buckets of drinking water drawn from the public well and reported me as the culprit who threw sand into her buckets, but honestly I swore I didn't do it. It was someone else she couldn't identify but I happened to be near her.

Fong Lup Wai took the law into his own hands. By western law or Chinese law, if the offence was committed outside school, he had no right to carry out the punishment in school. He could only make complaints to the offender's parents who in turn would take action.

When the communists took over in 1949, lots of complaints were laid against him, and these were given to the new regime to take action. As a result, he was sent for hard labour somewhere for many unjust doings.

In the year 2000, I visited my village for the first time after I left in 1950. I looked for Fong Lup Wai and wanted to confront him about what he had done to me. I was told he had passed away. Guess he would have been about 90 years old if he was alive.

CHAPTER 19

School Shanghai (Rubber band fight)

I was 9 years old, a member of the class 3 squad, rubber band fighting the much older boys of classes 4 and 5 in our village school in China.

For a week the school was supervised by a lone headteacher from Guangzhou.

One afternoon, he was away from school for more than an hour.

As previously planned for an opportunity like this our reps and their reps started a shanghai fight, paper bullets shot from shanghaies.

A rep from each side would confront each other in the little lane separating our classrooms. When they met, they shot each other and away they ran.

It was fun for a while until a smart alec from the older side shot a bullet made of thin wire inside the paper. Our rep got hurt and the game had to be stopped.

Our rep who got hurt became angry and reported to the headteacher soon after his return.

No punishment was carried out by the headteacher, maybe he thought it was his fault for being away leaving the school unsupervised.

CHAPTER 20
Lepers in my village in China

From the Qing Rule we learned there were 36 physicians in the palace who studied from the same book, and a few claimed to have certain skills inherited. However, they had no knowledge of curing those suffering from chickenpox, leprosy and venereal diseases. The irony is that sex enhancement drugs were commonly sold.

Firstly, a young man in his early thirties lived in a hut in the little vegetable garden beside his house in the north of my village.

One day, a mate of mine and I decided to roam around the north of the village and found him outside his hut. I asked him whether he knew me although we had never met before. He started shouting "Hit Oh Chor". Before my mate and I ran away we saw his younger brother hiding in the bush. Then I realised how he knew my name, his brother must have told him. Why he said kill the communist; my name is Fong Yuk Chor, and chor is a nickname for "Oh Chor" for a communist. The communists were not respected before they liberated the whole of China.

Secondly, a brother in his early thirties and sister in her early twenties lived in a house not far from mine. The brother soon passed away due to hunger. The sister was left to fend for herself by picking up pig waste around the village, sold as fertiliser to people who owned little vegetable gardens. Her whole body was infected with the disease, poor thing. Whenever she went to buy things from the only shop in the village, nobody would dare go along, as outside the shop there were displays of uncovered salted fish and dried vegetables which attracted flies all over the place. After a few weeks as far as I know she passed away. Amen.

Thirdly, an attractive old widow, tall and slim, lived in a house not far from behind my house. Her 14-year-old grandson lived with her. Her son and daughter-in-law were away working in the city. The boy was in class 5 and I was in class 4 in a room shared by two classes. One day a classmate of mine raised a question to him whether he got infected with the leprosy disease from his grandma as if so, he might pass on the infection to us. In her young days, his grandma had an affair with a notorious gangster who passed on the disease to her. He told us so far, he was clear and invited some of us to visit his home. Some of us went along with him and saw his grandma in their home. Part of her face showed signs of leprosy. We were concerned and left hurriedly. A month later the boy no longer attended school.

CHAPTER 21
On gambling

As a little boy in the village in China I learned to gamble.

One night in a house by throwing the dices I won the money from those present who could afford a little.

The last one was the village constable who had a little money left, challenged me to his last bet.

We threw the dices till daybreak and I won.

When I returned home early in the morning there was parliament with my mother, but she spared me of growling because I had won some money.

CHAPTER 22
Daring swim

I was about 10 years old in my village in Duntou, Zhongshan, Guangdong, China, when one day 4 boys including me wagged school and decided to make a daring swim across the village river more than 100 metres wide. This river leads to the high seas in Macau.

Of the 4 boys 3 of them were 12 years old.

Miraculously all of us managed to swim across the river and after a short break, swam back to where we started.

When I told my mother, she scolded me, but I escaped a big hiding.

Further up the river on the opposite side is the Lui village. Opposite this village lies a public graveyard on a hill, about 100 metres from the riverbank. A few Lui youths who braved themselves by swimming across the river (about 200 metres wide), were drowned about 10 metres before they reached the riverbank.

People believed that ghosts from the public graveyard up the hill were responsible for their fates.

A Lui youth who attended high school in Guangzhou (Canton City), a champion swimmer at his school, heard about the mishaps. He didn't believe in ghosts' activities, so he attempted to swim across the river. About 10 metres from reaching the riverbank, and on the exact spot where the said youths were drowned, this high school swimming champion felt cramps in his legs. He died from drowning.

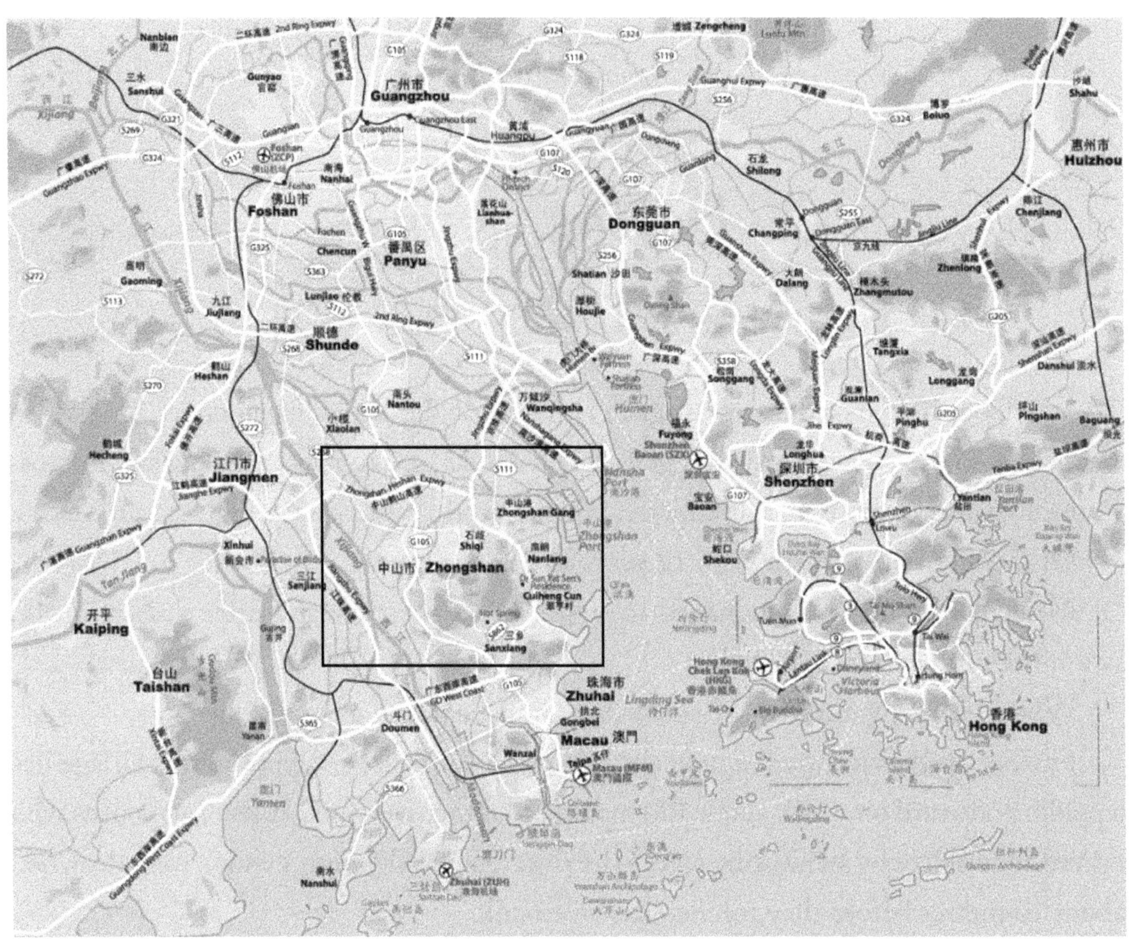

Detailed highways map of Hong Kong, Shenzhen, Guangzhou and Macau region, published under the Creative Commons Attribution ShareAlike 3.0 Licence from the Maps of the World web site at http://www.maps-of-the-world.net. You can see the outline for Zhongshan towards the middle bottom of the map.

CHAPTER 23
Sorry

My good friend, Michael Chiman Fang's stepbrother, David Chifoo Fong came from Fiji to my village in China, to study and stayed with his grandparents. He was a gentle giant and loved by all.

Then on the basketball court one day he deliberately bumped another player and said "Sorry".

All the spectators shouted out "Solly" and there was laughter. They were unable to say sorry because of the "R" tone.

He was a big and tall teenager. The opposition players could not match his height as he always won the rebound.

Then Fong Bing Kin (who later came to Fiji) from the opposite team, did a trick and stepped on his foot so that David Chifoo Fong could not jump.

CHAPTER 24
Stone-throwing battle

The big village next to mine in China has the same surname "Fong". It houses our male birth records.

There was a bunch of rich boys (fathers overseas) turned larrikins.

When they came across our boys doing something in their village, they harassed them.

Our gang leader Ernie Fu Kum Fong found out about this and arranged with their leader for a stone-throwing battle.

An empty block of land roughly 40 x 30 metres was chosen in our village for the battleground for both sides to face one another.

Broken bricks and enamel tiles were used to bombard one another.

This carried on for about 15 minutes, strangely no one was hurt.

Then the opposition side ran out of ammunition and started to retreat to a double story house in their village.

We pursued and bombarded the house with stones and whatever we could find.

In the end their gang leader stood outside the house upstairs and shouted, "We give up".

Just imagine how brave we all were but really very naughty.

With Ernie Fong at my 70th birthday party, Emperor
Garden Restaurant, Sydney City, 5 July 2008.
Ernie is chairman of the Sydney Hong Xi Guan Martial Arts Association.
Hung Hei-gun or Hong Xiguan was a Chinese martial artist who lived in the Qing dynasty.
He was also an influential figure in the Southern Shaolin school of Chinese martial arts.

CHAPTER 25

Night school in my village in China

I was 11 years old and in class 5.

There were only 5 pupils in that class that year. Two boys always competed for first and second place. A petite girl always came third; I always came fourth and leaving the fifth and last position for another girl. She wasn't dumb but because the first four were just better than her.

That particular year the school happened to have enough teachers. The headteacher and the school committee decided to run a one-term night school mainly for adult pupils not attending day school.

I enrolled and anticipating gaining further knowledge so that I could compete for a better position in my class.

As the term ended the results came out and I was first in the class.

I was happy but many came around and instead of congratulating me they jeered at me. They said I was lucky to be able to attend day school and so why deprived the second-place getter of coming first.

CHAPTER 26
The Qingming or Chung Ming festival

The Qingming or Ching Ming Festival, also known as Tomb-Sweeping Day in English, is a traditional Chinese festival on the first day of the fifth solar term of the traditional Chinese lunisolar calendar. This makes it the 15th day after the Spring Equinox, either 4 or 5 April in a given year. Other common translations include Chinese Memorial Day and Ancestors' Day.

I was 11 years old, a class 5 pupil in the village school in China.

Qingming time had arrived, and the school's scouts were chosen to represent the school to honour the village ancestors buried on a hill in a village nearby.

I was the only scout who could blow the bugle reasonably well, but we needed two bugle blowers, so the teacher on duty suggested another boy to hold the bugle while I blew.

As the worship commenced, I started blowing "dar dar dar da, dar da di", and the stupid boy holding the bugle got excited and blew "phat"; all the onlookers shouted out "Good music".

When we were leaving the cheeky onlookers commented "Two bugles with one sound".

CHAPTER 27
Gangsters in the Zhongshan District, Guangdong, China

On October 1, 1949, Mao Zedong proclaimed the establishment of the People's Republic of China.

The new government eradicated as much as possible opium smoking, prostitution, kidnapping, extortion, robbery at sight, burglary, etc.

Prior to that under the Guomintang (Nationalist) government, gangsters prevailed in the Zhongshan district I knew as a little boy, growing up in the village of Dun Tou.

North to Zhongshan City, there was a cave by the roadside between my village and the Sek Moon Wong village, a distance about a kilometre. A thug, holding his one-shot bullet rifle, waited to kidnap any child passing through.

Down south of the road to the Dai Chung Sue village, about 2 kilometres from my village, a similar cave was there also.

These thugs were under their gangsters' protection so the village constables and even the district government, in fear of retaliation by the gangsters, couldn't do anything to prevent such crimes happening.

A noted gangster nicknamed "Daring Hong" (大胆洪), lived in a diaolou he had built in the Lui village almost opposite to my village separated by the river flowing south to Macau. He had a gang of followers living with him.

Hong derived his income from illegal vices. He was very strict with his gang members, and I had never heard of any of his boys misbehaving.

There was an indoor basketball court in his diaolou compound, which staged friendly games with visiting teams from other villages.

I remember one afternoon, being a spectator at a friendly game in this court between my village team and Hong's team. Also present to cheer my village team was my good friend Michael Chiman Fong's 10th uncle Fong Wah Cheong, the vice-chancellor of the Zhongshan University. Wah Cheong was a very good basketball player whom our village team captain wanted him to play. He said let the boys have a go, and if the team was losing, he would go in. After half time, our village team was leading in the game, so Wah Cheong rode off on his bicycle.

The next gangster was Sue Pui Dai of Chow Ma Yin village, about 2 kilometres east of my village. Incidentally he was a relative of mine. His mother was an older sister of my grandmother, mum's mother.

Pui Dai lived in a house, no diaolou status. His followers were on call in times of need. He carried a pistol in a belt. He was more powerful than the first gangster Hong. As a kid I had no knowledge of what he was up to. Occasionally, his mother and wife visited my house, as her youngest sister whom I called Yee Po (grand aunty and widowed) lived with my mother and me.

The third gangster was Sue Tin Cheong, the most powerful in the Zhongshan district. He lived in his house in the Dai Chung Sue village (大涌鎮), the largest and richest in the district, no diaolou status. His followers were called in time of need. He also had in his possession the most machine guns.

I don't know much of him, but I heard that he would render assistance to needy people who approached him.

The three known gangsters got on cordially. Of course, they knew where they stood.

To round up this episode here is a side story.

The Ho Chung Fong village just next to mine once had a bamboo theatre built and contracted with a famous Cantonese Opera Troupe from Hong Kong to perform in this village. Things were going on very well until the third last day when rumours spread out that some unknown gangsters were out to disrupt the performances at night.

The big Fong organisers panicked, and immediately approached the most powerful gangster Sue Tin Cheong for help. Without delay he summoned 12 followers, all carried pistols in their belts, and ordered 6 machine guns and ammunition, 6 one bullet rifles and ammunition, and told them to be on guard around the Fong village bamboo theatre.

As a result of the armed preparations, there were no signs of trouble during the last three days of performance.

Nan Lou diaolou in Chikan, Kaiping, China sourced from Wikimedia Commons, a free media repository. Photograher: Hemis

CHAPTER 28
Boat thieves' burglary at night

Along the riverbank in front of my village lay a piece of fertile land. Owners planted rice and vegetables on their respective plots.

I was only 6 years old during a night in 1944 when the war of China/Japan was still on, when thieves in a rowing boat came to the riverbank, berthed their boat and helped themselves to vegetables that were ready for harvest.

Owners who lost their stolen possessions, reported the matter to the head of the village constabulary. He called a meeting with the elders, and a decision was made to guard and prevent would-be thieves from entering the village.

The 4 constables including the one in charge besides carrying pistols (handguns), had 4 one bullet shot rifles and limited ammunitions.

Instead of guarding the crop plots, the constables in fear of ambush, set up a little post about 100 metres from the village gate. With their rifles ready, the 4 stayed overnight waiting for thieves to enter through the village gate. They did that for 3 nights, but nothing happened.

I wondered whether the constables had been on guard or fell asleep while on duty during the previous 3 nights.

They were very happy and relieved after the post was called off.

CHAPTER 29
My last 8 months in the village in China

How did I spend my time between January to August 1950 in the village before leaving for Fiji?

Before the village school opened for 1950, word was out it would not be running class 6 as insufficient pupils were registered. Class 5 had 5 pupils the previous year but 2 were not prepared to start class 6.

So, during the last 8 months in the village I had been involved in the following:

- Firstly, there was no class 6 education for me, so I turned to my cousin for advice. He lived in a village near mine. He was 14 years of age, a very bright boy, dux of class 6 in his school the previous year, and even was admired by the girls in his class. He said he was going to enrol in a 2-month summer school class on Form 1 subjects conducted by the Zhongshan First Secondary (Forms 1 to 6), and he invited me to join him. I agreed and registered with the secondary school. After a school week of 5 days I ceased going back because I couldn't cope with the lessons. I had only attended school up to class 5 and missed the important subjects of class 6. Not only that; the students there were mainly boys whose fathers were overseas, and the manner they spoke, put me off.
- Secondly, before the beginning of the school term a Kungfu master came to start a 2-week course in an empty space near the basketball court. I wanted to register

and learn some skills, but my mother forbade me to go ahead. She told me I was already naughty enough, and if I joined and came out with some fighting skills, I would be more mischievous. I obeyed and did not register. However, I learned from the sideline, a trick that if someone (under 130 kilos) grabbed me from behind I can twist that person around and throw him on to the floor.

- Thirdly, I had the opportunity to taste dog and snake meat. I befriended a person whom I called uncle in the northern part of the village. He invited me to have some dog meat cooked with herbs. The dog meat with bones tasted like chicken/lamb stew, but the flavour was better. As for snake meat it was given to me by a rich man with a bad leg; it was believed that snake meat soup boiled with herbs was meant to improve his condition. He lived near a little lane where I often played marbles; and one day he gave me a small bowl of snake soup. It tasted like eel soup, but the flavour was so good, a very expensive dish.
- Fourthly, I learned how to ride a bicycle at night. My friend had a fairly new bike for carrying passengers. He charged a fee for teaching me. I sat on the trunk before the handles and he sat on the bike seat. We commenced riding; he was peddling, and we were doing well on the muddy highway, on either side lay muddy rice paddies. All of a sudden, I got excited and steered the bike into the muddy rice field. Fortunately, both of us didn't get hurt.

CHAPTER 30

Journey from China to Australia to Fiji

A Day that Shook the World: Mao's communists take over in China. On 1 October 1949, China's communist party, led by Mao Zedong, finally prevailed against the Nationalists and assumed power.

At the end of the year 1949 I completed class 5. The village school did not open class 6 in 1950 due to insufficient pupils for enrolment. In view of this, my mother was telling me the people were not sure of what was coming after the takeover by the new communist regime, so she decided that it was about time I went to Fiji to meet my father for the first time, to enroll at a school for further studies in English. My mum wrote to dad about the idea and he, without hesitation, agreed for me to join him.

My father went to work in Fiji when he was 18 years of age. At that time my eldest uncle Fong War Jue was working in Fiji. He later migrated to New Zealand.

My father at the age of 28, came back to the village to marry my mother aged 18. After about a month he went back to work in Fiji. When he was 38, he came back to the village, lay seeds and my mother started to expect me. Then about a month later he went back to work in Fiji, leaving a young pregnant wife behind. Fortunately, my grandparents were still alive, and they were around whenever my mother needed help.

In between the 8 months of January to August in 1950, application formalities were made. I can't remember who helped with these matters in the village. Permit to enter as a student to Fiji had been granted by August.

I went to Hong Kong to get used to circumstances of travelling, and to meet some 11 Syeyup boys who were going to Fiji.

For the first trip I went to Hong Kong by myself. I stayed free at the premises of Q Kong Knitting Factory whose manager was my father's friend whom I called Uncle Fong Sing Cheung (RIP). Day time working tables, night-time staff slept on them.

Once I went to use a men's public toilet containing 4 open cubicles; while people were doing their business inside, others queued up in front of them.

After 3 days I was missing Mum, so I caught a slow ferry to Macau and back to the village.

For the second trip, my Mum talked me into taking another trip to Hong Kong by myself. I stayed at my cousin's place. She was living with her partner in a dormitory space type of flat, just enough for a bed with curtains drawn in times of need. She arranged a bed in open space for me to sleep. A kitchen and a toilet were shared by 6 people.

Once a Lum Uncle from my Mum's village took me to an amusement park in Lai Chi Kok, Kowloon, Hong Kong. The Sydney Luna Park is nothing compared to it. The park had Cantonese opera performances, ferries wheels, a swimming pool etc. Lai Chi Kok Amusement Park was an amusement park on the west shore of Lai Chi Kok Bay in Lai Chi Kok, Hong Kong. It was once the largest amusement park in Hong Kong and attracted people from all walks of life in the territory. Again, I was missing mum so after 4 days I went back to the village.

Third time to Hong Kong: This time mum decided to go with me to Hong Kong and wanted to make sure that I would not come back to the village. While awaiting to join the group of 11 boys travelling to Fiji, mum and I visited many places of interest. A week passed and no sign of the group. I lost my patience, and still missing Mum at heart, I told her I wanted to go back to the village for the last time. Mum agreed and arranged a meeting with our agent; we told him we were going back to the village. Guess what. That agent was Mr Yee, younger brother of Mr Yee Hoy Shang, my father's boss at Kwong Tiy & Co. Ltd in Suva, Fiji. So off Mum and I went back to the village.

Sometime later the agent in Hong Kong sent word that I was to go to Macau, to meet up with my guardian (Captain) who would be accompanying me and the 11 young boys, 2 ten years old, some 14 years old, and the rest round about 18 years old. Incidentally one of the 10-year-old boys Yee Woi Ping is my son-in-law Sen Yee's father. He now lives in Homebush, Sydney. At that time missing mum was out of the question, so I picked up courage and said goodbye to her, then off I went to Macau.

The first and only night's stay at a cheap inn in Macau was quite an experience. Early that night we were told prostitutes would be parading past our inn. My guardian, the troupe of boys and I, stood outside our inn and watched a big group of young pros, young ladies aged between 15 to 19 going past slowly; only 1 man in charge. At that time prostitution was legal in Macau.

The next morning, all of us left Macau by a large but slow ferry for Hong Kong. The journey took about 3 hours. Nowadays a slow ferry takes one and half hours and a hydrofoil ferry would take less than an hour for the journey. There is now a Zhuhai to Macau to Hong Kong bridge and tunnel system that opened in October 2018. It runs for 55 kms, cutting the journey time by more than half.

We stayed at an inn in the Hong Kong Island side. During the next few days, travel formalities and photos for Certificate of Identity were organised. On the back of my photo my name was written as Fong Cook Cho, Syeyup dialect pronunciation, while in the Zhongshan dialect, it is pronounced as Fong Yuk Chor.

We went to a Notary Public (Lawyer)'s office to sign our Certificates of Identity.

From there the lawyer's office did the rest.

My birthday was 3 June Chinese Calendar, but my travelling document recorded 6 November, a bit of a mix up.

My father sent word for me to reduce my age by 1 year so that the boat ticket would cost half of 25 Fiji pounds, which was a lot of money in 1950. I was 12 years old at that time, bigger than all the 14-year-old boys. Fearing I might be caught falsifying my true age I reduced it by 6 months instead of one year. As a result, my father had to pay the full fare of 25 Fiji pounds. He was very disappointed.

Time to board a boat from Hong Kong to Sydney, Australia.

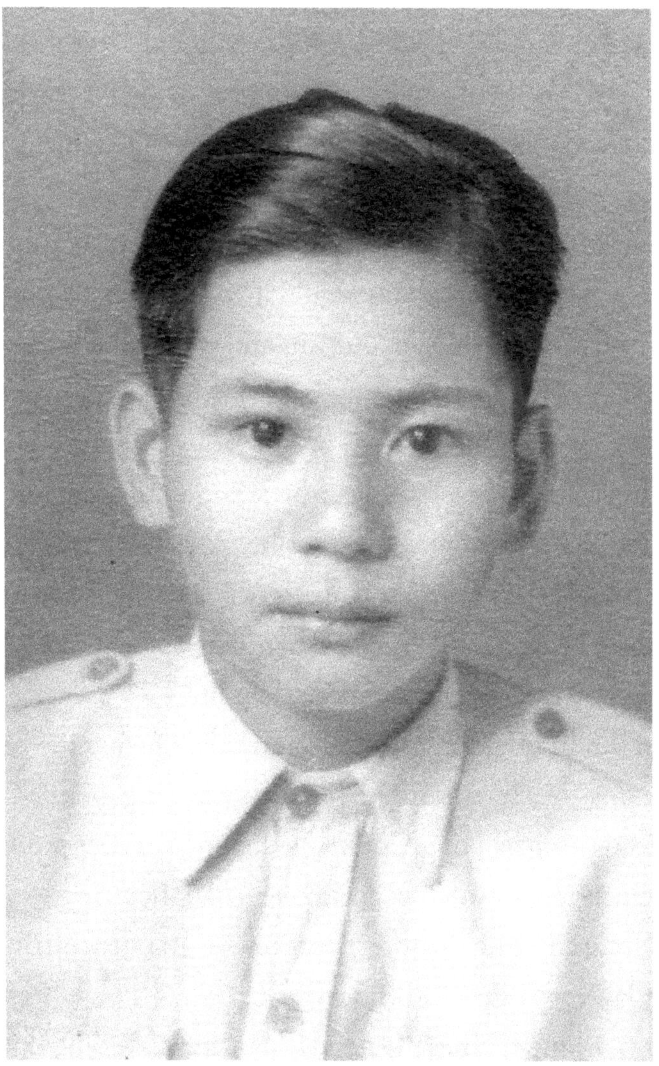

Me, aged 12.

CHAPTER 31
Boat journey, Hong Kong to Australia

I was already 12 years old in September 1950 when our guardian Mr Yee Wing Lee whom we called captain, accompanied the 11 Szeyup boys and me to board the old cargo boat "Tai Ping".

The passengers were placed in the cargo hold. Temporary partitions were erected and used for the steerage accommodation; weak spring mattress beds on the floor. To get down to the between-deck the passengers often had to use ladders, and the passageway down between the hatches were narrow and steep. The manner in which the ship was equipped could vary since there was no set standards for this. The furnishings could be easily removed, and not cost more than absolutely necessary. As soon as the ship had set the passengers on land, the furnishings were discarded, and the ship prepared for return cargo.

All the passengers men, women, and boys were led into the hull, each one was allocated a soft spring mattress bed, a little space in between. There were no infants. Partitions separated each section of 12 beds. Ventilation was reasonably good.

My friend Yee Lin Lum and I decided to put our Chinese lollies and snacks together so that we could share them during the voyage.

First night in the hull was interesting and enjoyable. At dinner time my gang together sat around a table, while the other passengers chose their respective tables. The dishes served were soup, rice, and 6 other dishes. All the passengers were happy with the first dinner on board, very tasty and a real treat.

Soon after dinner all the passengers from the hull and those on the upper deck, came out to the open deck to watch the boat leaving the Hong Kong harbour. The harbour scenery was quite an attractive sight, just beautiful.

I started to wander about. Has anyone been on a particular cruise before and experienced real problems with rough seas?

As the boat sailed through the passage, (as I was told all types of harbour passages have rough moments) huge waves splashed against the boat, and somehow water sipped into the boat near Lin Lum's and my area. He got seasick and started vomiting. He accidentally pushed our goodies into the wet area. That was the end of our snacks amen.

Two daily meals only were served, no breakfast nor lunch. The first meal around 11 o'clock in the morning, and dinner in the evening. As I mentioned earlier usual dishes were served: rice, soup, and 6 other varieties which consisted of a vegetable plate, beef, pork and fish. I couldn't remember any seafood being provided. Food was always tasty, and no complaints were raised by the passengers. Why should they because back in the villages we ate very simply.

It was difficult to recollect so many things happened during our 20 days inside the hull.

One day, Yee Jarn Yuen, a short man and well built in his early thirties, was returning on his second trip to Fiji. He rounded up our troupe of 12 boys to go up to the deck. He sensed that we 12 boys were very bored staying inside the hull, so he decided to teach us some kung fu movements. He told us he was a martial arts instructor in China. This practice was done on weekly basis and 3 sessions were held during the voyage.

It was extremely sad that he was murdered inside his store, which he rented from K. W. March Ltd in Amy Street, Toorak, Suva, Fiji. Mr Yee couldn't move around in a little space to defend himself. In an open space he could do a lot more in defence.

Similarly, I can tell you another tragedy which happened inside a cafe in the Suva Hotel opposite the Lilac Theatre in Suva, Fiji. A Chinese man believed to be skilled in kung fu, went into the cafe, where he found the owner was being harassed by a

Fijian man. This kung fu uncle intervened and a fight broke out between him and the troublemaker. After some movements the kung fu uncle with both his palms, pushed the opponent's chest in such a force that made the culprit run away from the cafe.

Soon he rounded up a gang of more than 7 to return to the cafe. The gang rushed forward, punched and kicked the kung fu uncle to death. He couldn't do a thing inside so little space.

Kan Lin, one of our gang, a young man in his early twenties, befriended a young lady. At the age of 19 she was travelling to Lautoka, Fiji, to meet her husband to be for the first time. It was an arranged marriage. One day she left a book on her bed when she went to the toilet. Kan Lin curiously picked it up and found it was a pornographic book.

One day Tony Jup Sing Yee, a 10-year-old boy in our group, urinated on the ground near the window. I happened to be near him; at that moment Mr Long Hong Tow, on his second return to Fiji, walked past and thought I had done the same naughty thing. He came and slapped my face. Strangely I didn't scream but told him it was Tony who urinated. Well, Mr Low was confused but he didn't apologise.

Tony, being a known naughty and cheeky boy in our group, made me angry one day and I gave him a slap on his face. Guess what… Tony was related to Mr Yee Wak Joong (RIP), a founder of Kwong Tiy in Fiji, father of Mr Yee Hoy Shang, manager of Kwong Tiy. Mr Yee Hoy Shang was my father's boss in Fiji. Mr Yee Wak Joong heard Tony's cries; came over and hit me on my thigh with his wooden shoe. In my reply I said "ni gor lou kai dai" literary means you old bugger. I told him Tony was cheeky to me.

A few days after arriving in Fiji my father questioned me about that incident. I said Tony teased me, so I went for him. My father did not punish me, but I presumed he would have apologised to Mr Yee Wak Joong on behalf of my disrespect.

On another occasion, I became friendly with a young man in his early twenties. He was from China's Shangdong Province, travelling from Hong Kong to Sydney, Australia. We had been sharing thoughts, then one day he all of a sudden said to me "my son". I didn't know what language he used so I left him and consulted Mr Low Hong Tow who knew some English. Mr Low told me if that guy said "my son" to you next time, you reply "fuck you". I forgot to ask Mr Low the meaning of f. y. Next time, that guy and

I met and immediately he said "my son". I was ready to return his ridicule. I said "fuck you". He wanted to hit me, but I ran away as fast as I could around the hull. Since that incident no more friends. End of another chapter.

The game of mahjong, gramophone records on Cantonese operas, were heard loud and clear until midnight every day.

The boat sailed past Luzon in the Philippines as we were told but we couldn't see any land at all. Looking down on both sides of the bow we saw two large fish swimming on either side of the bow.

The only port of call was Cairns. The boat arrived at Cairns, Queensland, Australia, in the morning. It berthed at the wharf. We spent one night there, and the boat sailed away the following evening. Passengers were not permitted to go ashore. One Chinese young man got off in Cairns. He had an open wardrobe showing many bula shirts. In the evening, when the boat was berthed at the wharf passengers came up to the deck and witnessed a regatta of little yachts, followed by little boats, sailing around the harbour. What a fantastic display of marine fraternity.

The boat continued its voyage to Sydney. Having lived in the hull for 20 days the passengers were relieved when the boat almost reached Sydney, Australia. Again, the passage to Sydney Harbour was rough but no one on board was seasick. On the 21st day the boat arrived at Sydney Harbour.

Some passengers bound for the Sydney destination got off, and others travelling to New Zealand and Fiji had to wait for transport by air. These passengers included us going to Fiji, were transported to an inn called King Nam Jang in the Rocks area in Sydney. The inn was owned by the Cumines family.

The first concentration of Chinese residences and shops was in lower George Street, in The Rocks. Men arriving to try their luck on the goldfields in the 1850's headed here to buy supplies for the trek inland, and soon rudimentary stores began providing more complex services to their countrymen, such as banking and letter writing. Some stores evolved into informal clan meeting rooms.

Many of the Chinese people who inhabited and worked in this area were interviewed for the 1891 Report of the Royal Commission on alleged Chinese gambling and immorality and charges of bribery against members of the police force, which provides an unexpectedly detailed record of this first Chinatown.

Some stores remained for many decades, including King Nam Jang, importers and ship providers. The King Nam Jang was still trading a century after it opened in the 1860's. In the later part of the nineteenth century, some of the most successful Chinese businessmen and their families lived in nearby streets. However, by the 1870's the centre of the Chinese trade presence had moved south to Campbell and Goulburn streets, with residential areas spreading into Surrey Hills.

Passengers bound for Fiji stayed at the King Nam Jang for about a week before they flew by TEAL to Fiji. During the week's stay our group guardian took us for a walk around the Rocks area.

I was lucky enough to be invited by my father's friend Uncle Fong Say Tin, who with his son Fong King Moo (King Fong), took me to Luna Park. We went by a return ferry. Mr Fong Say Tin was a very kind and generous man, who often went to the inn to render assistances to people in need.

In Sydney we saw many high-rise buildings. We assumed that since Fiji was further away the capital city would have many and taller buildings. After seeing Nadi and Suva we were disappointed.

After a week in Sydney, an aeroplane belonging to TEAL (Tasman Empire Airways Ltd) had seats available for passengers travelling to Fiji.

CHAPTER 32
Journey Australia to Fiji

After a week's stay at the King Nam Jang inn in the Rocks Area in Sydney, Australia, our guardian informed us (the 12 boys) that a TEAL's (Tasman Empire Airways Ltd) plane had seats to fly us to Nadi airport in Fiji.

We were very excited as it was our first aeroplane flight.

It was early in the morning and on arrival at Nadi, we found the weather was extremely hot; and we all wondered what the Fiji weather would be like all the year round.

As we got off the plane, we walked to the customs area; and saw a big and tall native policeman dressed in his blue shirt and white sulu. He had bushy fluffy hair, standing like a statue near the entrance. After going through customs, we were led to a waiting vehicle, which had wooden seats enough for 15 passengers. The driver drove us through the coral coast from Nadi airport to Suva, the capital of Fiji. The journey took several hours.

About 7 o'clock in the morning, we arrived at the Kwong Tiy & Co Ltd store in Suva.

I met my father for the first time, and as I was told by my mother to greet him as Look Sook, meaning 6th uncle, so I addressed him just that. Mum told me it was our custom to do so.

Our guardian and the 12 of us boys took our seats at a round table for breakfast. The resident cook served a minced beef tomato soup which I really enjoyed, as it was the first time, I had this type of soup. The MSG in it probably made it tasty. There were rice and other dishes which were tasty. No doubt we were all very hungry as we hadn't eaten since dinner on board the plane earlier.

Soon after breakfast, 4 of the younger boys were taken to meet the manager Mr Yee Hoy Shang. He asked each boy to write down his name on a piece of paper he had given. From the writing, he could tell who was smart, and better educated.

From there the 4 of us were taken to a house in Des Voeux Road. It was a big house with the sitting or common room in the centre, separated by amenities on both sides. I forgot whom we met there, but I vividly remembered a little boy riding a little toy car around the room. We stayed on for some time. A good lunch was provided for us although I couldn't remember what type of dishes they were.

From then on, we boys went our separate ways, and had no contact with one another for some time. The youngest of them, Woi Ping Yee who was two years younger than me, later became my in-law, as his son Sen Yee married my eldest daughter Geralyne.

I was taken to the Fong Quan Store in Flagstaff, where I was to stay till late December 1950. Uncle Fong Quan operated a general store and a sweets factory.

I wouldn't know what arrangements my father had made with Uncle Fong Quan in regard to my boarding there. While I was there, I lived with some employees in a large room, ate with them at a round table. Food was very good.

On Saturdays and Sundays, I helped by serving in the store.

I just couldn't remember where we took wash and shower, but I do remember the toilet facilities. A drum for wastes was provided in a closet, and the council waste management truck (topasi) came around once a week to clear the waste.

From late December 1950, and as arranged by my father, I went to board at Uncle Fong Hoy Sing's store premises in Samabula 3 miles.

CHAPTER 33
St Columba's primary school

The Marist Brothers' Primary School was established in 1888, at the request of Bishop Julian Vidal, initially to provide education for the children of European settlers. Very quickly, the brothers saw that the need for education was much wider than just this. At that time, there was no provision at all for the children of the indentured Indian settlers, and in 1897 a school for Indians was opened, though children of all races attended, so that it soon became designated as Marist Brothers' Cosmopolitan School. In 1913, the Felix College was opened, catering for Europeans and Part Europeans. In 1936 St Columba's Claudius Memorial School was opened. These two schools continued to run as separate institutions until 1963 when they were combined and named the Marist Brothers' Primary School. However, the school has always been more popularly known as "Marist Suva Street".

I boarded at Fong Quan's from October till late December 1950.

Albert Fong who was in class 7, took me to see Br McCormack, the head teacher of St Columba's Primary School. Without hesitation Br admitted me to the school. I was 12 years old then in late September 1950, and I was placed in class 1.

I went into class 1 and started to learn the alphabets a to z, simple arithmetic, and reading the premier book 1. I could speak only three English words namely "Solly (sorry)", picked up from a village basketball match, "My son", and two foul words I learned on the boat from Hong Kong to Sydney. I wasn't able to spell them though.

After a few days going to school, Uncle Fong Yuen asked me how I was getting on with pronunciations of words. I told him I found difficulties in counting wun dui flee (one two three), "lun (run)", the alphabets double yu (w), and z (yet). He told me I must first of all learn how to use the "R", because it would help with pronunciations.

With Uncle's advice and encouragement, I tried to learn the working of "R"s. During a lesson in class the next day I put a book in front of me, so as to block my face, and tried to pronounce te te te, telu, telu, and eventually tulu, tulu and finally ru, ru, ru, AHRU and succeeded.

Then trouble fell upon me. My teacher called upon little Jackson Mar, who might be 6/7 years old, a Chinese boy who could speak Zhongshan (Chungshan) dialect, to be my interpreter. Jackson said to the teacher "Checher, Ian was trying to learn how to pronounce the R alphabet". As a result, the teacher didn't punish me, but warned me not repeat the same offence. I could remember another boy called Narsley Lau, a quiet boy, in the same class. He was David King's younger brother.

At the end of the term I received my school report which indicated that I came 48th in the class out of 48 pupils.

Class 2 at St Columba's

I was boarding at Uncle Fong Hoy Sing's place in Samabula 3 Miles, from late December 1950 to late December 1951. He was operating a shop in the compound of Joong Hing Loong Co. Ltd. He lived in a room at the back of the shop. His son Albert and I shared a room nearby.

An old Chinese man in his sixties was manufacturing dried sausages in a wooden house in the compound. He wholesaled his products to Chinese grocery stores in Suva Town, the capital of Fiji.

Another Chinese man in his thirties, was employed by Joong Hing Loong. He cooked beef stew for the company's stevedoring labourers in the wharf.

A Fijian caretaker and his son also lived in the compound.

Albert and I caught the school bus to school every day. He always taught me how to pronounce words and spell them correctly. We had a friendly relationship. Then one day we had an argument and ended in a fight. As he was 18 and much bigger than me, he soon put me down and sat on top of me. He asked: "Have you had enough?" I replied, "Enough". We both stood up and laughed it off.

Trouble came one day before the first school term commenced. The caretaker's son came peeping into the bathroom where I was having a shower. He was just being cheeky and wanted to find out whether I was "boci", a Fijian word for non-circumcision. I swore at him in Fijian and said I would kill him. In the village in China when someone said "I will kill you", people would scatter and run away. Immediately, after drying myself, I took a wooden shoe and went after him. Just before I lifted the shoe to strike him, he punched my face which resulted a black eye. I gave up. He was 18 and almost a head taller than me. His father scolded him for being a bully.

The incident was reported to my father, so he came the next day. While pulling his wide belt out he demanded an explanation about the fight. I told him the truth and he put back his belt slowly. Next day, he came with a boiled egg to roll over my black eye spot, hoping to reduce the swelling. Such a caring dad.

At the end of the third term, Uncle Hoy Sing and Albert were migrating to Australia. He told my father to look for a place for me to stay. In no time my father found me a place in War Hing laundry in Amy Street, Toorak, Suva, where I stayed until the end of 1954. The laundry owner was Uncle Wong Chun, a Szeyup Xinhui man, a friend of my father, who became my guardian for the next three years.

My school report for the 1951 third term showed that I came 15th out of 48 in class 2.

Class 4 at St Columba's

I stayed the whole year 1952 at the War Hing laundry, Amy Street, Toorak, Suva. The proprietor Uncle Wong Chun, a Szeyup Xinhui man, was my father's friend. He gave me free board, a canvas bed in a room shared by two other employees. In return,

I helped with cooking and washing dishes. He gave me pocket money for ironing the Fijian soldiers' hard khaki shirts and short trousers. Every Saturday either morning or afternoon, Uncle Wong urged me to go to the movies. If it was in the morning I would go to the Regal theatre, asked the cashier for an upstairs ticket, but I was always given a downstairs ticket. If it was in the afternoon I would go to the popular Lilac theatre. I asked the cashier for either an upstairs ticket or downstairs ticket, no problems. The popular Lilac theatre was owned by the Grants family, a good Catholic family.

For passing time I often read Chinese language kung fu stories. While I was reading one by the laundry's side door stairs sitting down, a young Chinese boy approached me and asked me what I was reading. I told him it was a kung fu story book. He said to me that his father taught him quite a few kung fu movements. He also said he could read some traditional Chinese words which he learned at the Fiji Chinese Primary School. He later came to class 7b at St Columba's. We struck up a friendship ever since. Ken Seeto was my first friend in Fiji. Sometime later he introduced me to Ken Janson, my second friend in Fiji, and we are still in regular contact. On another occasion Ken Seeto introduced me to Lionel Low, my third friend in Fiji.

Ken Janson's father owned the popular Chung King cafe opposite the Burns Philip store downtown. When a warship came to port I helped out as a waiter in the cafe.

I was 14 years of age in class 4 and missing a good year in class 3. It was necessary for me to jump a class as my age was two years older than my contemporaries. Everyday after school during the year I had private coaching, in order to catch up with my lessons.

In school every afternoon the pupils were given a choice to learn Fijian or Hindi as a vernacular subject for an hour. I chose Hindi. It wasn't hard to learn the 52 alphabets a ma da da etc, but I soon lost interest, and opted to study on my own in the classroom.

An annual school raffle was held, and I won the prize, a box of chocolates. After the presentation, the box was handed around for quite a while before it reached my hands. When I opened it, the chocolates had been broken into pieces and also melted. It was the first time I had won a prize.

There were a few over age pupils in class 3, 5 and 6. One pupil, whose age was 21, made a request to the headteacher Br Columba, to let him in for another year in order to learn more English. Br said to him: "No, you are old enough to be married". In fact, he was already married, leaving his wife behind in China. All the old age pupils left school by the end of the year.

Before the end of the third term, the school report showed that I came 2nd in the class out of 48 pupils.

Class 7 at St Columba's

For the whole year 1953 I stayed at the War Hing laundry.

There were many activities during that year and my English had improved. I missed the 3 vital classes: 3, 5 and 6. I was 15 and had to jump classes from 4 to 7. I could cope with the class lessons reasonably well. The class teacher Brother Sebastian was a great teacher and very strict.

Brother Sebastian often made contact with the class 7 teacher of Suva Boys' Grammar School for softball games. Their team, comprised of all white boys, who won every game against our team. They brought their gear enough for both teams since we didn't have any in our school. Our school couldn't afford these expensive items, and the softball game was not our sport.

On one Saturday afternoon, Brother Sebastian and a group of 6 class 7 boys including me, went to cut grass and cleaned up at the Home of Compassion in Tamavua, Suva.

On another Saturday, Brother Sebastian and a group of the class 7 boys including me, went to climb Mount Korobaba in Lami. Located just ten minutes outside of Suva, it offers fantastic views across Suva Harbour. It is easy to get to and impossible to miss. Some like to describe as the smaller brother of the famous Pao de Suca (Sugarloaf) peak in Rio de Janeiro, Brazil. The time the walk takes to complete will depend on the size of the group that you are hiking with and how long you take for breaks, but some can complete it in less than one hour… or so they say. No matter how long you take and how many scenic (or catch your breath) stops you take, the payoff will certainly be worth it. You will see Suva from 400+ metres above sea level. Also, the islands of Beqa, Yanuca and Kadavu.

For religious lessons I went to Brother Herbert's class. Old Brother Herbert was born in Levuka.

I was baptised as a Catholic on 14 June 1953 by Father McDiarmed, and received holy communion on the next day 15 June. My Godfather was Bertie Mar.

I was confirmed sometime in September 1953. My Godfather was Francis Chong.

The 1953 earthquake occurred on 14 September at 00:26 UTC near Suva, Fiji, just off the southeast shore of Viti Levu. This earthquake had a magnitude of Ms 6.8. The earthquake triggered a coral reef platform collapse and a submarine landslide that caused a tsunami. Fish splattered outside Desai Bookshop in Victoria Road, Suva. Land was later reclaimed.

I was in the class 7 room when all a sudden the desks and the building started rocking. I asked our teacher, Brother Sebastian what had happened. As he was from New Zealand, he had good knowledge of earthquakes. He said it was an earthquake and told us to run outside. All the rest of the classes and their teachers also ran out, except old Brother Herbert and his class 6 remained in their room upstairs. Brother Herbert was very old, and he couldn't run, so he ordered his class to stay back in the classroom. The quake stopped after some seconds. Boy what a fright we had. We had never experienced such a shock before.

For some Saturday afternoons, Brother Bertrand coached Ken Seeto and me, by using the book "First aid in English" which consisted mainly of grammar. Brother was keen to learn some Cantonese phrases, so I coached him in return.

My friend, Ken Janson was made a prefect of the school. I was very proud of him since he was the first and only Chinese who became a school prefect.

I spent a lot of time with Ken Seeto. We often hung around outside Lionel Yee's uncles' shop while he was studying inside. Ken and I used to think he was a crammer. He was very good at mathematics, but he also came first even in English. We were convinced he was really clever.

Most Sunday mornings during the year I went to the Chung King cafe and helped Ken Janson to butter the bread, set the tables and chairs, before the waitresses came on duty. Soon after, Ken and I put on our boxing gloves and belted it out in the dining room. I was heavier than him and tried to give him a beating, but he was more scientific in his moves, so he got away from my strikes. Afterwards, I had lunch and went home.

There was a classmate called Shankar Singh who said he was the nephew of Tiger Singh, the wrestling champion of Fiji. My gang including Ken Seeto and Victor Harrison, arranged for me to have a wrestling match with Shankar on the path near the upstairs in the flat where Ken Seeto lived. Shankar and I were almost the same height but he was fatter. No more than 10 seconds after the beginning of the wrestle I had a break and threw him down near the stairs. He was lucky because he didn't fall down the stairs. Thank God.

On another occasion, Victor Harrison and the gang arranged a heavyweight boxing contest between big Bola and me. It was held at Marks Park. I was stupid to accept the contest because Bola was so much taller and bigger than me. As soon as we started moving towards each other, Bola with his long reach, punched my neck so hard that made me give up. End of the contest.

The school athletic competitions were held in Albert Park. Although the event was termed athletics, it was just one race, and that was the 100 yards sprint. Everyone present thought big Eliza would win since he was a known fast runner. In the end I won comfortably and became the champion runner for 1953.

When the school report came to hand, I came 25th out of about 35 boys in the class.

I attended St Columba's for 3 years and 2 and half months, and missed important lessons of classes 5, 6 and 8. I had to jump classes because of age.

If I didn't jump classes I would be completing primary school at the age of 18, and high school at the age of 22.

According to record, Ratu Mara was 22 years of age after he left Sacred Heart College, Auckland, before he went to study medicine at the University of Otago, New Zealand. I am an old boy of Sacred Heart, represented the college in athletics and rugby union. Ratu Mara still holds the college high jump record of five foot eight inches (5'8"), but he couldn't represent the college in the Auckland Inter-secondary School competition as he was over 19 years of age.

Goodbye St Columba's. I was going to Marist Brothers' High School the following year.

St Columba's Primary School's champion athlete Ian Fong, 1953.
I was 15 years old.

St Columba Primary School's Assembly, 1953.
Brother Sebastian standing behind Class 7A.

J.M.J.C.
Box 86, Suva.
Phone: 22137

Marist Brothers' Primary School,
Suva Street,
Suva.
8th May, 1974.

R. No. 1392 IAN DAVID FONG DATE OF BIRTH 11 - 11 - 38.

1950 - CLASS 1. C. PRASAD. (CLS. TEACHER).

ENGLISH:-

Recitation	-	0	
Reading	-	30	TOTAL MARKS.
Spelling	-	0	
Formal	-	0	
ARITHMETIC:-			361.
Mental	-	40	
Written	-	100	
GENERAL SUBJECTS:-			
Hygiene	-	30	POSITION IN CLASS.
Nature Study	-	30	
Handwriting	-	38	
Handwork	-	35	48th.
Drawing	-	38	
Moral Inst.	-	20	

1951 - CLASS 2. SHRI RAM. (CLS. TEACHER).

ENGLISH:-

Recitation	-	29	
Reading	-	60	
Spelling	-	50	TOTAL MARKS.
Formal	-	59	
ARITHMETIC:-			650.
Mental	-	50	
Written	-	100	
GENERAL SUBJECTS:-			
Geography	-	30	
History	-	25	
Hygiene	-	29	POSITION IN CLASS.
Nature Study	-	25	
Handwriting	-	59	13th.
Handwork	-	59	
Drawing	-	25	
Moral Inst.	-	50	

..........2.

My school report for class 1. I came 48th out of 48 students.
My school report for class 2. I came 13th out of 40+ students.
LOL just noticed that the date of birth they had on record was 11 November 1938. Wonder where they got that. My Chinese birthday usually falls on a day in July (Western calendar) each year. The date in my passport is 6 November 1938.

J.M.J.C.
Box 86, Suva.
Phone: 22137

Marist Brothers' Primary School,
Suva Street,
Suva.

1952 - CLASS 4. ALFRED DAYA PRASAD. (CLS. TEACHER).

ENGLISH:-	
Recitation	40
Reading	66
Comprehension	32
Spelling	50
Formal	80
ARITHMETIC:-	
Mental	45
Written	95
GENERAL SUBJECTS:-	
History	75
Hygiene	35
Nature Study	41
Handwork	75
Drawing	39

TOTAL MARKS. 675.

POSITION IN CLASS. 2nd.

1953 - CLASS 7. BROTHER SEBASTIAN. (CLS. TEACHER).

ENGLISH:-	
Recitation	28
Reading	65
Comprehension	32
Spelling	41
Formal	71
Composition	80
ARITHMETIC:-	
Mental	32
Written	50
GENERAL SUBJECTS:-	
History	32
Hygiene	-
Geography	34
Nature Study	31
Handwork	F.
Drawing	26
Handwriting	36

TOTAL MARKS. 596.

POSITION IN CLASS. 25th.

The above marks are a true copy of our records concerning the examination results of Ian David Fong.

B. Owen
Headmaster.

My school report for class 4. I came 2nd out of 40+ students.

My school report for class 7. I came 25th out of 40+ students.

CHAPTER 34

Suva earthquake and stay at my Uncle Wong Chun's laundry

The 1953 Suva earthquake occurred on 14 September at 00:26 UTC near Suva, Fiji, just off the southeast shore of Viti Levu. This earthquake had a magnitude of Ms 6.8. The earthquake triggered a coral reef platform collapse and a submarine landslide that caused a tsunami. Fish splattered outside Desai Bookshop in Victoria Road, Suva. Land was reclaimed later.

I was boarding for 3 years with my father's friend Mr Wong Chun of War Hing Laundry, Amy Street, Toorak, Suva. Free board, free pocket money and guidance. Uncle Wong was a wise and generous man.

My repayment to him was to iron Fijian soldiers' thick khaki shirts and short trousers, helped in cooking dinners, washing dishes etc.

My father was living with his bachelor workmates on free board/accommodation provided by his employer Kwong Tiy Co. Ltd.

Mr Yee Kam Chee the managing director of Kwong Tiy from his house at the top of St Fort Street, was really scared for his life, spent that whole night playing mahjong in the laundry, Amy Street, Suva.

Uncle Wong got hold of a cat and with expensive herbs cooked a pot of soup, supposed to provide energy. I had a small bowl of soup and after a bite on a piece of cat meat I stopped. The soup was okay, but the meat was tasteless.

The room shared by 3 of us was used by the mahjong players so Uncle Wong let me sleep in his room. I slept on the floor. I didn't want to interfere with his comfortable bed that was positioned on the same space used by one of his previous partners (deceased). Believe it or not every Ching Ming period for a week his bed rocked at night. Uncle Wong wasn't scared and continued placing his bed in the same space.

Sometime late that night while awake I felt I was being raised slowly. So, scared I tried to shout for help, but my mouth could not make any noise. Afterwards, I felt my body was lowered slowly. I then fell asleep.

Next morning, I related the incident to Uncle Wong. Then came this tale. He said his worker who was of unsound mind, slept on the ironing table, had a knife beside him, and he would chase a ghost around the laundry some nights.

Hard to believe this one.

CHAPTER 35
My time at the Marist Brothers' High School

1912, Brothers Augustine, Alphonsus and Loyola began secondary classes in St Felix College, also on the Suva Street property. In 1936, after a considerable struggle with the civil authorities, who opposed secondary education for locally born children, the Brothers could reopen their secondary classes to all races. Thus, the Marist Brothers' High School had its beginnings in Suva Street. The High School was built at Bau Street during 1948, ready to begin the year there in 1949.

Notable Alumni:

- Ratu Sir Kamisese Mara, Former President and Prime Minister of Fiji
- Voreqe Frank Bainimarama, Present Prime Minister of Fiji

Due to lack of space there are also many outstanding old boys who cannot be named here. Go to google for more details.

After 3 years and 2 months in St Columba's, and skipping classes 3, 5, 6 and 8, I passed the secondary school entrance exam by only 1 mark. Being a Catholic, I was lucky to be admitted to the MBHS starting form 3. The principal Br Cassian asked to see my father, and in the interview, Br wanted to know if my father could support me through to form 6. He said several boys had passed the entrance exam with higher marks, and he didn't want the place given to me to be wasted. My father assured Br Cassian that he could do it.

During form 3 in 1954, I stayed at my guardian Uncle Wong Chun's laundry, Amy Street, Suva. As usual I was given free board, and in return I helped in the cooking, washing of dishes and ironing soldiers' thick khaki shirts and short trousers. I was given pocket money regularly.

I couldn't remember exactly what I had done in 1954. Because I wasn't up to scratch in English. I struggled with the new subjects, Mathematics and Chemistry. I had no problems with French and Latin as they were memory subjects.

I had lost all the school reports for the 1954 year. My position in class could be not far from the bottom list.

1955, I reckoned was the best year of my life as the principal Br Cassian, took me in to live in the school as a house boy. I wanted to improve my English and requested him to give me that chance. In those days the school dormitory had not been built for boarders. There was a room with 4 canvas beds for the 4 house boys (meant for students from the Fiji outer islands and other Pacific islands).

I was given free board, free school fees and ten shillings pocket money for a week.

My daily duties Monday to Friday were to sweep the front stairs in the mornings and clean the toilets in the afternoons.

During the second term school holidays, we house boys painted the school's external walls in the back. Our pay of 10 shillings for the week still stood.

On Sundays when the cook had his day off, we house boys took turns in preparing breakfast, lunch and dinner. Roast mutton leg was for dinner every Sunday.

We house boys played a lot of table tennis on Sunday afternoons. Occasionally on some fine Sunday afternoons, Henry Manueli and I teamed up against young Br Placid and the school gardener's son, for a game of rugby, played on a make-shift area. We had fun tackling Br Placid, but his partner the bigger Fijian boy was a mighty threat.

We could go to the movies every Friday night. On one Friday night, when we came back from the movies, and on reaching the school ground, we (Francis Hong Tiy, Henry

Manueli and I) heard loud Indian music coming from an empty plot opposite Fong Quan's in Flagstaff. We became curious and went over to join the crowd.

An Indian wedding was taking place. We overstayed, and when we came back to our room, Br More was sitting on my bed, waiting for us. He didn't say a word and left us.

We presumed he didn't report our late return to the principal Br Cassian, because Br Cassian didn't send for us to be disciplined.

The Inter Secondary School Athletics Championship was staged in Lautoka. I represented the school in the Intermediate sprints in both the 100 yards and 220 yards, but I didn't get anywhere. Competitors from Queen Victoria School (QVS) and Ratu Kadavulevu School (RKS) were far too strong. For the meeting we travelled by bus to Ba and stayed overnight at the Xavier College. Desktops were given to us to sleep on, but the majority slept on the floor. The following morning, we travelled to Lautoka for the competitions.

In the evening, senior students from St Thomas Secondary School and some working girls put on a social dance for us.

I was in the 1st fifteen rugby squad but due to my underweight problem I had to withdraw from the team. Br Placid warned me that the big and tough QVS boys would give me a hiding if I played against them.

As for schoolwork I seemed to have settled down, but I doubted I had done well. At the end of the 1955 school term I had been given my school reports, but I had misplaced them. My position in class might not be far from the bottom list.

I passed the Fiji Junior School certificate with a second-grade pass.

In 1956 I started school at the Sacred Heart College, Auckland, New Zealand.

Old boys from our Catholic Amateur Athletic Club.
From left John Seeto, Frank Bainimarama (eighth Prime Minister of Fiji who was first elected into office in 2007), Ian Fong.

CHAPTER 36

Catholic Amateur Athletic Club (CAAC)

Words came to St Columba's Primary School that the club was seeking good athletes.

As I had just won the 100 yards race at St Columba's, I decided to enter the 100 yards competition for juniors, which was held at the Marist Brothers' High School ground. I won the race, but I didn't know what time was clocked, it might be 12 seconds or less. As for the prize I was given a Parker fountain pen.

On the same afternoon, a young Chinese man in his mid-twenties, about 5'5" in height, came with a pair of expensive running shoes. He claimed that he was the champion sprinter at the University of Hong Kong.

The fastest runner at that time was Charles Lew Gor who clocked 11 seconds for that race of 100 yards, and this former champion of the University of Hong Kong was ten yards behind the finishing line. We didn't see him again.

When I was in Form 3, I didn't do any running but concentrated on studying the new subjects. During the following year in form 4, I took part in the 100 and 200 yard races, and as an Intermediate athlete, represented the school and CAAC in both these races.

As for an annual event of competitions with Queen Victoria School (QVS) and St John's College (Cawaci), the club athletes and officials, Br More (Coach), Bill Ragg (President) and Vincent Chong Hop (Treasurer), travelled to QVS and Cawaci.

The tour party travelled by bus to QVS and stayed for the night. Some boarders gave up their beds for us guests. That was the first time I slept on a spring mattress bed and it was a big difference compared to the canvas beds I had in Fiji before I got married. The next day breakfast served to us were fresh bread, block cheese, jam and tea. The school had a dairy farm which produced cheese, a bakery for bread, and milk from the cows.

The competitions were staged in the afternoon. I have forgotten what the results were. QVS was always a strong competitor.

After the competitions with QVS we moved on and travelled by boat to Cawaci. For the night we were provided with desks in a classroom to sleep on. Dominico Valebulu and I found it hard to sleep on the desks, so we used the floor instead. I can't remember what breakfast was served to us.

In the afternoon, the competitions were held. I had no recollection of the results. Usually we won over Cawaci as they didn't have the number of athletes as compared to QVS.

Finally, the CAAC had a great number of members, who provided fierce competitions to the other clubs in Suva.

Queen Victoria School (QVS) is a school in Fiji. It was established in 1906 in Nasinu to provide education to the sons of Fijian Chiefs. It later moved to Nanukuloa in Ra when World War II broke out, then the school was moved to Lodoni where the two schools QVS and RKS operated side by side, before eventually moving to its current site at Matavatucou, Tailevu. It then accepted students from Fijian villages based on their results in a secondary entrance examination.

The school is run as an academic college, but there is an adjoining farm which provides food to the school and serves as a training ground. Students are taught basic skills like crop and livestock husbandry, and there is a small dairy unit. These sessions usually last for about three hours and take place on Saturday morning. There is a farm manager and some permanent labourers who live on the compound.

The school is equipped with a library, chemistry and biology laboratories, computer lab and playing fields. This school takes part in cadet training and march for the pass out parade. In Fiji, it is well known for high discipline.

St John's College is one of Fiji's oldest Catholic mission schools, established at Nasarete (Nazareth) a small hill within the Cawaci Catholic Mission land in 1894. The school catered first for native Fijians of chiefly rank. This class-based enrolment was later abolished. The Marist Brothers were responsible for teaching the boys. Brothers Maurice, Vincent and Cloman were the first teachers. The school opened with 12 students and by 1906 there were 80 boys from all parts of Fiji. By 1929, there were 100 pupils and in 1938 there were 300. In 1937, the boys aged 6 to 16, were required to pay £1 on entry to pay for their sulu, soap, textbook and exercise books. They were taught in Fijian and then in English.

Cawaci is a piece of land which the Fiji Catholic Mission bought from a European settler and cattle grazer, Thomas Perry King Wilson in 1890. On 26 April 1890, the lands of Cawaci and Cicia were formally transferred to the trustees of the Catholic Mission by the Registrar of the Supreme Court of Fiji, Mr John Langford, in Suva. The trustees of the Catholic Mission were Fr. Jean Baptiste Bréhéret; Fr. Joseph Laberre, and Fr. Ephrem Marie Bertreux. They were all Marist priests and Fr. Bréhéret was in charge.

On 22 May 1890, Mr Wilson, a grazer, planter, stockholder and former property owner of Cawaci and Cicia sold his cattle to the mission. This included 4 branded Toro bulls, some cows and twenty pigs. He also entered into an agreement to lease the property and to pay a yearly rental.

There is not much information as to when Mr. Wilson left Cawaci or where he went to after that. The Catholic mission in Cawaci was firmly established by 1893 when the Catechist School was established having moved from Loreto. In the early 1990's the Fiji Archdiocese sold a small portion of the land in Cicia to the Government who needed to relocate their Public Works Department (PWD) section in Levuka as its present site was congested. The land in Cawaci belongs to the Archdiocese.

Today St John's College is co-educational boarding school catering also for non-Catholic students.

Suva Centre Junior Champions 1954, Catholic Amateur Athletic Club.
I'm wearing a dark singlet and white shorts, standing on the furthest right of the photo.

Some Catholic Amateur Athletic Club members at St Johns School ground, 1955.
I'm standing on the furthest right.

Some Catholic Amateur Athletic Club members and some
QVS prefects in the QVS compound, 1955.
I'm standing near the middle.

CHAPTER 37
A thousand lines on…

I must not disturb David Fong while he is cleaning the toilets.

This punishment was dished out by Brother Cassian to Vincent Peter (Tovata) in 1955. 1955 I reckoned was the best year of my life as the principal Brother Cassian, took me in to live in the school as a house boy. I wanted to improve my English and requested him to give me that chance. In those days, the school dormitory had not been built for boarders. There was a room with 4 canvas beds for the 4 house boys (meant for students from the Fiji outer islands and other Pacific islands).

I was given free board, free school fees and ten shillings pocket money for a week. My daily duties Monday to Friday were to sweep the front stairs in the mornings and clean the toilets in the afternoons.

Vincent was a clever Fijian student but very proud and boastful, who would argue and argue about anything with anyone.

One afternoon after school while I was cleaning the toilets, Vincent came into the toilets and started flushing them one by one.

I confronted him and he was about to strike me, but before he could do anything I struck his face with the brush full of disinfectant, and I ran as fast as I could with him chasing from behind till I reached Brother Cassian and lodged the complaint.

Brother Cassian ordered him to write a thousand lines on "I must not disturb David Fong while he is cleaning the toilets".

Vincent revenged during a 1st fifteen rugby squad practice under Coach Brother More. I happened to be his partner practicing tackles, so when the turn came for him to tackle me, he torpedoed my back with his head.

In later life we met occasionally and became friendly to each other.

After leaving Marist Vincent went to study at the Corpus Christi Teachers' College and was a classmate of Frances Wong. After the second year he left to marry Father Raselala's sister Sereana. She passed away leaving behind 4 very young children. He then married Sereana's younger sister Anna, and together they had 2 children. Vincent had worked for W. R. Carpenter (Fiji) Ltd and the Government's Audit Dept for co-operative stores.

CHAPTER 38
My three years in New Zealand, 1956 to 1958

My friend Hampton Mar's father Mr Mar Chin Leung, was very happy to know that his son was admitted to study at the Sacred Heart College, Auckland. He accompanied Hampton and me to Nadi, and he took us to visit his old friend Mr Wong, a storekeeper. We also visited his nephew Gordon Mar, who was operating a poultry farm. We stayed for a night at my village friend, Horley Fong's place.

The next morning, Mr Mar farewelled us at the Nadi Airport, and Hampton and I were on our way to Whenuapai airport, North West of Auckland, by a TEAL plane.

From the airport a bus took us to the Auckland City office of TEAL, where my cousin Bill Fong and his mother's worker Sue Hing, were waiting. It was so nice to meet my cousin for the first time. From there, the four of us sat on the front seat of an open truck and travelled to Panmure where my Aunty Fong Low Shee and her family lived.

On arrival, I introduced Hampton to Aunty and her two daughters Jean and Nancy, and they greeted Hampton and me cordially. I told Aunty that Hampton would stay for the night with us, and on the following day he would look for his friends for accommodation.

I was shown to a bedroom which was vacated by my eldest cousin Lois, who had just got married. A double bed was also in the bedroom. Hampton and I shared the same bed for the night.

The next day, Sue Hing took Hampton and me to 8 Sussex Street, Grey Lynn, where we met Bentley Lee-Joe and John Rounds, Auckland Uni students from Fiji. Hampton found accommodation there until school commenced.

I lived with my Aunty and family until the beginning of the third school term in 1957. She and my older cousins Jean and Nancy, and younger cousin Bill, treated me very well, just like one of them. Whenever Aunty and family were invited to parties, I was always included.

During the school holidays I worked at two places. First one was at the Everest Bedding Factory in Onehunga, where I used the rolling machine, rolling edges of cheap mattresses, making spring mattresses, and blowing kapok into pillowcases. The last one was full of dust. The pay was 12 pounds a week. The second job was at Mrs Chong's market garden in Mangere, where I was given free accommodation and a pay of 12 pounds a week.

When the Von Trapp Family singers visited New Zealand, and performed at the Auckland Town Hall, I was there to witness their marvelous voices.

When the famous Harlem Globetrotters Basketball Teams came to Auckland, I made a point of attending their demonstrations, which were held at Western Springs. Two teams were brought over to play each other, and the displays were terrific.

Sue Hing, Billy and I were active members of the Auckland Chinese Youth Club. We often went to the social dances organised by the youth club.

Every Saturday night, Sue Hing who was provided accommodation, drove Billy and me to the city to see a movie at the Civic Theatre.

During some Sunday mornings in winter, the three of us went to swim in the heated Tepid Baths in the city.

Every Sunday afternoon, the three of us would go to Sue Hing's parents' house in Onehunga, where he unloaded his laundry for his stepmother to wash and picked up the washed and ironed clothes.

Every Sunday afternoon during summer, the three of us ended up playing basketball at the Victoria Park in the city.

Aunty was very generous for giving me free accommodation. In return, I helped to serve in the shop after school and Saturday mornings.

For the third term in 1957, I boarded at the Sacred Heart College.

For the year 1958, I managed to find a part-time job at the Wing Jang Fruit and Vegetables Supermarket and Ship stores, opposite the post office in the city. The company offered me free accommodation and wages, which were sufficient for my incidental spending except for school fees which were supplied by my father. I worked after school Monday to Friday and Saturday mornings.

In 1959 I was supposed to study Accountancy at the Seddon Memorial Technical College, but my father was beginning to suffer more health problems, so he told me to return to Fiji, and look for a job.

The Seddon Memorial Technical College is now the Auckland University of Technology.

With Aunty Fong Low Shee and Cousin Bill Fong, Auckland, 1956.

With cousins Jean, Nancy and Bill Fong, Auckland, 1956.

With friends in Auckland.
Sitting from left Gordon Fong, Jun Sue.
Standing from left Ian Fong, Alan Young.

Taken at a wedding, 1956.
Lily Chong and me. She was 16 and I was 18.
During the 2 weeks school holidays I worked for her mother who owned a vegetable garden and lived in their house. She and I became friendly and we would yarn till 2.30 am on some nights in the sitting room without disturbing anybody, as bedrooms were away from the sitting room.

Taken at a wedding. The bride was only 16.

Part of the Auckland Chinese Cantonese Opera Troupe helpers during Easter in Wellington. The amateur troupe was on a charity performance in Wellington.

Chinese Presbyterian Church Youth Club members at a picnic, Auckland, 1956.
All the youths were aged between 16 to 18, except 2 who were over 20.
Unusual, as no romances blossomed among them.

Catholic Pioneer (Non-Alcoholic) club picnic at a venue in Auckland.
On the left front of me was my friend Helen Gilbert of Mangere. Met her again at the 1957 annual debate St Mary's College Ponsonby/Sacred Heart College Glen Innes. Helen was a great debater. And of course, every year the judge awarded St Mary's the winner. There was some fun. After the debate those boys and girls who were good at piano and other musical instruments assembled and started playing fast jiving music, but when the nuns left the band changed to slow music. (You can guess what happened next. Hehehehe.)

CHAPTER 39
The double tenth sports tournament in Auckland

The National Day of the Republic of China, also referred to as Double Ten Day or Double Tenth Day, is the national day of the Republic of China (ROC). It commemorates the start of the Wuchang Uprising of 10 October 1911 (10-10 or double ten), which led to the end of the Qing Dynasty in China and establishment of the Chinese Republic on 1 January 1912.

During the course of the Chinese Civil War, the government of the Republic of China lost control of mainland China, fleeing to the Island of Taiwan in December 1949. The National Day is now mainly celebrated in ROC-controlled Taiwan but is also celebrated by some overseas Chinese.

The Auckland Chinese Youths Club played hosts to teams from Hamilton, Wellington, Christchurch and Dunedin, who took part in sports of Soccer, Indoor Basketball, Table tennis and Athletics (4 x 100 yards relay only).

The soccer team comprised of Fiji students Ian Fong, Ming Fong, Willie Fong, Gilbert Lee-Joe, Wilfred Lee-Joe, Yee Hing Sue, and together with some local youths, won the soccer competition.

The Athletic Relay Team of Fiji students Ian Fong, Ronald Fong Sang, Robert Mar, and local Bobby Wong, won the relay competition.

At the end of the sports meet, a social dance was put up for all the youths and friends.

The social occasion was memorable, and some romances blossomed. A notable result was Ronald Fong Sang who married a beautiful girl called Marina Wong from Wellington.

Marina was captain of the Wellington Chinese Youths Club Team's Indoor Basketball Team.

Auckland Chinese Youths Athletic Relay Team for 1956,
winner at Double Tenth Competition.
From left Ian Fong, Robert Mar, Ronald Fong Sang, Bobby Wong.

Some Chinese students from Fiji at a social dance in Auckland, October 1956.
On 10 October every year, Chinese youths from major cities in New Zealand meet for a sport gathering at a chosen venue, to celebrate the Double Tenth.
Standing from left Maureen Fong Sang, Tom Lee-Joe, Tesley Sohn, Wilfred Lee-Joe, Gilbert Lee-Joe, Conrad Honson, Willie Fong, Ian Fong.
Squatting from left Jimmy Lum, Yee Hung Sue, Ming Fong.
Conrad Honson and Jimmy Lum were not students.

CHAPTER 40
Sacred Heart College, Auckland, New Zealand

Sacred Heart College is a secondary school in Auckland, New Zealand. It is a Catholic, Marist College set on 60 acres of land overlooking the Tamaki Estuary in Glen Innes.

The college was opened in 1903 in Ponsonby, by the Marist Brothers. It is the oldest continuously existing Catholic boys' secondary school in Auckland although it has changed its location, moving to its current Glen Innes site in 1955. St Paul's College was founded on the old Sacred Heart College site in that year. The Marist Brothers continue to be a presence in the school community, with both teaching and maintenance of school grounds undertaken in part by the Brothers. The Headmaster role at the college was served solely by Marist Brothers up until 1993, when Brendan Schollum took the role, the college's first lay principal. In 2003, the college held its centennial celebrations, which included the opening of a new administration building, technology block and Year 7 and 8 Department, and in 2005 it celebrated 50 years of being at the Glen Innes site. At the end of 2006, Jim Dale became the third lay Headmaster at Sacred Heart College, taking over from Phillip Mahoney.

Sacred Heart offers a wide range of sporting options to its pupils, though it is traditionally a school with a very strong rugby culture. Sacred Heart won four titles in the 2006 season, with its 3A, 3B, 5A and 5B teams victorious. The Under-15 Open team won the North Island Catholic Boys Under 15 Tournament, held at Francis Douglas Memorial College in that year also. The Sacred Heart 1st XV remains the only team never to have been relegated from the 1A grade. The 2011 1st XV was one of the more successful teams in college history and went unbeaten in the 1A competition round robin and won the Moascar Cup, Fitzpatrick Kirckpatrick cup, Hibernian Shield and the Marist Quadrangular Cup. Other Sports include: Football, Cricket, Water Polo, Tennis, Cycling, Basketball, Hockey, Badminton, Rowing, Swimming and Athletics.

For 2007, a new Sports Institute has been opened for boys in years 7-10. Currently, the only sports on offer for this academy are Cricket, Football, Rugby union, Tennis and Water Polo, though this is likely to expand to include other sports in subsequent years.

I would like to mention here about Brother Theophane, as for many years he was a great teacher, master of discipline, and athletic coach of the college. Brother was born in Levuka, Ovalau, Fiji. After he left Sacred Heart College, he became the Brother Provincial for Fiji, Samoa and Tonga for two four-year terms. Before he retired, he taught at the Marist Brothers' High School, Suva, Fiji.

Notable alumni:

- Reginald John Cardinal Delargey (10 December 1914 – 29 January 1979) was the Roman Catholic Bishop of Auckland, and later Cardinal, Archbishop of Wellington and Metropolitan of New Zealand. His title was Cardinal-Priest of Immacolata al Tiburtino.
- Ratu Sir Kamisese Mara – former Prime Minister of Fiji and President of Fiji
- Sir Anand Satyanand – former Governor-General of New Zealand
- Sean Fitzpatrick – former rugby player, All Blacks captain
- Greg Davis – former Wallaby captain
- Gregory Victor Davis (1939 – 1979) was a New Zealand born, national representative rugby union player for Australia. He played at flanker and made seven international tours with Wallaby squads. He was the Australian national

captain in 47 matches from 1969 to 1972 and led the Wallaby side on three overseas tours.

- Nili Latu – former Tongan Rugby International and captain

Other old boys from Fiji:

- David Houng Lee, Maharaj, Suki Chand, Leo Sohn, Ming Fong, Willie Fong, Ian Fong, Hampton Mar, Robin Storck, Dominic Wong, Norman Chan.

From Auckland:

- John Wong Toi

From Western Samoa:

- Philip Muller, Julius Mathis, Pat Ah Koy

I have a special mention here of Willie Fong who was an outstanding student of the college. Willie Fong was a winger of the college's crack third grade A rugby team which won the championship for 1957. Normally the third grade A players will return the following year to play for the first fifteen. Halfway through the winter season, Willie fractured his leg in a game and was on clutches for 8 weeks. Willie was very good in mathematics. He solved a mathematics problem during class in Form 6 UE. He was the only Fiji student granted the UE certificate in the early years. Normally Fiji students, after Form 6 from the Marist Brothers' High School in Suva, were required to repeat Form 6 UE, and had to sit for the UE examination.

I am privileged to be an old boy of Sacred Heart College which is similar in many ways to St Joseph's College in Sydney. On leaving the college, the Director Brother Morris said in the reference he gave me, that I was of good average intelligence, took an active part in all the college's sporting activities.

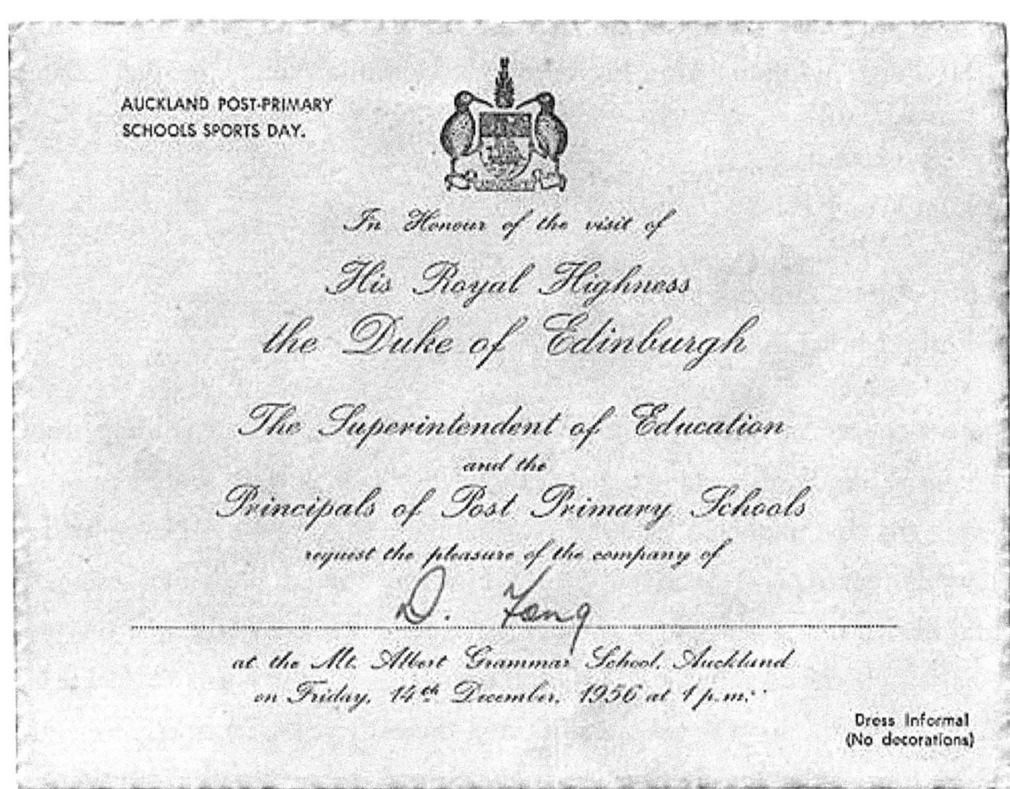

AUCKLAND POST-PRIMARY
SCHOOLS SPORTS DAY.

In Honour of the visit of

His Royal Highness
the Duke of Edinburgh

The Superintendent of Education
and the
Principals of Post Primary Schools
request the pleasure of the company of

D. Fong

at the Mt. Albert Grammar School, Auckland
on Friday, 14th December, 1956 at 1 p.m.

Dress Informal
(No decorations)

Invited as a sprinter (100 yards) to perform for His Royal Highness the Duke of Edinburgh when he visited Auckland, 14 December 1956. Phillipa Gould only 15 then from Diocesan Girls' High School, was in the swimming demonstration. Earlier in the year she swam in the Melbourne Olympics and won 3rd place in the 220 backstroke.

CHAPTER 41
Fights at the Sacred Heart College, Auckland, New Zealand

This morning, I spoke to Hampton Mar in Brisbane and obtained his okay to write about his fight at the college.

I too had a fight at the college. I was a day boy and Hampton Mar was a boarder. Most mornings the Fiji boarders and I would meet, and they would ask me what's happening in the outside world. They were Hampton Mar, David Houng Lee, Ming Fong, Willie Fong, Tesley Sohn, Suki Chand, Maharaj and lastly big Philip Muller.

After one year, Hampton left for St Bede's College in Christchurch.

One morning as soon as I arrived at school, I was told that Hampton fought a boy and lost the contest.

At a dinner in the dining room the previous night, Hampton was served by the head of his table, the smallest piece of steak. Hampton disputed with the head of the table, his surname Haybittle, why the smallest piece of steak was served to him. There was an argument so they decided in order to resolve the problem they would go for a physical fight at the handball court. All the Fiji gang for Hampton was present and so was a few supporters of the other guy. No referee was arranged. The fight started and Hampton tried a kung fu trick on his opponent's leg, hoping to down him. Instead the opponent pushed Hampton to the ground and sat on him. He asked Hampton: "Have you had enough". "Yes", was the reply. You know this guy was one and quarter times Hampton's size, and a head or more taller. End of the story.

Now it comes to my turn. At a school assembly, the Master of Discipline Brother Theophane (born in Levuka Fiji) was the speaker. Just before everyone assembled this cheeky brat standing behind me, and for no reason called me a chink. I tried a back kick on him, but he moved away. I wasn't satisfied and told him I would fix him up after the assembly. Straight after the assembly when Brother Theophane and most of the boys had left, I went straight after that rascal, no punches were given as both of us about the same size ended up in a wrestling match. This lasted for a few seconds and a prefect present, separated our fight. We were reported to the Master of Discipline, who in turn reported us to the Director (College Principal Brother Maurice). I was called to the Director's office and told him it was not my fault. Brother Director let me off. I didn't know what had happened to my opponent. His surname was McCleod, a boarder.

Notable alumni:

- Ratu Sir Kamisese Mara, former Prime Minister of Fiji. Former President of Fiji. He still holds the high jump record of 5'8". After MBHS Suva Fiji, spent a year at SHC before he went to study medicine at Otago University.
- Sir Anand Satyanand, former Governor General of New Zealand. Born in New Zealand and son of migrants from Fiji.

Some famous All Blacks:

- Keith Davies, Half Back
- Pat Walsh, Full Back
- Terry Lineen, Second Five Eight
- Xavier Rush, Wing
- Sean Fitzpatrick, Hooker and Captain who made a teasing remark in the year 2000 College Magazine about Guy Davies, a Marist Brother then, that he could hardly speak English. Guy was his teacher and could be speaking English in a Fiji Accent.

Other old boys:

- Ian David Fong, Athletics and Rugby. Ran in the Relay against Peter Snell in the Auckland Secondary School Athletic Championships in 1956. Peter once held world records for 880 yards and the mile. First Fifteen in 1957, played against Tony Davies (First Five Eight) of King's College, Waka Nathan (Break Away), Mack Herewini (Full back) of Otahuhu College. All three became famous All Blacks.

With classmate Hampton Mar at Sacred Heart College Auckland, 1956.
I was a day boy and Hampton was a boarder.
Most mornings, the Fiji boarders and I would meet, and they would ask me what's happening in the outside world.
They were Hampton Mar, David Houng Lee, Ming Fong, Willie Fong, Tesley Sohn, Suki Chand and Maharaj.
After one year, Hampton left for St Bede's College in Christchurch.

CHAPTER 42
Groomsman to Sunny Chiu Sun Fong

For my first summer school holidays in 1956, I was helping out my village friend Sunny Fong who owned a market garden in Pukekohe, a town in the Auckland Region of the North Island of New Zealand. Located at the southern edge of the Auckland Region, it is in South Auckland, between the southern shore of the Manukau Harbour and the mouth of the Waikato River.

Pukekohe is a rural service town. The fertile volcanic soil and warm moist climate support a large horticultural and dairy farming industry.

Sunny got engaged to a Chinese girl from a market garden nearby. He presented a whole medium size roast pig to the girl's family.

His fiance's grandfather who lived away from her, had flavoured and roasted the pig inside a brick oven specially built for roasting purposes.

Sunny asked me to accompany him to pick up the already roasted pig, to be delivered to his fiance's house.

At the grandpa's house, we found the pig was beautifully done. Its skin colour looked so sumptuous.

We used a wooden rod and hung the pig in the centre and carried it to the car. We were so excited and before we reached the car, the skin cracked and came off the meat.

Sunny was so disappointed but his fiance's family didn't show any sign of disapproval. The girl's father jokingly said the pig had just been cooked and needed time to cool down. All ended well.

The wedding day came, my cousin Bill Fong was best man, and I became the groomsman.

The party was held at Sunny's home, and food was mainly cooked by the bride's family. The wedding was beautiful, and the reception was friendly and intimate.

On a weekend I went to see a movie at the local town theatre. Beforehand Sunny told me I could only buy a ticket to sit downstairs, as the upstairs seats were for the white people. I couldn't believe it till I approached the cashier for an upstairs seat but was given a downstairs one.

The same occurred at the Regal theatre in Suva, Fiji, in the 1950's. When I asked for an upstairs ticket, I was given the downstairs one.

The Lilac theatre operated by the Grants family (Catholics), sold seats upstairs and downstairs to anyone. Cheers for this amicable family.

Sunny Fong's Wedding, Pokekohe, 1956.
From left Ian Fong, the bride's younger sister, Sunny Fong,
the bride, Bill Fong, the bride's younger sister.

CHAPTER 43

My employment history in Fiji

I started full-time employment, after my studies, when I was about 20 years old. My first job was as an Accounting Clerk at Mobil Oil Australia Pty Ltd in 1959. I held this job for 4 years before moving to be the Assistant Accountant at Cathay Hotels (Fiji) Ltd. Over the years, I worked in other accounting jobs at W.R. Carpenter & Co. Fiji Ltd, Austral Motors Limited, Choy's Food stores and the Government Supplies Department for Fiji.

I taught Book-keeping at the Mahatma Gandhi Memorial (MGM) High School in 1968.

At the age of 29, I was about the youngest in Fiji, to start an accountancy and tax agent practice in 1969. I registered with the Government before the formation of the Fiji Institute of Accountants. I offered convenient assistance to my Chinese clients by signing their tax returns. Some other small businesspeople did not want to leave their old friends (for sake of token money), who translated their records from Chinese to English, and then took them to Pearce & Co Ltd for signature, prior to lodging with the Inland Revenue Dept.

When I first started my practice, all the shopkeepers in Flagstaff (except two, Mr Yee Suit's brother's Store and Ko Foo Store), became my clients. They were Bill Apted

T/A Fong Quan, Yee Suit Store, Fong Sing Store, Mee Lee Store and Tom King Store. Soon I had clients from Labasa and Savusavu.

On 18 December 1985 my family and I migrated to Australia.

In 1986, I went back to Fiji to round up my practice. I was already practicing as a public accountant and tax agent before I joined the Civil Service. The Chief Accountant in the Treasury, Mr H.W. Tennet, gave me special permission to carry on for a year until I made up my mind to stay on or leave.

In 1967, the Income Tax Dept. employed 4 retired senior assessors from New Zealand. Investigations were carried out on many businesses for not lodging tax returns, and no doubt my new market gardener clients were targeted. I saved them many thousands of dollars by each offering a token tax payment and assured the Tax Dept. I would start afresh by lodging their tax returns in the future.

One of the Senior Assessors questioned me why I could go for an interview only at 3.30 pm on Friday. I told him I worked for the Government, and on Fridays I knocked off at 3 pm, so I could come by 3.30 pm. He said you were not allowed to work for the Government and run a private practice. In reply I told him I had special permission from the Chief Accountant, Mr H. W. Tennet, to do so. He said "I see, it's strange".

On another occasion when I accompanied a market gardener client for an interview, an assistant Fijian assessor told me to stay outside the office, and he could interview my client in Fijian. After a short while, the assistant assessor had to call me in to assist in the interview because my client did not understand what he had been asked.

CHAPTER 44
My voluntary work in Suva, Fiji

This is some of the voluntary work I did.

1. English/Chinese Cantonese Interpreter in the Supreme and Magistrate Courts. Once I ended up as interpreter for two brothers-in-law on a business transaction dispute in the Supreme Court.
2. Relieving English Secretary and Committee Member, China Club.
3. Secretary, St Vincent De Paul Society Suva Branch. I visited the sick in the CWM hospital, and the old people in their homes.
4. Treasurer, Fiji Scout Association. Commissioner Ben Janif, Assistant Commissioner Norman Lee-Joe
5. Treasurer, General Electors Association Fiji. President Wesley Barrett, Committee Member Roger Probert.
6. Auditor, Suva Fire Brigade Staff Association.
7. Convenor, Suva Chinese Catholic Association.
8. Auditor, Loreto Ex-students Association.
9. Committee Member, Fiji Chinese Association. President CL Cheng, Secretary Frances Wong.

CHAPTER 45

Night fishing near Nukulau Island

It was sometime in 1961 when Douglas Houng Lee and I first met in the Chinese Grocery Section of the Kwong Tiy store in Cumming Street, Suva.

We became acquainted, and he invited me to board with him. He was a widower and had two young daughters aged about 8 and 10. I moved in with his family and found his daughters very pleasant. A space without partition and a bed in the sitting room, were provided for me to sleep.

In the evening, Douglas and I shared the cooking and I normally washed the dishes. After a year, he got married to Shirley Gock, so I had to move out.

My stay with the Douglas Houng Lee family had been a very happy one.

One day, Douglas saw an advertisement in the Fiji Times regarding a second-hand boat for sale. He and I went along to see the boat which was berthed at the Suva wharf. We found a white man in his mid-thirties on the boat, and to our surprise he said he was the new owner. Douglas was so disappointed as he had wanted for a long time to buy a small boat to go fishing.

Douglas started a conversation with the man. He said he was the American Vice Counsel. He bought the boat for leisure use, but he told Douglas that he didn't know how to operate the boat. Douglas said he was a motor mechanic and he knew how to run the boat.

The American said he was lucky to be acquainted with Douglas, so he told Douglas to look after the boat and to use it whenever he wanted. The owner would like Douglas to take his family out on the sea whenever required. A very good deal for Douglas.

Then, one fine night, Douglas invited his father George Senior, younger brother Edward and me, to go out fishing. He berthed the boat off Nukulau Island, and we threw our lines into the water. Everyone had good catches, but much to our disappointment the fish caught were yellow khaki species which were not good for eating. Midnight was approaching, so Douglas and his father decided to get rid of the yellow khakis. Off they were thrown back into the sea.

After that, we took our spears with us, baskets hung on our backs, and we went to the nearby reefs. Our intention was to catch crayfish. As we walked around, we speared them on the spot.

The crayfish shells showed green colours, so it was easy to spot them. We caught 12 and shared them with George Senior and Edward. Douglas and I took our share and cooked them but found little flesh inside. They were very young crayfish. It would have been early in the morning by the time we returned home.

George Houng Lee Senior was a familiar figure with his motorbike and sidecar carrying his wife around the streets of Suva Town. He could be the first and only one who owned a motorbike with a sidecar in his time.

Wedding reception of Douglas Houng Lee and Shirley Gock, at their home in Nasese, Suva, 1961. From left Sparkle Chan, Everett Harrison, Douglas Houng Lee, Shirley Houng Lee, Ian Fong.

CHAPTER 46

My part-time work at the Golden Dragon Night Club

The opening date of the night club was around December 1961. The first night club in Fiji surely attracted so much attention. Both the dragon floor and the restaurant downstairs were filled with guests. Prominent guests were Ratu George Cakobau who was the district commissioner then, and Ratu Penaia Ganilau, the commander of the Fijian Military Forces.

I had started part-time work since the opening day. I was the proprietor, Mr Harry Janson Ho's left-hand man, as his right-hand man (his son Ken), was away studying overseas.

Mr Ho and I had no experience in managing a night club, but he was fortunate to have two voluntary advisers, namely Vic Hugo (Co-founder and President of the Fiji Marching Girls' Association), and an Officer of the New Zealand Air Force and his wife, advising us what to do. Mr Ho was willing to pay for other services such as entertainment requirements like the MC, the bouncer, the band, and the entertainers.

The advisers recommended me to be the MC, and that saved the extra expenses. I also had to take over the duties of hiring the bouncers, the band and entertainers.

The first band, Mick Heatly and his serenaders, played at the Dragon for some time before Tom Mawi and his 3 other brothers took over, and they continued to be the musicians for many years at the dragon. I remember there was so much excitement when the dragon staged the first Island Night when a cruise ship berthed for the night. Well-known hula dancer Finau Hanson and the Lulu sisters performed beautifully that night.

The night club carried on business as usual with the bar handled by the experienced barman Ram Singh, and the food from the restaurant downstairs.

However, it lacked the lustre management of Ken, who came back from overseas. With his Elvis style singing, he brought the dragon up to a fantastic standard.

It's hard to believe how I survived. Monday to Friday I worked full time at the Mobil Oil Australia company Monday to Saturday, I worked at the dragon 8 pm to 2 am. I rested full days on Saturday and Sunday. I had been on a token pay, and free lunches and dinners Monday to Sunday.

After about three years, I decided to study Accountancy, and resigned from my part-time work at the dragon.

During my stay at the Dragon things of note were as follows:

1. One day, Mr Ho received a surprising phone call from a prominent businessman. He asked Mr Ho to ban his wife (already separated from him), and her new partner, from entry to the Dragon. The man heard that the two concerned had been to the Dragon. Mr Ho told the man that could not be done, as he had no good reason to ban people from entry as long as they paid for it.
2. When the Oronsay cruise ship stopped overnight on a Sunday night, the club, obtained a special liquor licence to operate from 12 midnight till 6 am Monday morning. Both the dragon and the third floor were full of customers. Within the hour a sad and tragic event happened. A crew from the Oronsay had stabbed to death another crew member inside the men's toilet. Police were called and they stopped the business operations for the morning.
3. The bouncer had resigned, so I hired a young Fijian man who was working with me at the Mobil Oil Australia company. He was of big built and did his job well for a while, and then he started to play up. I fired him and left the Dragon without a bouncer. This guy took advantage of the situation, and on the same night he brought his gang to cause trouble. Luckily, two-part Chinese friends of mine, namely Tom Seeto and Chang Sau were present, and they intervened. They were muscular and

controlled the situation. Instead of trouble inside the Dragon, the sacked bouncer and Chang Sau made an agreement for a fair fight in the park. After a few blows, Chang Sau dropped him on his knees and asked him if he wanted to carry on the fight. Peni said he had trouble with his knees and couldn't carry on. No more trouble after that.

4. For a short while Tom and Chang came to the Dragon a few nights until a new bouncer was hired. They didn't ask for remuneration, but just to keep them a little happy, I suggested to Mr Ho to give them free beer while they were around. Another time when a bouncer resigned, and a new Futunian man was hired. He was about my height, 5'8", almost twice my size. He controlled law and order for some time in the Dragon. Then one evening, about 40 crew members from the Cable and Wireless Repair Ship Retriever, came to the Dragon. Some got drunk and started causing trouble. The new bouncer could hit anybody while he was standing, but he was rushed by many of the crew who put him on the ground. A truce was called by Mr Ho, and the matter was solved.
5. On a rather quiet night when the Dragon was fairly empty, but some crew from a cargo boat was present. The band boys Tom Mawi, and his three brothers enticed me to sing a song in front of the microphone. I chose the song "Lovers in the Sand", by Pat Boon. Before I finished singing the first verse, one of the sailors shouted "Shut up you bastard" to me. I had to stop singing immediately. I couldn't blame him because I was no singer. Might be he wanted some fast music.
6. Ken came back from his studies. What a relief. Then I was almost hurt badly by a huge size Canadian sailor who was near the bar. I was cashier inside. There was trouble downstairs, and I saw Ken running towards me, asked me for an empty bottle. He cracked it and ran downstairs with the cracked bottle. The sailor leaned forward and grabbed me by my collar, and he said "You bastard, why did you give him the bottle? He could kill somebody." I told him he was my Boss. I panicked but I thought of something to get him to release his grip. I pulled his little finger and got released from his hold. He was very surprised, and said you were lucky I didn't hurt you badly.

Those were some of the happenings in the Dragon which I could remember.

Golden Dragon Night Club and Restaurant, opposite the old Grammar School, near the Government Buildings, Suva, Fiji.

Ian Fong and Ken Janson.

From left Willie Mar, Mr Harry Janson Ho, Ian Fong, at the Golden Dragon Night Club bar.

Mr Harry Janson Ho and Ian Fong at the Golden Dragon Night Club.

Receiving guests on opening night in December 1961.
From left Margaret Janson Ho, a friend, Catherine Janson.

Ian Fong and waiters.

Ian Fong presenting Helen Reiher, Miss Hibiscus 1967.

Sitting from left Julie Yee, Ian Fong, Rosie Seeto.
Standing from left Shirley Kwan, Lorna Kwan.

Ian Fong with guests.

Mr Janson Ho, the owner, wearing glasses, Ian Fong and visitors.

Ian Fong with the house band.

CHAPTER 47
Unpaid escort to the Catholic Debutante Balls and Hibiscus Ball

I was not a casanova but a friendly young man when I escorted two young ladies to the St Joseph's Convent school break-up dance.

I was also invited to escort two young ladies on separate Catholic Debutante Balls.

The last one was something of note when I escorted Miss Morris Hedstrom Miss Emily Fong, to the Hibiscus Ball in 1959, which was held at the Grand Pacific Hotel.

Miss Robin Ann Riemenschneider was about to be crowned Miss Hibiscus for 1959.

From the hotel balcony, just before she was about to be introduced to the crowd in Albert Park, she suddenly screamed out. Her long gown was accidentally stepped on by me, which stopped her from walking forward.

In shock I immediately apologised to her. What an embarrassing moment.

Escorting Miss Morris Hedstrom Miss Emily Fong, a Miss Hibiscus Candidate, being presented to the guests in the main hall of the Grand Pacific Hotel, 1959.

At the Catholic Debutante Ball, Club Hotel, 1960.
From the middle Ian Fong, Evelyne Ah Jack, Mariam Fong.

At the Catholic Debutante Ball, Club Hotel, 1962.
From left Michael Oey Wong, Frances Fong, Douglas Yee, Anne Wong, Ian Fong, Carmela Vue, Keith Yee Joy.

CHAPTER 48
My restaurants in Suva

In April 1969 I started operating a restaurant in the Procera House, Waimanu Road. I named it Geralyne's Restaurant.

After two years, I found a very good upstairs location in 160 Renwick Road. I had the premises renovated and moved from Procera House to the new location.

Geralyne's Restaurant at Renwick Road was very popular. The steak and dalo dish was much appreciated by the Fijian young men from the Government Buildings, who came often for lunch.

After operating Geralyne's for a year, and in 1972 I sold it to a market gardener tax client. The new proprietor and his wife have since passed away, but their son is still running the restaurant business.

While I was operating Geralyne's Restaurant, an opportunity came when I discovered an excellent location for business. It was upstairs a retail store owned by a Gujarati businessman. It was located in the entrance corner of Cumming Street, the busiest street in town. The vacant upstairs premises was out for rent. Without hesitation I rented it and arranged for my carpenter and his team to carry out renovations for a restaurant. With the help of the Bank of New Zealand and huge monthly credit limits from Burns Philp and Morris Hedstrom, I managed to get the premises ready for business. David's Restaurant was born.

David's was a popular liquor licensed restaurant for locals and crew members of tourist ships. It had seating for about 110 diners, an a-la-carte menu of many dishes. There were full houses for lunches Monday to Saturday.

After operating David's for about 10 years I sold it to Ming Fong, who changed the name to Shanghai Restaurant.

There was an underground premise for rent in Carnarvon Street, back of the Carnegie Library. I rented it and arranged for my carpenter and his team to carry out renovations for a new restaurant. I did this to provide employment for a young friend who had just returned from Hong Kong. He was married with a 5-year-old son. I brought him in as a shareholder without contributions and made him a shareholder and director of the company Jade Restaurant Ltd. I spent F$28,000 on renovations, and that was a big sum of money at that time.

About two months later my friend got into marital problems with his wife, and he left the restaurant.

I was left alone to operate Jade. Soon I approached my Fijian cook to take over as manager/cook.

He applied for a liquor licence on his own name.

Jade was poorly run and lost heavily.

I fiddled around with it for a couple of years and eventually had it closed.

On 18 December 1985 my family and I migrated to Australia.

Geralyne's restaurant in Renwick Road in Suva.

Niece Jean Wong Baever on duty at the David's Restaurant in Cumming Street, Suva, Fiji.

CHAPTER 49
Geralyne's Restaurant

Procera House was situated in Waimanu Road, Suva. It housed the well-known Procera Bakery in the back, 2 shops in the front, and offices on the second and third floors. When one of the front shops became vacant, I negotiated a lease with the landlord Mr B Seeto.

After receiving the keys to the vacant premises, I immediately hired my carpenter friend, Jagat Ram and his gang of helpers to put up the shelves needed to operate a grocery store. These people were working full time for Marlow Construction, and they did the renovations after working hours.

I used the back part of the store for my accountancy practice. It was about this time the principal of Marist Brothers' High School Br Eugene, started book-keeping lessons at the school. I heard that he studied this subject at Miss Free's St Lawrence Commercial School.

Br Eugene approached John Seeto after his return with a BCom degree from New Zealand, to teach form 6 (year 12) at the Marist Brothers' High School which he did that year.

The following year, Alfred Mow and Peter Mar, with their BCom degrees, returned to Fiji. They worked for Carpenters Fiji Ltd. All three of them taught at Marist for a year.

Paul Ellis who was studying for his final accountancy exams took over and taught there for many years.

I was quite surprised when Miss Free sent her assistant with the accounting books to me and requested me to be her tax agent. I happened to be very busy, so I introduced her to Tong Yee, who had just started his practice.

The store was away from the main shopping areas in town, but I thought that with so many houses up Waimanu Road to the CWM hospital there was bound to be business for my store. My estimates were totally wrong, as people living in those houses were good Gujaratis, who were vegetarian. They bought vegetables and spices from their Gujarati shops.

In view of the above, the store business was not operating satisfactorily.

I always held the never say die attitude. I thought of an idea from a change of store to a restaurant. I arranged kitchen equipment to be made, and bought dining tables and chairs.

Geralyne's Restaurant had begun business, and in order to keep it afloat, I also ran two mobile canteens. The drivers sold cooked food such as curry chicken and rice, beef chop suey and tapioca, roti and curry, meat pies, sausage rolls, cakes, cigarettes, sweets and soft drinks. They ran two sessions at 10 o'clock (morning tea) and at 12 noon (lunch), in the wharf and the industrial areas in Walu Bay. In addition, the restaurant wholesaled lamingtons and cupcakes to the Morris Hedstrom cafeteria. At the same time, the restaurant served morning tea, lunch, afternoon tea and dinner.

One day, the proprietor of a fancy goods store in 160 Renwick Road, approached me to rent his upstairs premises for a restaurant. That was a much better location than the Procera House. It was right opposite the ever-busy Peter Fong Shop and the Sundarjee clothing shop.

Immediately, I accepted his advice. In between lease formalities, I obtained the keys to the premises. Again, I called my carpenter friend Jagat Ram and his gang of helpers to carry out the renovations.

When renovations at Renwick Road had been completed, I arranged for all the removables to be transferred from the Procera House restaurant premises to Renwick Road.

Geralyne's Restaurant at Renwick Road, being in a good business location, started operating well right from the beginning. The restaurant had a seating of 40, and it was always full during lunch hours Monday to Friday.

It was popularly known for stir-fry curry chicken and steak and dalo. Young Fijian Civil Servants from the Government Buildings, often came for lunch Monday to Friday.

For 2 years I was enjoying the running of this little restaurant, then my tax client Mr Joe Tow, who wanted a change from market gardening, approached me to sell the restaurant business to him. I agreed to let him buy it at a cost I had incurred. I made a quick decision to sell because I had found an excellent spot to start a new restaurant, situated at 30 Cumming Street.

I understand that Mr Joe Tow and his wife had passed on, but his son Yew Wah Joe is still running the Geralyne's Restaurant.

My mother's 60th birthday, 31 January 1971, Geralyne's Restaurant, Procera House, Waimanu Road, Suva.

Geralyne's Restaurant, 160 Renwick Road, Suva, after the lunch hour rush.

New owners Mr and Mrs Joe Tow and their son Wah Joe.

CHAPTER 50
David's Restaurant

While I was operating Geralyne's Restaurant in Renwick Road, an opportunity came when I discovered an excellent location for business. It was upstairs a retail store owned by a Gujarati businessman. It was located at the entrance corner of Cumming Street, the busiest street in town.

I believe my father and two Gock uncles had operated a fancy store partnership about 30 years ago on the ground floor and could be on the same spot as the retail shop. The premises were in a wooden building, like the rest of the buildings in the same street, which were made of a wooden structure. Their partnership business was doing fine, but a huge fire destroyed the whole street of wooden buildings.

Since then my father had no interest to go into business again. For many years he worked as a clerk for Kwong Tiy & Co. Ltd.

The vacant upstairs was out for rent. Without hesitation I rented it and arranged for my carpenter friend Jagat Ram and his team to carry out renovations for a restaurant.

With the generous loan from the Bank of New Zealand (loan without securities), and huge monthly credits from Burns Philp and Morris Hedstrom, I managed to get the premises ready for business. About this time I sold Geralyne's Restaurant in Renwick Road to my tax client/friend.

David's restaurant was fully air-conditioned, thanks to the good work done by the well-known Ah Tong Bros.

David's Restaurant was born.

For a year the restaurant was very fortunate to have Mr Tong Chew Len as Chief Cook, and his wife as Cashier. This couple was running the popular Lilac Cafe for many years until the cafe lease expired. Mr Tong's Roast Belly Pork, Cha Siu (Red Pork), and Won Ton dishes were extremely popular.

After Mr Tong's resignation (he was preparing to migrate to Canada), and to replace him, I employed Jackson Low as chief cook.

He was the chief cook of the Grand Pacific Hotel before he came to David's. Jackson worked for a number of years and resigned to run a taxi business. I bought a second-hand car which I gave as a bonus to him.

The person who took over as chief cook from Jackson Low, was Miss Laisani Dau from Koro. She was our first house girl until I transferred her to work as a kitchen hand in David's. She learned all the Chinese cooking skills especially roasting belly pork, cha siu (red pork), and making won ton pastry.

David's Restaurant was a popular liquor licenced restaurant for locals and crew members of tourist ships. It had seats for about 110 diners, an a-la-carte menu of many dishes. There were full houses for lunches Monday to Saturday.

On two occasions Br Raphael dropped by for a nib of whisky and a chat. During a conversation, he told me Steve Gammon of Gammon & Co, Chartered Accountants, said there were too many pirate accountants in public practice. These were non-chartered accountants but were accepted by the Commissioner of Inland Revenue. I knew a Gujarati import and Export Agent Mr Umaria, who with his assistant, were looking after the tax affairs of more than 400 Gujarati customers. Just imagine what fees they had paid if they went to the chartered accountant sharks (all Europeans in practice at that time).

According to the words of Robert Wendt, an employee of Fiji Times, and almost the dux of Marist Brothers' High School in 1953, when Ken Harrison became dux. Robert said as an individual I owned more than enough restaurants in Suva.

After operating David's for about 10 years, I sold it to Ming Fong (RIP), who changed its name to Shanghai Restaurant. That was the end of my restaurant era.

Since then my family and I were working towards our immigration to Australia.

On 19 December 1985 my family and I migrated to Australia.

Family's nightly dinner at David's Restaurant.

Son Gerard's birthday at David's Restaurant.

Lunch at David's Restaurant.
From left father-in-law Wong War Sik, Frances Fong, Magdalene Fong, my mother, Aunty Au Yang Wong Sau Fong, Geralyne Fong.

Entertaining relatives for lunch at David's Restaurant.

Eldest daughter Geralyne's birthday at David's Restaurant.

CHAPTER 51
Jade Restaurant

It was situated in the basement of a building in 10 Carnarvon Street, Suva. It was owned by Ram Charitra.

The rental lease normalities for his premises were done smoothly due to the fact that we both were registered licenced accountants of the Fiji Institute of Accountants. He was confident that I would keep up the rent payments.

A little more about this man Ram Charitra. His son Binod was my classmate at the Marist Brothers' High School, Suva. Ram, a retired Senior assessor of the Inland Revenue Department; that was the highest position in the tax department held by a local. After retirement from the government, he started a public accountancy and tax agent practice. When he was with the Income Tax Department he worked zealously, even after normal working hours. He told me that for some years, he received a Christmas hamper every Christmas, from a well-known businessman, whom he had investigated and sorted out the man's tax problems. This arose from a night visit to the taxpayer's house while he and his family were having dinner.

I spent F$28,000 (2017 F$130,252) on the renovations of the rented premises, registered a private limited company Jade Restaurant Limited, offered my young friend whom I treated as my younger brother, Christopher Chung free equal shares in the company and provided a job for him to manage the restaurant when he returned from

Hong Kong with a wife and little son. After a short while, two months, he resigned from his responsibilities. He had marital problems with his wife, who took their son and left with her new lover, to the United States. Chris went to the US, and after a year or so, he came back for a visit. He told me he managed to get a green card which enabled him to work in the United States. As for his missing wife and son, he said he didn't know their whereabouts. My family and I put up a dinner for him on the night before he returned to the United States. That was the last time we saw him.

Early 1971 when I was operating Geralyne's Restaurant in Procera House, Waimanu Road, Suva, an elderly Chinese Lady came to me and asked me to give her son a job, and to discipline him. Her son was in bad company, motorbike riding, going out with his gang often. I agreed and told her that although I didn't need extra staff at that time, but I would create a new job for him. I said I could use him on a mobile canteen. The mother was very happy and thankful for my offer. The next day, her son Christopher Chung came to start work. After a day's orientation he started driving my mobile canteen and did well with his job. It went on for about a year until his mother passed away. Chris was in his early twenties then, and he decided it was time to get married. He took his father for a holiday in Hong Kong, got married, and sent his father back to Fiji. He continued to work in Hong Kong.

After Chris left Jade Restaurant, I then appointed the head waitress to be a cashier/waitress, and I dropped in casually to check on a few things. At that time, I was still operating David's Restaurant in Cumming Street, Suva, besides practising as a public accountant/tax agent.

In the beginning, Jade Restaurant was operating satisfactorily, but soon starting to lose money. I found a solution and decided to rent the restaurant premises to the chief cook young Bogi Ledua. He learned how to cook Chinese dishes well. He and his wife were happy to give it a try.

I suggested to Bogi to apply for a liquor licence for the restaurant, and he did. Previously Chris had applied for one which had been rejected. On the hearing day at the District Commissioner's office in Nausori, the secretary of the Liquor Licencing board was trying to discourage the grant of licence to Bogi's application. Fortunately, it happened that the District Commissioner was James Vei, my school mate of Marist Brothers' High School, Suva. He said to the secretary: "What's the fuss? If the application is in order, just grant the licence to him". The licence was granted.

After three months, things didn't turn out well for Bogi and his wife. For a short while they worked hard, and doing well, but they started to have problems. His wife took off with their young daughter, and Bogi was left with frustration. As a result, I had to take back the restaurant. Bogi continued to work as chief cook.

The restaurant continued to lose money, so finally, I decided to have it closed. Furniture, fittings and equipment were left behind in the premises. No doubt rent was owed, but I can't remember how I got out of it, especially from a tough guy like Ram Charitra.

Jade Restaurant Ltd was registered as a private company. It hadn't been liquidated before I migrated to Australia. Presumably the Fiji Government must have discharged it due to non-compliance of annual returns.

In conclusion my mother and wife Frances had been very unhappy about opening this restaurant because they had not been consulted. I went behind their back for doing this, just because I had wanted to help somebody, and as a result I lost a lot of hard-earned money.

Dinner with Chris' family at Jade Restaurant, about 1978.

Part of the staff having dinner, about 1978.

Geralyne with some of the kitchen staff at Jade Restaurant, Carnarvon Street, Suva, about 1978.

CHAPTER 52
My duties as master of ceremony

I had been MC for three weddings, on two occasions in Fiji and one in Sydney, and two birthdays in Fiji.

In Sydney, I proposed a toast at Thomson Fong's wedding at the Emperor Garden Restaurant in Chinatown.

I delivered the eulogy at the late Lim Wong's funeral in Sydney.

I also delivered the eulogy of the late Wong York Lun in Sydney.

In Auckland, New Zealand, I delivered the eulogy at my cousin Bill Fong's funeral.

On 18 February 1963, this first MC duty was at the wedding of Everett Harrison and Margaret Young in Levuka.

The reception was held at the Levuka Town Hall, and all the doors were opened, so anybody could gate-crush the party. Many uninvited guests came dressed up with shirts and ties.

Quite a number of guests came from Suva, for the wedding in church and the reception.

After the formal speeches, I informed the guests that there was a lot of food for everybody, and they could take their time to enjoy.

The caterers had prepared more than enough food for the party, but due to the presence of some uninvited guests, the food soon ran out.

However, the party carried on, and all the people present had a great time, dancing to the tunes of a great band.

With Everett and Margaret Harrison at the Levuka Town Hall, 18 February 1963.

Guests from Suva came to Margaret and Everett's wedding in Levuka.

MC at Maria Goretti Wong's wedding, Club Hotel.
From left Sai Choy Wong, Ian Fong, Father Hannan.

The 50th wedding anniversary of my father-in-law and mother-in-law, Club Hotel, Suva, Fiji, 1974.
From left Sai Len Wong, Wong War Sik, Wong Ung Sau.

MC at the Wedding Reception of Melanie Lee and Richard Gock, Marigold Restaurant, Sydney, 1997.

At the Wedding Reception of Melanie Lee and Richard Gock, Marigold Restaurant, 1997. Sitting left Gerard Fong, Clare Kent, Magdalene Fong, Louise Faymon Valentine, Patrick Wong, Iris Wong, Marion Wong, Geralyne Fong Yee. Back standing Jun Ping Gock, Richard Gock, Melanie Lee Gock, Lily Lee, Sam Lee, Sai Sing Wong, Laisani Dau, Sen Yee.

CHAPTER 53
My godsons

In 1953, I was in class 7 in St Columba's Primary School, Suva Street, I became Godfather to an Indian boy named Vincent in Baptism. We eventually lost touch with each other.

Fortunately, I am still in contact with my other four godsons, Sydney Chong, Clement Paligaru, Christopher Wong and Paul Cheer.

I was also godfather in baptism to Paul, son of Ian Cheer, who is the son of my good friend Patrick Cheer. Ian was named after me, but he is not my godson. Frances and I, both being godmother and godfather to Clement, went to attend his 50th birthday celebrations in Melbourne, on 20 May 2017. Clement worked for the ABC for many years.

In the party, I was very happy to have met up with MBHS classmate Michael Thoman, and other old boys.

Frances and I were entertained by Clement's parents Johnny and Rosemary, who are our very good friends. We were invited to lunches and dinners at their home.

I was Godfather to Sidney Chong, Sacred Heart Cathedral, Suva. Baptism date 17 October 1965.
His father Francis Chong was my Godfather in Confirmation.

I was Godfather to my nephew, Christopher Wong, dinner at home in North Ryde, NSW, 11 June 2016.

I was Godfather to Clement Paligaru. He was celebrating his 50th Birthday in Melbourne, 20 May 2017.

Marist Brothers old boys at Clement Paligaru's 50th birthday celebrations in Melbourne, 20 May 2017.
From left Clement Paligaru, Ian Fong, Amroh Amputch, Michael Thoman, Gregory Eyre, David Prasad, Newtown Yuen, Reynold Paligaru, Ralph Paligaru.

My Godson Paul Cheer. Baptised at the Hunters Hill Catholic Church.

CHAPTER 54
Frances Wong's 21st birthday in Levuka, Ovalau, Fiji

It was about the year 1961 when I was a boarder at Choy Wong's house at Pender Street, Suva. His younger sister Frances, who was a final year student at the Corpus Christi Teachers Training College, came visiting. She and I met for the first time.

Frances came out once a month to spend Saturday and Sunday with us, namely Choy, her younger sister Anne and me.

When Frances was in town, Anne and I would round up our gang of friends and go to the movies or social dances in the China Club on Saturday nights.

Little did I realise that 6 years later Frances and I fell in love and were married in 1968. I will elaborate on this happening in my writing on my courting days later.

After completing three years at the Corpus Christi Teachers' Training College, this young lady had sacrificed her five golden years, teaching at the Natovi Catholic Mission Primary School, Tailevu. Her mother was worried she would become native, so she urged her to make a change by finding a teaching position in Suva. Frances agreed, applied to, and was accepted by the Fiji Chinese Primary School, (now Yat Sen Primary and Secondary School). She commenced teaching there at the beginning of the 1967 school term.

During the years 1967 to 1985, Frances was fortunate to be given government in services training. She completed a one-year Junior Secondary School Teaching Certificate, and two years at the University of the South Pacific, gaining a Bachelor of Education Degree. In 1984, a UNESCO scholarship was offered to her to study Mandarin at the Beijing University of Languages. After three months she had to discontinue her studies and return to Fiji for migration purposes.

Apart from her times at Yat Sen and away on studies, Frances also spent 5 years as Deputy Principal at the Laucala Bay Secondary School. Her last three years were as headteacher at Yat Sen before migrating to Australia.

29 April 1962 was an awesome day for the guests from Suva, Natovi Catholic Mission, and the local kai Levukans. It was Frances Wong's 21st Birthday.

Henry Fat Kow Yee, a good cook, and I the assistant, cooked the chow mein dish for the party. A fabulous roast pork dish was prepared by Frances' eldest brother Len, who used his bakery oven heated by firewood. Many other dishes were also prepared by the family and friends.

I was told about 200 guests were invited.

Frances' older brother Choy was the capable MC, and the well-known and ever-popular Dr Erasito, proposed the toast to Frances, and she replied.

A special present was given to Frances. A large box wrapped up with 21 boxes within, and eventually in the last little box she found a little doll inside it. There was an uproar.

After dinner, the dance started with music from an old gramophone. Although there was little space in between, the guests made the most of it.

Many photographs were taken by our friend Ross Yee.

There were memories galore.

From left Frances' best friend and Corpus College mate Carmela Vue, Frances' mother Wong Ung Sau and her father Wong Wah Sik, and older brother Choy Wong.

Frances with her parents.

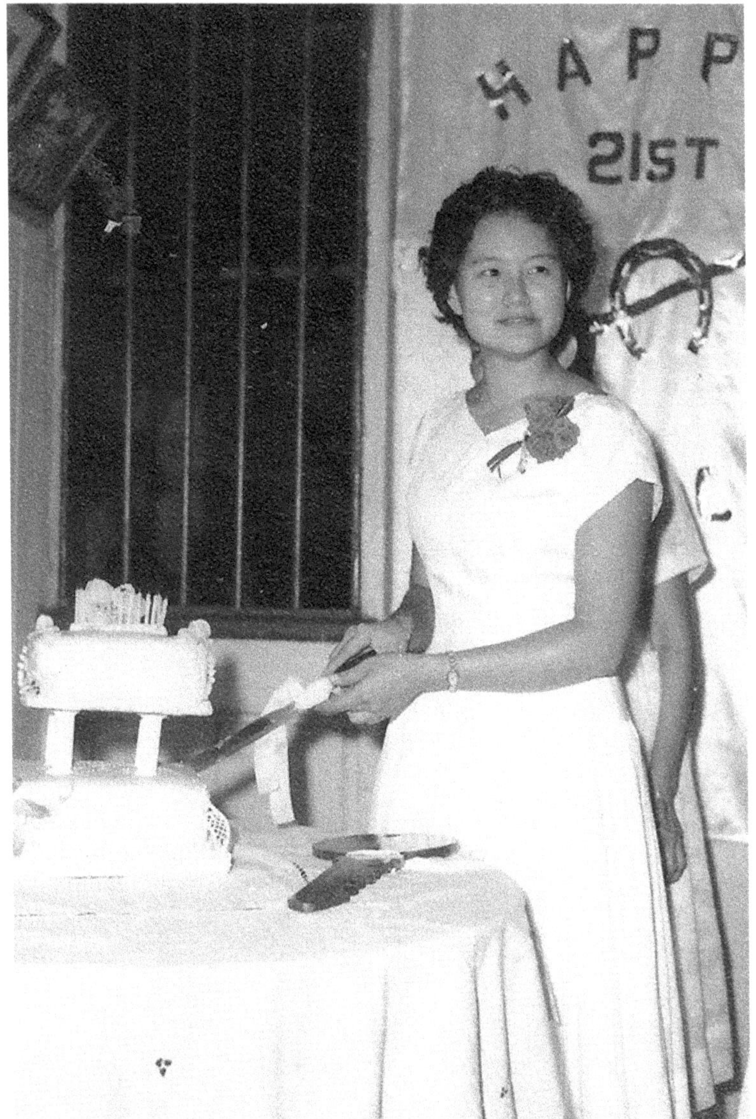

Frances cutting her 21st birthday cake.

A fun present. A box wrapped with 21 boxes within.

Middle row Frances' sister-in-law Lina Wong was holding baby nephew Paul.
Her younger sisters Emily and Anne were in the front right.
Others were friends from Suva.

CHAPTER 55
Sporting activities during my bachelor days

At the Marist Brothers' High School Sports Day in 1969, a 100 yards sprint race was set between the present and old boys.

I took my running shoes with me and off I went to the school grounds, ready for the race. By the time the present student finished the race, I was not even three-quarter way to the end. No doubt I have had my used by days, as without training, I was not capable of running fast as I used to do at school. It reminded me of a guy who came to a CAAC meeting at the MBHS school ground. He said he was the sprint champion of the University of Hong Kong. By the time Charlie Lew Gor reached the finishing line with a time of 11 seconds, not bad in those days, this guy was just over halfway on the ground. The old saying, used by date is really true.

As I had played rugby union at school I wanted to play rugby union in the Cadets team, with some members I had already known, like big Tom Seeto and big Chang Sau in the forwards, and Bill Apted and Jim Ah Koy in the backs. Outside the dressing room in the Albert Park, I heard the twin brothers of another team talking to their members, about how to hurt opposition players. I was very surprised to hear these threats, so I decided to leave the ground. No more rugby union for me.

As a member of the China Club, I represented in table tennis. In those days there was no organised association on this sport. There was a competitive team from the Fiji School of Medicine in Tamavua, and the China Club. Lockson Mar was our team captain. We enjoyed playing against the medical students, who always beat us. It seemed that ping pong was their only recreation.

When I was working for Mobil Oil Fiji Ltd, I had been involved in 2 friendly games between employees of Mobil Oil Fiji Ltd and Shell Co Ltd. First one was a rugby union match captained by Jed Peterson, who played for the Levuka Old Boys in the European competition. He played at first five eight and I played wing. During the match I made a tackle to a charging Shell forward and hurt my right shoulder and further down the chest. The match was won by Shell. I was told later he was a rep of the Fiji Rugby Union. My wounded chest brought me a lot of pain and needed treatment. I was also working part-time at the Golden Night Club, where I came to know a hula dancer Finau Hanson. She told me to contact her mother who was a massage specialist. With her expert hands, Mrs Hanson Senior massaged my wounded chest back to normal. At a Hibiscus Night fixture, a soccer match between Mobil Oil and Shell was played, in the presence of a large crowd in Albert Park. I was at the wing but never touch the ball as the centres were greedy with the ball. In the end Shell won.

Indoor basketball was a sport I played most at centre and wing. Mr Peter Seeto, the manager of the Black and White team admitted me to the team. The game was played on Sundays at the St Anne's court. Sometimes we played friendly games with the New Zealand Air Force team, and we really enjoyed playing them, besides forging friendly relationship. I didn't stay long with the B and W team because I couldn't make the starting five, as the older and better players were always chosen first.

As a result, I joined the China Club team which was short of good players. While there we also had friendly games with the NZ Air Force team. The Eastern Basketball teams of boys and girls from Wellington, New Zealand, consisted of Chinese players. Both the touring boys and girls' teams beat the China Club teams.

I got married on 4 May 1968, and since then I retired from playing sports, and concentrated on my businesses.

Friendly game with the NZ Air Force team, 1959.

CHAPTER 56
The China Club I Leong For Ye

At a wedding party in China Club Ratu Sir Kamisese Mara was proposing a toast to the groom Leong and bride Yee.

His opening words were "I leong for ye" meaning "I long for yee".

The bridegroom Leong and bride Yee had their party in China Club sometime after the 1968 wedding receptions of Tasman Sohn and David Fong, who had no choice but to rent the St John's hall which proved to provide better facilities.

Tasman's father was a founding and life member of the club. I was a committee member in 1968, also rep member for basketball and table tennis, frequent poker/card social gambler.

The president ARANZ, ACIS, in 1968 refused to let the club premises out while he was in office. Bloody mean bugger for no good reason.

Lots of members voiced out about that.

I think it was in 1969 when Sang Yee Joy (RIP) became president and he and his committee made a decision to let the club out for functions. Sang was an extremely sociable gentleman, always greeting people that he met.

My gang of 12 friends had recommended me and Patrick Cheer (RIP) to go into the election, me for Chinese secretary/committee member, and Patrick for a committee member. It happened every year only a handful of about 20 members were present at the annual general meeting.

One guy twice my age was also nominated for Chinese Secretary by his relatives and supporters. Okay fair enough. Judging by the statistics before the election date I was sure to win.

Then on Election Day all the inter-related Honsons, Houng Lees and Lee-Joes turned out to vote. As a result, my opponent won, but I was still voted into the committee.

At a committee meeting early in the year, a member present made a suggestion that the club should rent the club hall out to members for functions. The president strongly objected to the idea; a decision was made to have a vote. There were 6 presents, the English Secretary Greg Yee was away so I deputised for him. The result 3/3. Three votes came from the president, his brother-in-law and a supporter, while the other votes came from me, Patrick and another supporter. In view of the tied result the president cast his vote and won.

Here were things happened in the club.

I remember a simple poker machine was introduced; then one-night people were queuing up to play. There was a Chinese lady in the middle of the queue, although desperate for the toilet, remained in the queue, otherwise she might miss her turn to play. What happened: urine came down from her panty.

During most of my bachelor days I spent Saturday and Sunday nights on social gambling/poker games in the club. There was a guy who always won and left at 11 pm each session, leaving the poor bugger losers to play it out through the night. It was told to me that one night he won a huge pool by producing the 5th As. The pack of cards had only 4 As of different colours. There were 3 silly players, 2 (RIP): after the first 2 cards had been delivered, first bat begun, these 3 would top bats for as far as 50 times until the rest of the other players withdrew one by one.

One night in the room at the club upstairs, 8 of us were having it out- on a poker game of course. I was extremely lucky and won/dried up 7 of the players except one who still had some money left to play. I wanted to go home, but the losers complained that it was bad sport, so the one, a rich boy who still had some money left, suggested I stay back and play on accepting credit, and that he would guarantee for payment. You know what happened: eventually the group dried me up to the last cent, and I had to walk home.

I attended lots of social dances and Hibiscus Dragon Night banquets held at the club. One night at a Dragon Night function my wife and I were invited by the organising committee, to sit at the Official Table; other guests were Mr CL Cheng, The Governor General Ratu Sir Penaia Ganilau, Chief Justice Timoci Tuivaga and wife, James Ah Koy and wife. During the night Jane Fong Wing Chee who happened to be in Suva visiting, came over to exchange greetings with Ratu Sir Penaia. People around were surprised, not knowing that Jane knew him before. Jane's mother was the sister of the Tui Ba. I heard Jane's mother was the most wonderful person.

The China Club, Suva.

At the China Club in 1968.
From left Bill Fong, Janice Fong, Frances Fong, Ian Fong.

Island Night for the Eastern Indoor Basketball Team from Wellington, at China Club.

Island Night for the Eastern Indoor Basketball Team from Wellington at China Club.

Adults from left Francis Hong Tiy, Ian Fong, Ken Janson,
Emily Yee Joy, Pam Yee, Sang Yee Joy.
Children from left Christopher Yee Joy, Roderick Yee.

Dragon Night at the China Club, August 1972.

From left Frank Yee, China Club singer Simione, Ian Fong.

China Club basketball team. I played wearing shirt number 5.

China Club basketball team in action.

CHAPTER 57
My carefree bachelor days 1962 to 1966, Age 24 to 28

If my parents were rich, they would have helped me to settle down with a wife in between the above years. But I had to paddle my own canoe until such time when my job was secured.

During the above 5 years I had been involved with lots of happenings. You could guess I was lonely at night when I was alone living in a rented room. It wasn't too bad during the day when I went to work during the working day week. In the weekends, I played indoor basketball and table tennis in the competitions.

Fortunately, I had been to many social dances at the St Anne's Hall organised by Father Tang, and the China Club, and attended some weddings.

With Micky Columbas's gang of 5, I also attended monthly dances at the old town hall, organised by the Suva Girl Guides' Association. Before we went to the town hall dances, we would go to the Club Hotel public bar and drank a few beers to prime ourselves up. I couldn't take beer much, but I obliged with a glass or less. I was lucky to be attached to the gang, who protected me and made things safe for me. Often when a couple was on the floor, someone would come around and ask the male dancer to be excused. If any of my gang was dancing, no one dared interrupt, because my gang of 5 were big strong boys.

Micky's reputation was well known to people in the town hall dances.

Micky, a MBHS old boy, later took over as General Secretary of the Fiji Oil Workers' Union from the noted James Anthony, another old boy of MBHS.

I had seldom been in contact with Frances Wong and her family, but more often since early 1967. Her family settled in Flagstaff next to Fong Quan's about 1964.

I joined the gang of young men and ladies for picnics to Nukulau Island. We went out to Deuba Beach once but found the distance too far for future outings.

I am always grateful to Patrick Sui Wing Cheer and his wife Agnes Hansen Cheer, for the way they helped me to get away from social/habit gambling at the China Club. Between the period 8 June 1964 to 31 March 1967, Patrick, Henry Yee Joe and I, were working at WR Carpenters & Co they were in the Shipping Dept, and I was Branch Accountant for Austral Motors Ltd, Cicia and Lomaji Cobra Plantation Estates. The three of us became very good friends.

Patrick's younger brother Johnson Cheer worked with me as my assistant at Carpenters.

Patrick and Agnes with their infant daughter Karen, lived in a unit near the Albert Park. Every lunch break Patrick drove the three of us to his home for lunch. The three of us were fanatics on chess playing, the winner stayed for the next challenger. We played during the little time we had during lunch break, and after work we would go back to Patrick's home and passed our time playing chess until Henry and I left for home late at night. The only time we stopped playing was while we were having our dinner.

Those days were truly happy days for us. Patrick's wife Agnes was very caring. For lunch we had canned fish, bread and tea. Curry mutton and rice was one of our most favorite dinner dishes.

On a boat returning from Nukulau Island, 1967.

At a social dance in the Fiji Chinese Primary School (now Yat Sen Primary and High School), 1959.
From left Ian Fong, Winnie Low.

Chinese New Year, China Club, 1966.
From left Emily Wong, Ian Fong, Anne Wong.

Indian Night at the Grand Pacific Hotel, 1963.

Wedding reception for Francis Chong and Theresa Fong at the St John's Red Cross Hall, 21 November 1964.
Seated from left Ian Fong, Maylin Cheer, Jeannie Lui, Irene Mow, Belina Bing, Lydia Fong, Miss Mow, Helen Cheer.

With Far Eastern Indoor Basketball team members from Wellington at a reception in the China Club.
From left visitor, Leslie Houng Lee, Ian Fong, Everett Harrison, visitor.

At a wedding reception in St John's Hall, Suva.
From left Agnes Cheer, Ian Fong, Judy See, Joan Cheer, Patrick Cheer, Jessie Lee, Symond Cheer, Johnson Cheer, a friend.

Social dance at the China Club, 1966.

Double Tenth Celebrations at the China Club, 1966.
From left Ian Fong, Douglas Yee, George Lee Joe, Frank Yee, Harry Fong, Keith Fong.

Social dance at the China Club, 1966.
From left a friend, Ken Low, Wing Kangwai, Ian Fong, Catherine Wu.

From left Ian Fong, Lily Wong, Sparkle Chan, Ester Cheng.

Picnic in Deuba Beach, 1966.

Nukulau Island, 1967.
I couldn't play anything, just for show.

Social dance at the China Club, 1966.
Seated from left Elizabeth Mar, Frances Wong, Emily Wong, Marjorie Sahay, Queenie Kangwai.
Standing at the back Ian Fong, Philip Wong, Edmond Chang.

Chinese New Year Eve, China Club, 1966.
From left Mariam Fong, Ian Fong, Loretta Mar, Elizabeth Mar, Patsy Mar.

Dancing with Anne Cheng.

From left Ian Fong, Vivian Yee, Elizabeth Mar.

CHAPTER 58
My courting days and engagement

On two occasions in early 1966, an old boy of the Marist Brothers' High School, Suva, and I met outside the Fong Quan's store in Flagstaff. He was a staunch Catholic who had married a good Catholic girl.

On the first occasion, he asked me "How are you getting along?", I answered "okay".

Not long after, we happened to meet again. He said to me to stop floating along, just get to know a good Catholic girl and settle down. I told him it was difficult to find one. To this he joked "Why do you have to look far? There are two good Chinese Catholic girls living upstairs next door." I couldn't remember what else was said between us after that.

On the above two occasions, I happened to be visiting the Wong family. Usually Frances Wong, her sisters and her mother (Aunty Wong Sau Ung), greeted me cordially and made me feel at home. I had always regarded the girls as "sisters".

After a little while, the girls would excuse themselves, leaving their mother and me alone. It was easy for Aunty to have a conversation with me as I was, and still am fluent in the Zhongshan (Chungshan) dialect. She and I could talk about anything but not about her daughters' futures.

Thanks to a hint I got earlier, so I took the idea up, hoping to get the opportunity to woe Aunty's daughter Frances, whom I regarded as a suitable wife. To me she appeared to have a healthy disposition, pleasant manners, natural good looks, intelligence and so on.

Since then, I visited the Wong family every week.

Frances, at a stage, was wanting a change for an office job from teaching. She enrolled for a Book-keeping course at the Derrick Technical Institute. She sat for the London Royal Society of Arts Book-keeping Stage 1 Exam and passed. That was not good enough to apply for an office job. I told her she had to learn short-hand and typing as well. After considering the options, she decided to stay put on her teaching job.

During one of my visits to the Wong family, Frances' mother and I were left talking to each other. She told me that during the past 5 years, Frances had received proposals from boys in Suva, Lautoka, Ba and Rakiraki. One had offered to build a new house, and another had offered to buy a new house. She didn't want her daughters to marry into rich families. Then she spilled out that she was worried about her two daughters already reaching the coming of age to be married, and told me if I was interested, talk to any of them to be my life partner.

Her frank approach was a big surprise to me, and I told her I would be extremely happy to marry Frances and left the matter at that.

I remembered 5 years ago, Aunty Wong Sau Fong from Levuka, had hinted to Frances' mother that I was a suitable husband for Frances. At that time, I didn't have a good and secure job, so I had not thought of settling down then.

I was trying to work out a way to approach Frances on my desire to marry her, but how? Then it happened after a picnic trip to Nukulau Island. On reaching home about 6 pm that evening, I phoned Frances asking her out for dinner at the Grand Pacific Hotel. At first, she hesitated but agreed only on her terms. I was so happy and went by taxi to take her out.

We sat by a table in the GPH dining room, in the presence of candle lights. Before we ordered our meals, I nervously proposed to Frances for her hand of marriage. I didn't know it was customary to have a ring for the proposal. She laughed. She thought it was a big joke as she didn't expect this to happen.

I told her I meant every word I said, but she told me she won't accept my proposal of marriage. However, she agreed to be my steady girlfriend for the time being and decide what to do later.

After enjoying a good and happy dinner, we walked to her home through McGregor Road to Knolly Street, to Flagstaff.

People whom we knew drove past and calling out: "Something's cooking".

During our courting days, we enjoyed many outings such as picnics, Loreto High School Ex-students' social dances at the Metropole Hotel, functions at the China Club, and weddings.

In early January 1967, Frances and her beloved mother went to Sydney for a holiday, and visited her older married sister Judy who was expecting her second child. While they were there, Frances was very shocked to receive a registered article with a bank draft plus a short note saying, "Since you are in Sydney you may as well shop for an engagement ring as the shops have many varieties. If the money I sent is insufficient I will repay you the balance". Frances was furious as she had not agreed to marry me yet.

Her sister Judy was very excited, so she rang her very good friend to take them to have a look at some diamond rings.

After a few days, Frances had cooled down and agreed to go shopping. Judy's friend took them to an exclusive diamond dealer in the city, and then Frances chose the setting.

We finally got engaged in October 1967. Her family celebrated the occasion with a party at her home.

On 4 May 1968, we were married at the Sacred Heart Cathedral, Suva, Fiji.

Courting days, China Club, 1967.

Loreto High School Ex-students' social dance at the Metropole Hotel, 1967.

Dragon Night at the China Club, 1967.

On a boat returning from a picnic at the Nukulau Island, 1967.

CHAPTER 59

Part-time book-keeping teacher at the MGM High School

Mahatma Gandhi Memorial High School (founded 1960) is a mixed high school situated in Fletcher Road, Suva, the capital of the Fiji Islands. It is a school which is named after Mohandas Karamchand Gandhi, an Indian political leader.

MGM High School was founded by the Gujarat Education Society in 1960. The society's first school was MGM Primary. MGM High School was opened in mid-1960 with Mr. Satya Narayan as the Head Teacher. A year later, the late Mr. Gopalbhai Patel became the principal since Mr. Satya Narayan had gone overseas to continue his studies.

In early 1968 while I was practising as a public accountant and tax agent at home, I saw an advertisement in the Fiji Times, seeking a part-time Book-keeping teacher at the MGM High School. I went to see the Principal Gopalbhai Patel and applied for the position. At the meeting he said it was okay with him, but he had to send me to the Secretary of Education the late Mr Joe Gibson, for a check and approval.

I went straight away to Mr Gibson for an interview. I knew he was an old boy of the Marist Brothers' High School. He asked me to introduce myself briefly and wanted to know what sort of accounting qualifications I possessed. I told him I was a MBHS old boy, and I was practising as a public accountant and tax agent at home. I was hoping to sit for the Accounting 2 and Auditing Examinations of the University of Wellington

Grants Committee, and Stage 2 Examinations of the Australian Society of Accountants. Without hesitation he said I was more than qualified enough to teach book-keeping at secondary schools. On the phone, he gave approval to the Principal of MGM to take me on.

I commenced my teaching job at the beginning of the first term in 1968 and continued until the end of the third term.

By then my tax clients had considerably increased in numbers. In view of this I resigned from my future teaching jobs at MGM.

MGM's Principal Mr Gopalbhai Patel, MA (Auckland Uni)), was the highest qualified secondary school principal at that time. He was assisted by Mr Satya Nand as the Deputy Principal. Mr Nand had graduated with BA from the New Delhi University in India.

Before he came to MGM, Mr Patel was running secondary school classes at the league hall in Toorak, for boys who were not accepted into the secondary schools in Suva.

While I was at MGM, I got to know two teachers. The first one was the late Mrs Irene Jai Narayan, MA from India, who was Head of English. She later became a famous parliamentarian. The second one was Bessie Ng Kumlin Ali, BA (Auckland Uni), and later MA (Hons in English, Auckland Uni), who started her teaching career at St Joseph's Secondary School, Waimanu Road, before coming to teach at MGM. From there she went on to teach at the Marist Brothers' High School and was Head of English. She was the founding principal of Yat Sen Primary and Secondary School and remained there from 1986 to 2002, except for two stints overseas. She is the author of the book "Chinese in Fiji".

I would like to tell you an amusing incident in my classroom at the MGM. A teacher who was walking past the classroom, found two boys sitting at the back playing draft. It happened during the time I was writing something on the blackboard. The teacher came into the classroom and told me about their misbehaviour. He told me that he would report the matter to the principal.

I taught 4 different book-keeping classes for the whole 1968 school year. Each class had about 48 students of boys and girls. It was satisfying teaching them.

Yum cha at the East Ocean Seafood Restaurant in Sydney city.
Seated from left is Bessie Ali, Frances Fong, Ian Fong, Benson Wong.
Standing at the back is Queenie Wong.
Bessie Ali was the Founding principal for Yat Sen Secondary School and worked there for 16+ years.
I taught Book-keeping at Mahatma Ghandi High School for 1 year when she was teaching there.

CHAPTER 60
The wedding of Frances Wong and Ian Fong

After our engagement in October 1967, Frances and I were thinking and thinking where the wedding reception would be, the preparations and the actual date. First of all, I moved from my room in Toorak to a rented two-bedroom partly furnished granny flat in Carew Street, close to the Marist Brothers' High School. It had a sitting room, kitchen, separate toilet and bathroom. Next, Frances had curtains made to cover the windows. In the meantime, I enjoyed the comfortable living compared to the previous room.

After living in Carew Street for less than three months, Frances and I found a newly built three-bedroom house for sale in 18 Tanoa Street, a two-minute walk to the Fiji Chinese School. We thought it would be a good home if we could buy it. This address would be convenient for our future children when they attend primary school. We approached the owner of the house, and he agreed to let us buy it. Frances and I asked the Bank of New Zealand for a loan. Fortunately, the manager approved our application since we both had secured jobs. When mortgage formalities had been completed, I moved into the new house. Frances was again busy preparing curtains. We both decided on what to buy to furnish the house. Our sister-in-law Lina Wong was very proud of us as it was the first family home bought in Suva.

Originally, Frances and I had decided to get married over the Christmas holidays in 1968, as that would give us more time to prepare. However, her younger sister and her fiancé also wanted to get married that same year. Frances' mother wanted us to be married first because Frances was the older sister. So, we had no option but to get married earlier in the year. We then decided on the 4 May, the beginning of the first term school holidays.

To add security to our house, we ordered grills to be installed around all the windows. The house also needed to be painted. Our next-door neighbour, who was a painter by trade, helped paint the internal and external walls of the house.

Frances' parents generously bought a new beautiful set of sofas and gave it as a present to us. Her mother asked her brother Sai Choy who was on business in Sydney, to buy a set of Chinese teapots, and matching cups and saucers for the Tea Ceremony. It was a beautifully decorated set, very fine and delicate. Frances' mother's friend Mrs. Mar Gun was very kind in organizing the tea ceremony after the church service. Gong cha (tea ceremony) was served to David's eldest Aunty Fong Low Shee, eighth Uncle, and Aunty Fong War Kit, Uncle and Aunty Fong Yuen, and Cousins Bill and Janice Fong.

A marriage ban was obtained from the Catholic Church. The priest Father Kavuru, was to give us marriage instructions. On our first meeting, Father told us there was no need for us to be instructed, as he knew we understood the marriage related matters regarding a Catholic couple as we had been educated at Catholic High Schools. However, we were not aware of the civil authority side of the law. We had not applied for a marriage licence from the government. Father O'Neil, who was to perform the marriage ceremony, pointed this requirement to us, after the church rehearsal the evening before the wedding. He told us he couldn't conduct the wedding ceremony without a civil marriage licence. He was quite annoyed with Father Kavuru for not informing us about the civil marriage licence. Fortunately, Father Kavuru was very good friends with the registrar of marriages, so Father rang him to arrange for a private civil ceremony consultation in the government buildings at 10 am the next morning.

At 9.30 am in the morning, I came by taxi to pick Frances up to accompany me to the government buildings. That was a very important trip. Her mother and family said we were not supposed to see each till the church ceremony. Frances said she would explain later. She then hurriedly went downstairs to the waiting taxi.

At the government buildings, a civil officer attended to us. He was on the veranda and we were separated by a grill. He had the documents with him, and he asked us for our names, birthdays and addresses. He asked me the most important question, "Do you Ian David, take Frances to be your lawful wedded wife?" to which I replied, "I do". Frances had to answer a similar question and replied, "I do". Then we both signed the civil marriage certificate. God saved us.

Three months before 4 May, we had ordered red Chinese traditional invitation cards which were printed in Hong Kong, and they arrived in a good time. We invited over 500 guests. Cards were sent to adult guests only, and verbal invitations were given to Frances' class 7 pupils of the Fiji Chinese Primary School, and also to the girls of the Loreto High School Girls' choir, who came from Levuka to sing at our wedding in the church. Frances was then the president of the Loreto High School Ex-students' Association.

Frances and I were surprised that my eldest uncle's wife, Aunty Fong Low Shee, my cousin Bill and his wife Janice, told us that they were coming from New Zealand to attend our wedding. It was a big honour for us to have them attend. We were very thrilled.

For my best man I chose Philip Wong, a good friend, and Frances organised her bridesmaid, her younger sister Anne and their nieces Lily and Evelyne were flower girls.

The beautiful bridal bouquet of white orchids was arranged by our good friend Margie Wong. She also arranged corsages and sprays for members of the bridal party and immediate family members. All the flowers and accessories were donated by Margie. She personally did everything fantastically herself.

As for the wedding cars, my Indian tax client who owned a big taxi business in town offered free of charge, two big cars for the bridal entourage. The cars were decorated with fresh flowers and white ribbons.

Cooking for the reception was done in a specially built shed at the back of our house. I bought two 44-gallon empty drums, had them halved to make stoves. I hired large woks, large pots and other utensils from the Sikh Temple in Samabula 2 Miles. I approached three village uncles, Fong Kow, Willie Kin Man Fong and Fong Bo Wah, to do the cooking, and thankfully they willingly obliged. They did an excellent job.

Frances had called on a gang of helpers to help the cooks. They were a friend Enola Nielson, her eldest brother Sai Len's children Michael, Catherine, Jean and Lily, all from Levuka. A few of her friends in Suva also helped. As far as I can remember Uncle Fong Yuen's children Amy, Jacky, Jack On, Jack Keung, Jack Ping, and their two sisters came to help. Also, in those days, there were no frozen chickens available in the Supermarkets or elsewhere. I bought 100 live chickens, which had to be killed, bathed in boiling hot water, cooled and their feathers plucked. All this work was carried out on the afternoon before the wedding. It was very good of our relatives and friends to help us.

On the wedding day morning, the cooks sent the 2 pigs and 50 chickens (already flavoured the previous night) to our baker friend's oven in Rewa Street for roasting. We retained 50 chickens and used them in other delicious Chinese dishes such as Chicken chow mein, Stir-fry chicken and vegetables, Chicken mushroom etc. I was told that the roast pork was very crispy and tasted yummy.

On the morning of the wedding day, Frances' class 7 pupils brought flowers from their gardens to decorate the church. Her younger sister Emily Wong, friends Charlotte Fong Toi, Maria Wong, Lily Yee and some other friends, decorated both upstairs and downstairs floors of the reception hall. In the evening they also served food to the tables.

When all the food for the reception had been prepared and ready, my good friend and future brother-in-law Sai Sing Wong, who was in charge of the transport, took the food and drinks to St John's Hall in Rodwell Road in the city.

Frances's father, Wong War Sik escorted her into the church, which was well attended by relatives and guests. Sister Irene of St Joseph's Secondary School played the organ, and the choir sang beautifully.

At 5 pm, 4 May 1968, Frances and I were married at the Sacred Heart Cathedral, Suva, Fiji.

As we came along the church aisle, Frances was very emotional when she saw so many people greeting us.

Frances, just before leaving home for Suva Cathedral.

Frances with her flower girls (nieces Evelyne Wong, Lily Wong), the bride to be Frances Wong, younger sister Anne the bridesmaid.

Leaving home for Suva Cathedral.
Front are the flower girls Evelyne and Lily Wong.
Back is Wong Wah Sik, the father of the bride to be, the
bridesmaid Anne Wong, the bride to be Frances Wong.

Arriving at Suva Cathedral.

Signing our marriage certificate.

Signing our marriage certificate.
Standing at the back are Philip Wong, Best man and Anne Wong, Bridesmaid.
Standing at the front is Evelyne Wong and Lily Wong, flower girls.
Sitting at the front are Ian and Frances.

Wedding photo taken at photography studio.
Ian and Frances.

Wedding photo taken at photography studio.
Ian and Frances.

Wedding photo taken at photography studio.
From left Evelyne Wong, Philip Wong, Ian Fong, Frances Fong, Anne Fong, Lily Wong.

Chinese tea ceremony.
From left, Aunty Lee (eighth Uncle's wife), Fong War Kit (eighth uncle), Frances Fong, Mrs Mar Gun (who organised the tea ceremony).

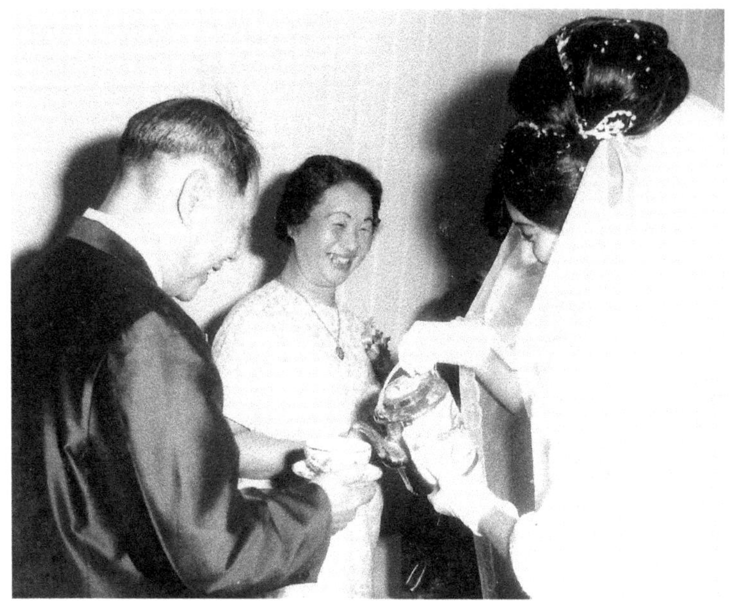

Chinese tea ceremony.
From left my eighth Uncle Fong War Kit, eldest uncle's wife Aunty Fong Low Shee, Frances Fong.

From left Frances Fong, my eighth Aunty Fong War Kit, eldest uncle's wife Aunty Fong Low Shee, eighth Uncle Fong War Kit.

Frances offering tea without kneeling as her wedding gown was long. From left Frances Fong, village neighbour Uncle Fong Yuen, bridesmaid Anne Fong, Cousin Bill Fong and his wife Janice Fong.

Receiving guests at the entrance of the St John's Red Cross Hall. At the back is my new father-in-law Wong Wah Sik. At the front is my mother-in-law Wong Sau Ung, Frances and I.

My cousin Bill Fong, his wife Janice Fong, Frances and me.

Sitting from left Aunty Lee (eighth Uncle's wife), Fong War Kit (eighth uncle), Aunty Fong Low Shee from New Zealand. Standing from left Aunty Fong Yuen, Uncle Fong Yuen, cousins Bill Fong and Janice Fong from New Zealand.

Cutting our wedding cake.
Empire Cafe Toorak baked and decorated our beautiful cake.

CHAPTER 61

My father-in-law Wong War Sik and me

I always greeted him as Ah Bak meaning Older uncle before and after I married his daughter Frances. His children addressed him as Ah Sook meaning younger uncle. It was a kind of custom to some people. I didn't mind greeting him as Dad.

There was a special bond between him and me. While I was courting his daughter Frances, he was happy and had no objection to that. Then one afternoon, when I was visiting the family, he came home and ignored me completely, and went straight to his room without saying a word. Everyone present was very surprised and wondered why he behaved in such a manner. In view of that, I said good-bye to the family members who were present. They were Frances' mother, Frances, her younger sisters Anne and Emily.

I lived in a room rented from Mr Jeung So Chong in the corner of Amy Street and Toorak Road. Not long after arriving home I received a phone call from Frances. She told me to go back and reason with her father.

When I arrived at her home, her father and the three sisters were waiting for me. The girls asked their father why he had ignored me. He said the shop keeper down the road, told him I was a gambler and he ought to be careful in choosing a person like me to be her daughter's husband. The girls explained to him that I was not a regular gambler who gambled in the gambling house, but for past time I played poker cards with some members in China Club.

Since then he was happy with me courting his daughter.

About six months before my wedding I rented a room in a flat next to the flat where Frances lived. In the evening I started cooking at 6.30 pm, and by the time I finished cooking, eating and washing my dishes, the time would be 10.30 pm. Some nights Frances cheekily peeped through the kitchen and see what I was doing. I invited her to come in and help with the washing of dishes. She refused because of the scandal.

Frances felt sorry for me and sought approval from her family for me to eat dinner with them and paid a token monthly amount of money.

At night, I often worked on my clients' books (as I had just commenced my Private Accountancy Practice). I piled extra books on my dining table to attract Mr Wong's attention. From there he could see that I was a hard-working young man.

That was all between my father-in-law and me.

Busy day for my son Gerard's birthday at Tanoa Street, Suva, 1977.
Left seated was my mum Fong Lum Oy Wan.
Right seated with hat was father-in-law Wong War Sik.
Front was Geralyne Fong.

CHAPTER 62
My mother-in-law Wong Ung Sau and me

I always greeted her as "Bak mu" meaning older uncle's wife before and after I married her daughter Frances. It was customary, but I wouldn't mind greeting her as Mum. She was such a nice person, not only to me but also to the people around her.

We first met in her son Sai Choy's house when I was boarding there. As usual, I soaked my clothes in a bucket and washed them when I got home after work. When I got home one day, the clothes in the bucket had been washed and dried.

This was still at Sai Choy's house: One day Aunty Au Young Hin from Levuka came visiting and stayed back for dinner. It was about 2 o'clock in the afternoon before I went to play cards (poker games) with my usual gang in China Club. I told Bak Mu and Aunty Au not to do any preparation for dinner, as I would do the cooking when I came back later. I came back at about 7 o'clock in the evening and immediately apologised for being late. No worries they said, dinner had already been cooked and they and the family had also eaten their dinner. I felt horrible. The fact was that this Aunty Au, to whom Bak Mu's daughter Frances' last Chinese name Fong, was named after her, had in some stage, recommended me as a suitable husband for Frances. Anyway, my misconduct didn't get me into trouble. Aunty Au said young people always learned from mistakes and 100% points for me. At that time, there was no chemistry between Frances and me. We both were not ready to settle down yet. We both remained friends.

The Wong clan moved into a flat in Flagstaff, and I was a frequent visitor. Frances' mother loved to talk to me and vice versa. On one occasion she sounded out to me that she didn't want her daughters marrying into rich families.

She often spoke about her worries about Frances and her younger sister Anne, not getting married. Frances was then 25 and her younger sister Anne was 22. She said if I didn't mind, just ask any one of them. This not only gave me a hint but tremendous encouragement, and I took up the challenge. After a picnic in Nukulau Island, I invited Frances for a dinner at the Grand Pacific Hotel, where I proposed to her. She didn't accept my proposal but agreed to go steady with me.

About six months before my wedding, I was staying in a rented room next to the flat, where Frances' family had moved into. Frances and I were going steady and getting ready to be married.

After a little while Frances felt sorry for me, for I had to cook, eat and wash dishes. She raised the question to her family to take me in for dinner, at a moderate sum of payment. Her family agreed and it was a pleasure to join them for dinner.

During this period of stay, Frances often worried about me getting up late for work so she arranged for her nephew Patrick, about six years old, to come through the balcony to wake me up in the morning.

Lastly my mother-in-law had a lot of love for her children. She loved and treated every child equally and showed no favouritism to any child.

My mother-in-law Wong Ung Sau and my wife Frances Fong.

CHAPTER 63

The 50th wedding anniversary of my father-in-law and my mother-in-law

In the year 1974, my father-in-law and mother-in-law celebrated their 50th wedding anniversary at the Club Hotel.

The family nominated me as the MC for the occasion.

Geralyne's Restaurant (owned by me), did the catering and supplied the food to the hotel for the guests.

My wife Frances and her younger sisters Anne and Emily took control of the guests' list and the printing of invitation cards.

My eldest brother-in-law Sai Len, his wife Lina and their children from Levuka, came to Suva to join in the celebrations. Their second daughter Catherine was on a Government Scholarship studying in New Zealand.

My sister-in-law Judy Wong Leong, the second eldest in the family, with her two sons Edmund and Winston, came over from Sydney to attend the celebrations. Her husband Henry Leong couldn't come due to business commitments.

My mother and son Gerard were in Hong Kong on family matters.

Many guests attended the party.

Mr CL Cheng proposed the toast of the evening to my father-in-law and my mother-in-law and was full of praise for them. My brother-in-law Sai Choy on behalf of his parents thanked Mr Cheng for the many kind words, and the guests for their presence and the valuable gifts they brought.

It was a wonderful party, and the good food was enjoyed by all.

The presence of so many grandchildren contributed a fantastic atmosphere to the party.

Club Hotel, Suva, Fiji, 1974.
Mr CL Cheng proposing the toast of the evening and speech.

Sai Choy Wong replying on behalf of his parents, to the toast proposed by Mr CL Cheng.

My in-laws blowing the candles.
From left Sai Len Wong, Wong War Sik, Wong Ung Sau, MC Ian Fong.

My parents-in-laws with their children.
Front row Sai Choy Wong, Sai Len Wong, Wong War Sik,
Wong Ung Sau, Judy Wong Leong, Sai Sing Wong.
Back row Michael Sai Oey Wong, Frances Fong, Anne Fong, Emily Wong.

My parents-in-law with their children and spouses.
Front row Lina Lui Wong, Sai Len Wong, Wong War Sik, Wong Ung Sau, Sai Sing Wong, Yuk Kin Woo Wong.
Back row Richard Fong, Anne Fong, Judy Wong Leong, Ruth Wong, Sai Choy Wong, Frances Fong.

CHAPTER 64

My favourite brother-in-law Sai Len Wong and me

When I think or talk of Sai Len, I just love him. He had very pleasant manners. He treated everyone with respect. He was well-liked by the people around him. He was very supportive of my wife Frances in her young days. My children held high regard for him. Sorry, due to old age he went to rest in God's land.

Sai Len was born in 1922, in Cheong Chau, near Seiki (Zhongshan City), Guangdong, China.

At 10 years old he travelled to Fiji with his mother Mrs Wong Sau Ng, to live with his father Wong War Sik. The family lived in Levuka at Cokacala, opposite the Fijian village of Levuka vaka viti.

Sai Len went to school at the Sacred Heart School in town for a few years. It was difficult for him as he had to learn English for the first time.

As more younger siblings were born, he left school to help his father in the bakery and grocery business.

When he was a teenager Sai Len inherited a shop in Namacu, Koro, from an old man called Uncle Wong whom he had befriended. He helped his father run the shop in Koro for a few years to supplement the income needed to bring up 7 younger siblings in Levuka.

On 27 November 1953 Sai Len married Lina Lui. Together they raised a family of 8. They ran the Levuka vaka viti shop and bakery for many years till all the eight children had completed high school, and three of them attended university. Sai Len and Lina lived in Levuka all their life. In 2014 they were recognised as the longest surviving married couple in Levuka. They were also the last remaining members of the old Chinese community in Levuka.

Sadly, Sai Len passed away on 4 October 2015 at the ripe age of 93.

He left behind 7 children (Lily RIP in 1986), 24 grandchildren, 14 great-grandchildren. His surviving wife Lina still lives in the home he built beside the old shop and homestead.

Cousin Kinman Fong brought dinner to Len's house when the two sisters Frances and Emily visited their brother in Levuka in June 2015.

Watching TV after dinner supplied by cousin Kinman Fong, Levuka, June 2015.

CHAPTER 65

My brother-in-law Sai Sing Wong and me

Sai Sing now lives in Sydney. He once owned Wong's Shipping Co. Ltd, Suite 6. 1st floor, Epworth Arcade, off Nina St, Suva, Fiji. Wong's was the biggest domestic shipping company in Fiji. All the fares included meals, but cabin passengers got better facilities.

Before he moved his Wong's Shipping office to Nina St, he shared an office with me at 30 Cumming St, 3rd Floor, for about a year.

He left school after class 7 at the Sacred Heart Convent in Levuka. He went to help his father in the shop in Levuka, and later in Namacu, Koro.

He married Yuk Kin Wu from China, an arranged marriage, when he was 20 years old on 6 June 1956.

In the shop in Koro he baked bread, dried copra, planted yagona and dealt in trochus shells. Later his father and he moved to Natena in Gau.

His wife had 2 children Patrick and Evelyne in Levuka. The two children spent their childhood in Gau. When Patrick was 6 years old, Sai Sing and his father ceased trading in Gau, and moved to Suva so the children could attend school.

Sai Sing and his younger brother Sai Choy combined and opened Choy's Food stores in Flagstaff. Later his wife bore him two more sons Christopher and Stephen.

Sai Sing left his partnership with Choy's Food store and founded Wong's Shipping Co, and later Wong's Shipping Co. Ltd.

I was his accountant/tax agent for a number of years until his business expanded. He then consulted Gammon, Chau & Co to look after his accounting/tax affairs.

Sai Sing and I meet at our homes alternatively two to three times a week. He has always been a very good brother-in-law (Frances' older brother), and friend. He takes great interest in what my children are doing. He is a very popular uncle.

He is a very pleasant person, likeable to those who come into contact with him.

With Sai Sing Wong at the Suva wharf, farewelling relatives Agnes Lum Wong and family, who were migrating to Canada, 1967.

3 brothers-in-law, close friends too.
Me and wife Frances' older brothers Sai Len and Sai Sing Wong at our house.

At the Sydney airport farewelling youngest daughter Magdalene, leaving for the first time to work in London, 2006.

Brother-in-law Sai Sing Wong's 50th wedding anniversary party, King's Seafood Restaurant, 2007.
From left Ian Fong, Dr Kam Young, Winnie Young, Frances Fong, Patrick Wong.

Brother-in-law Sai Sing Wong's 50th wedding anniversary party, King's Seafood Restaurant, 2007.
Sitting from left Patrick Wong senior, Marion Wong, Frances Fong, Henry Leong.
Standing from left Patrick Wong junior, Iris Wong, Joshua Vigano, Matthew Wong, Alex Chang, Ian Fong, Sai Sing Wong, Yuk Kin Wong holding Zack Wong.

Good brother-in-law and friend Sing and wife's 60th Wedding Diamond Jubilee at the Harvest Buffet, Star Casino, 11 June 2016.

CHAPTER 66
My brother-in-law Sai Choy Wong and me

Sai Choy was the Manager of the popular Suva Co-operative store, situated at the back of the Golden Dragon Night Club restaurant. He was a frequent lunch hour customer at this restaurant. I too often went there for lunch.

One day in 1961, we happened to be sitting on the same table and became acquainted. During our conversation he found out from me that I knew how to do Chinese cooking, He made a proposal to me to move into a three-bedroom house in Pender Street which he had rented; free accommodation on rent and food, sundry items included, and in return, I would do just the cooking for the both of us. I was so happy and accepted his proposal right away. I moved into his house the next day.

After graduating from Loreto High school, his younger sister Anne came from Levuka to Suva, and became the third person living in the house. She and I often cooked together in the kitchen, and baked mutton chops were our favourites. We had a cordial friendship, no chemistry between us but we enjoyed talking to each other and I always treated her as a sister. On Sundays, we went to Mass together, but we never thought of going to the movies.

Soon, Sai Choy's mother came from Levuka to join us. She was very kind to me, even washed my clothes. As I was fluent in the Zhongshan dialect we talked to each other a lot.

Another member of the family from Levuka came to join us in Pender street. It was Sai Choy's younger brother, Michael Sai Oey.

As a result, there was no room for me to continue to stay in the house, so I found a room in a boarding house owned by a Mrs Hurley (one of the well-known Barrett sisters). The house was situated near the Merchant Club and the Defence Club. After leaving the Wong family, I still kept in touch with them.

Sai Choy completed class 8 at the Chinese Primary School (now Yat Sen Primary and Secondary School). When he went to school from class 5 to class 8 in Suva, he was offered free accommodation by Joong Hing Loong Co Ltd, a company with which his father had business dealings. Though he passed his exam to go to the Marist Brothers' High School he decided to find work. He realised that his father needed his help to provide finance for his 3 younger sisters to attend high school.

He worked for the Joong Hing Loong grocery store for three years and received free accommodation.

When the Suva Co-operative store opened in Carnarvon Street, Suva, Sai Choy became its first manager.

After he left Suva Co-op, he went for a holiday in Sydney. While he was there, he went around consulting manufacturers, hoping to become an agent for them.

After his return from Sydney he opened a shop called Choy's Food stores in Flagstaff, and at the same time started an Import and Export agency. He was in a partnership with his older brother Sai Sing in the Food store section, wholesaling goods mainly to outside islands of Taveuni, Savusavu etc. Not long after, Sai Sing left the partnership to run his own shipping company.

Sai Choy was a clever man, had a good business brain, and one who was extremely generous too. He was a fervent member of the Assembly of God Church. I believe he gave 10% of his earnings to the church, and for some time, paid for his church pastor's house rent.

Sadly, he was drowned in the sea in Lakeba (Lakemba), Lau, Fiji, in 1986, aged 49.

What had happened? See the brief story below. The Prime Minister of Fiji, Ratu Sir Kamisese Mara, a keen golfer himself, had invited many golfers for a tournament in the Island of Lakemba where he was also High Chief. The people who lost their lives in the drowning tragedy did not want to stay overnight in the island, so they hired a punt to go back to sleep onboard the boat.

After my family had just moved to our home in North Ryde, Sydney, tragic news reached my wife Frances that my brother-in-law Sai Choy Wong, our niece Lily Gibbons (Nee Wong), her husband, Dr John Gibbons and their two young children, Robert and Talei, had drowned in the sea off Lakemba. A good family friend's son Gerrard Fong was also lost in that tragedy. Their long punt powered by a putt putt engine had overturned in the "breakers" off Lakemba Island in the afternoon as they travelled to the Wongs Shipping Company's ship.

Nobody knew about the capsized boat and the eight adults and 2 toddlers who struggled in the ocean. They managed to turn the punt upright a few times, but the strong waves capsized the punt. The family, with 2 friends and 2 Fijian sailors, hung onto the punt for several hours.

Soon night fell and all were darkness. One of the Fijian men decided to swim ashore, 2 kms away, to alert the villagers.

Cold and exhausted he managed to pass on the message of the struggling family in the sea to Prime Minister Ratu Sir Kamisese Mara, who quickly ordered all able-bodied men in punts to search for the survivors. They used bright torches and called out across the ocean. It was about 4 am when they found the remaining survivors, 1 Fijian man and 2 teenage friends. The others had been swept away one by one – too exhausted to continue hanging on. It was a great tragedy Fiji had, and a tremendous loss for the Wong family.

The only survivors were my nephew Stephen Wong and his friend Jeffrey Lin and the 2 Fijian sailors.

Bodies recovered were Sai Choy Wong, his niece Lily Wong Gibbons and her infant daughter Talei, but the bodies of Dr John Gibbons and his 6-year-old son Robert were never found.

To those who had drowned RIP.

Taken outside the Pender St house, March 1961.
Front Anne Wong, Frances Wong.
Back Sai Choy Wong, Michael Sai Oey Wong, Ian Fong, Henry Fat Kow Yee.

CHAPTER 67

Mr Au Yeung Hin and Mrs Wong Sau Fong Au Yueng

Aunty Sau Fong was also called big Fong (Fong Levu), and my wife Frances was called little Fong (Fong Lailai), whose last Chinese name Fong was named after her. When I was boarding with Sai Choy Wong in Pender Street, Suva, Aunty came to visit, and it was then we first got acquainted.

I always stayed at Uncle and Aunt's house whenever I visited Levuka. If mud crabs were available at the market, Aunty would buy them and cooked for dinner. The flavours and method she cooked the crabs were second to none. When she was stir-frying the crabs and the ingredients in the wok, the whole house was filled with aromatic smell.

Uncle Hin was equally good with his Chilli Lairo (Small Land Crabs) dish, so says Margaret Harrison who had enjoyed this.

Uncle and Aunty operated a bakery in the early days in Levuka. He delivered bread on a shoulder pole with two baskets. Their friendliness and generosity were well known to all the people, and were well-liked by all in Levuka.

According to Margaret Harrison the lovely couple looked after Melvyn Harrison (aged about 1) when sadly his mother passed away suddenly. Melvyn was always grateful and appreciative to the old friendly couple.

In their later years Aunty and Uncle brought their grand nephew from Hong Kong to join them in Fiji.

Aunty's closest friends in Levuka were: Mrs Chang Yet Pore, Mrs Young Yet, Mrs Kang Kee Tong, Mrs Wong War Sik, Mrs Mar Ghee Ho, Mrs Yuet Wan Wong, and Mrs Henry Shey.

She and her dearest friends loved mahjong and nearly every night, had a game with Mrs Kang Kee Tong, Mrs Young Yet, and Mrs Mar Ghee Ho.

Aunty strongly recommended me to Frances' mother that I was a suitable husband for Frances. She also was a match maker to a few couples whose marriages are still rock solid,

Uncle passed away many years ago, and Aunty became a widow.

When my eldest daughter Geralyne got married in Sydney, my wife Frances arranged for a visa for Aunty to come over to attend the wedding. She stayed at our home for a few days.

After a few years at the Home of Compassion in Tamavua, she passed away on 17 December 1994.

The beautiful tombstone was completed on 6 December 2017.

Standing is Aunty Sau Fong.
Sitting from left is my mother-in-law Wong Ung Sau, Mrs Young Yet, Mrs Cheer.

With Uncle Hin and Aunty Sau Fong in front of their home, 1967.

My youngest daughter Magdalene celebrating her birthday at the David's Restaurant in Cumming Street, Suva, which I once owned.
From left Magdalene, my mother Fong Lum Oy Wan, Aunty Sau Fong, Aunty Fong Sue Kee.

Mrs Wong Sau Fong's gravestone in Levuka, Fiji.

After Father Pedero's blessing of the tombstone, 6 December 2017. From left Sister Veronica Lum, Emily Au Yeung, Mavis Leong, Fr Pedero, behind is Kwok Wai's son, Diane Chan, Kinman Fong, Annie Young, Kwok Wai Au Yeung, Margaret Harrison, Sam Young, behind Sam is Michael Young, Marjorie Sahai, Akata Wong.

CHAPTER 68

My mother from Hong Kong to Fiji

My father passed away on 10 March 1969, leaving my mother alone in Hong Kong. The last time I said goodbye to her in the village in China, was in September 1950. Frances and I decided to bring her to Fiji, so that we can look after her. Of course, we did but it also turned out to be the other way around because she looked after us as well.

In December 1969, after spending two weeks with my eldest uncle's wife Aunty Fong Low Shee in Auckland, New Zealand, mum arrived at Nadi where she was lovingly greeted by Frances and me.

When our 3 children were attending the Yat Sen Primary School, which is about 3 minutes' walk from our home, mum cooked lunch every school day and our house girl would deliver to Frances and the children. Not bad having fresh and warm lunch every day.

When mum was young in China, she was educated through private tuition. She was well liked in our village in China. She had an open mind and had an excellent relationship with Frances.

Our children learned to speak the Zhongshan dialect as mum taught them.

Mum lived with us in Fiji and migrated with us to Australia on 19 December 1985 until she passed away on 2 January 1989, just short of her 80th birthday on 31 January 1989.

Sitting from left Geralyne Fong, Fong Lum Oy Wan, Ian Fong.
Standing from left Laisani Dau, Frances Fong carrying Gerard Fong.

Sitting from left Fong Lum Oy Wan carrying Gerard Fong, Frances Fong carrying Magdalene Fong, Geralyne Fong.

Sitting from left Gerard Fong, Fong Lum Oy Wan, Magdalene Fong. Standing from left Frances Fong, Ian Fong, Geralyne Fong.

CHAPTER 69
Our eldest child Geralyne

Following our wedding, Frances fell pregnant. For 4 months she suffered from extreme morning sickness. She couldn't eat, drink nor teach. Strangely any noise made her sick. She was seen by different doctors and had to be admitted to CWM Hospital in Suva. In the fifth month Frances returned to her beloved teaching role and was able to consume food every three to four hours. If her meal was late her morning sickness returned.

You will laugh when you read this. One weekend, Frances tried to catch a large crab that came loose in the kitchen. The mud crab nipped her finger. She called out loudly to Teresia to help. I ran into the kitchen and at the same time calling Teresia to boil some water quickly, as I thought Frances was having the baby. Frances called out: "It's the mud crab biting my finger, you stupid". Teresia hurriedly tapped the crab and it released its grip. What a relief! Teresia Siata was Frances' friend and live-in housekeeper, a very good cook of Chinese dishes.

In Hong Kong, my parents were thrilled to learn of the birth of their first grandchild. Sadly, my father passed away 4 days after Geralyne was born. However, he was able to give her the Chinese name of Fong Gar Yook which translates to treasured family jade.

A nine pounds 4 oz baby girl was a bundle of joy, and a great surprise to the whole family. Thank God she was big and strong. At Geralyne's one-month-old party, relatives and friends commented that she was the size of a three-month-old baby.

After her maternity leave, Frances returned to teach at the Fiji Chinese Primary School (now Yat Sen Primary and Secondary School). Her mother came to help for the remaining two school terms. She lived in Rewa Street, Flagstaff. Every morning she walked down to our house and bathed baby Geralyne. She was a big baby, but Grandma Wong told me she was anxious about dropping her into the water because she had poor eyesight.

Geralyne was a healthy baby and hardly got sick. She often winked at me when Frances brought her to my office while I was working late at night. During her toddler years, she liked sitting under our mango tree in the front of the house, and watched the cars and people passing. At that time Grandma Fong had come from Hong Kong to live with us. She enjoyed looking after her first grandchild.

Geralyne attended the Fiji Chinese Primary School from Kindergarten to Class 8. She came first in the class from 1 to 8. From years 3 to 8, she took a very active part in the school's cultural dances. She was appointed the school's head girl by the teachers and senior pupils.

When she was in Form 5 at St Joseph's Secondary School in Suva, she was selected as a member of the Fiji Chinese Youth to accompany the Fiji contingent to the South Pacific Arts Festival in Tahiti. The Chinese youths performed Chinese dances which were very well received. Geralyne and the Chinese youths enjoyed their few weeks' stay in Tahiti.

On 19 December 1985 she and the family migrated to Australia. She spent many hours searching newspaper advertisements to assist her mother to look for a house to buy.

In Sydney she attended Marist Sisters' College in Woolwich. After completing her Higher School Leaving Certificate Exam (HSC) she went to study at the University of New South Wales. After a week, she opted to study at Macquarie University as it was much closer to home. She graduated with Bachelor of Economics majoring in Accounting.

During her years at high school and university, she worked part-time in the weekends and full time during the school holidays and earned enough to become quite independent.

She married Sen Yee, the love of her life and has two beautiful and loving children Jonathan and Tiana.

She is now working as the Financial Controller of a reputable Australian privately owned company, leading a centralised team in Sydney.

Before this job she worked as an accountant at two other big companies.

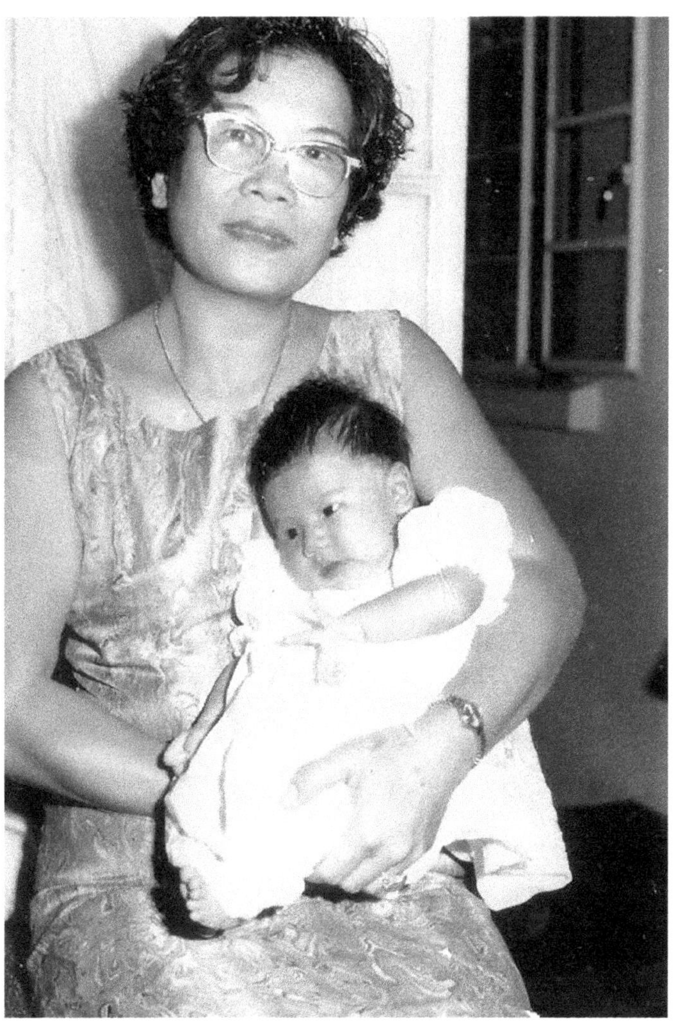

My eighth Aunty Fong War Kit holding baby Geralyne.

Geralyne at her First Holy Communion at Suva Catholic Cathedral.

Our 3 children at our home in Tanoa Street, Suva, Fiji, early 1980's.
From left Gerard Fong, Geralyne Fong, Magdalene Fong.

On a float for a parade, Chinatown, Sydney.
Geralyne is wearing the cheongsam (Chinese dress) on the furthest right.

Geralyne's wedding day in 1991.

Our 3 children at my 70th birthday party in 2008.

CHAPTER 70

Our second child son Gerard

Gerard was a 9 lb 7 oz baby, a bigger one than his older sister Geralyne. He attended the Fiji Chinese Primary School (now Yat Sen Primary and Secondary School) from kindergarten to class 8. He came first every year from class 1 to 8.

The teachers and senior pupils from class 5 to 8, voted him to be the head boy of the school in his final year. His mother Frances, who had just been appointed headteacher through a transfer from the Laucala Bay Secondary School, ruled him out of the position, because Gerard happened to be her son. She made the decision to avoid mischievous talks by parents.

No doubt Gerard was bitterly disappointed, but his school mates still regarded him as the unofficial head boy for that year.

At home I taught Gerard how to play the game of chess. As soon as he had learned to play the game, he was capable of winning whenever he and I played.

Two Yat Sen pupils achieved brilliant results in the Fiji National Mental Abilities Tournament in July 1983. Gerard took firsts in Current Events, Geography and Abstract Learning, and was declared the 1983 champion in the Fiji Primary School Chess Tournament. Meanwhile Gerard's classmate Estelle Fong, won firsts in Mathematics and Scientific Knowledge in the same competition.

In another competition in 1983, Gerard was the winner of the Five-Minute Lightning Chess Tournament held in the University of the South Pacific. He beat Jaiwant Singh (second place) and Dr Virgilio De Asa (third place).

Gerard attended Forms 3 and 4 at the Marist Brothers' High School in Suva.

He migrated with his family to Australia on 19 December 1985.

After passing his Higher Leaving Certicate Exam (HSC), Gerard studied at the Sydney University of Technology, and graduated with a Bachelor of Business (Commerce) Degree.

My wife and I were happy and proud of him for working part-time during weekends and school holidays at the Flemings Supermarket (part of Woolworths) in Gladesville, earning enough pocket money for his needs. On Sundays he worked as a store manager.

Gerard is now working as an Information Technology (IT) manager.

He married the love of his life Clare Kent, who is a solicitor.

They have two lovely daughters Chloe and Rachel.

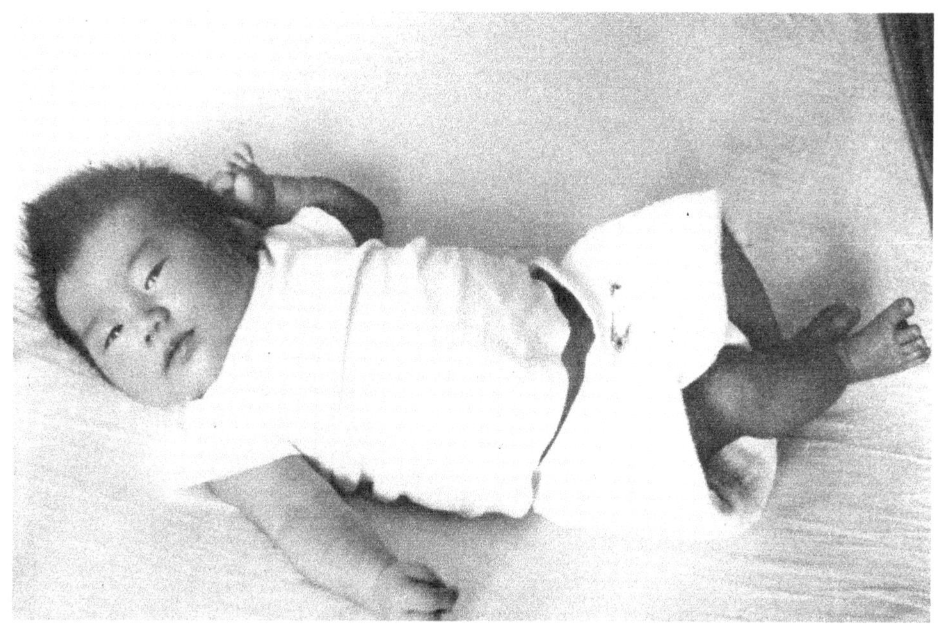

Gerard Fong, 1 month old.

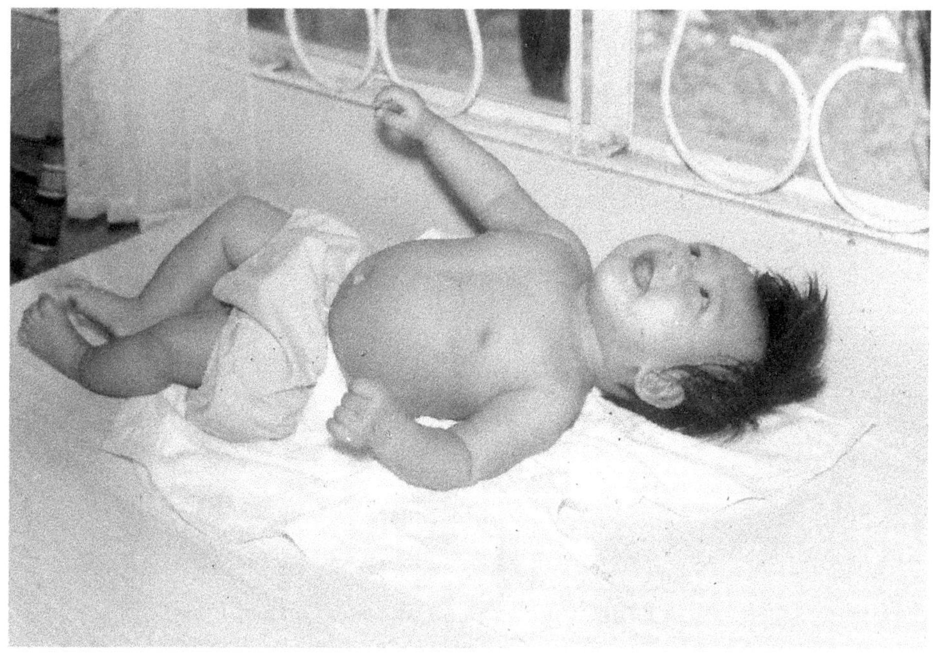

Gerard Fong, 3 months old.

My Mum Fong Lum Oy Wan and son Gerard Fong.

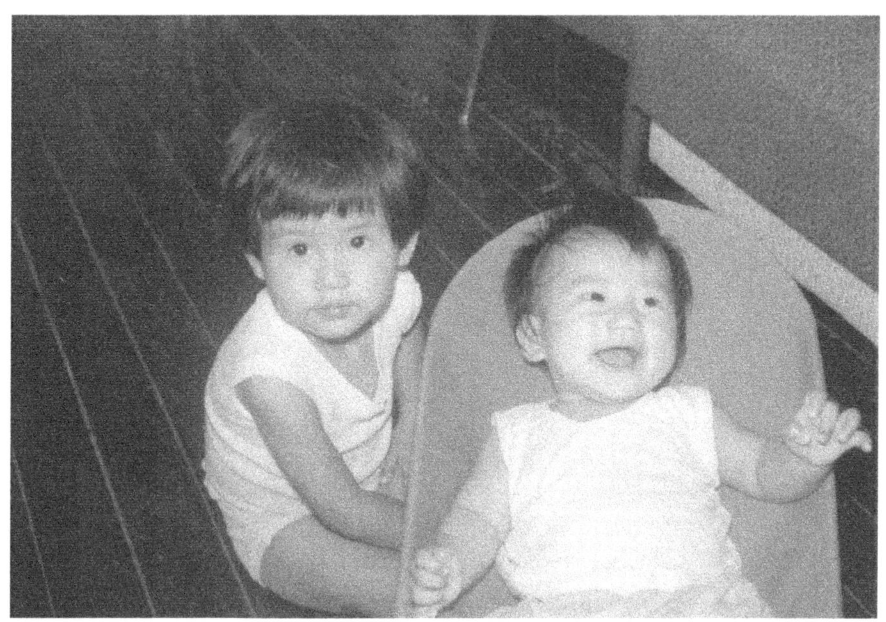

From left Geralyne Fong and Gerard Fong.

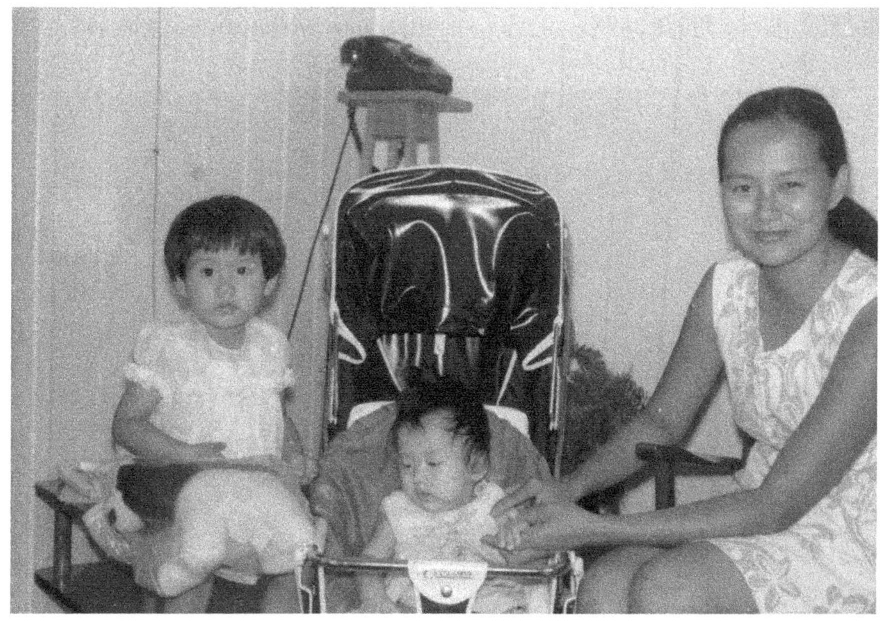

From left Geralyne Fong, Gerard Fong and Frances Fong.

Gerard Fong, receiving trophy for winning the five-minute Lightning Chess Tournament held at the University of the South Pacific in November 1985.
He was 15 years old.
Many thanks to The Fiji Times for providing permission to publish this image.

In church at our son Gerard and daughter-in-law Clare's wedding, 1999.
From left Geralyne Fong Yee, Magdalene Fong, Frances Fong, Ian Fong.

Son Gerard and his family.
From left Gerard Fong, Clare Kent, Rachel Fong, Chloe Fong.

CHAPTER 71

Our third and youngest child Magdalene

Magdalene was an 8 lb 8 oz baby, a little smaller than her eldest sister Geralyne and elder brother Gerard.

Immediately after she was born, she didn't cry out until the nurse on duty smacked her bottom.

Then she cried.

When she came home from the hospital, she seldom made any noise. Frances and I were very worried and thought we would have a dumb child. After a week she started to cry, and that was a relief.

As a little child of 3 and a half years old, Magdalene loved school. Frances was teaching at the Laucala Bay Secondary School. She made a request to the headteacher, Sister Paula for Magdalene to be admitted into kindergarten for half a day. Magdalene ended up loving her time in kindergarten, so we got permission for her to continue to attend it aged 3 and aged 4, moving up to Class 1 at age 5.

Magdalene came first in every class from class 1 to 5. Starting from class 3 at school, she started performing Chinese Cultural dances on numerous occasions.

On 19 December 1985 she migrated with the family to Australia.

In Sydney, she attended class 6 at Our Lady Queen of Peace Catholic Primary School in Gladesville, and from year 7 to 12 at the Marist Sisters College in Woolwich, graduating at the young age of 16.

Frances and I were very happy and proud of her for working part-time in the weekends and during the school holidays, earning enough pocket money for her needs.

On her first payday at the Top Ryde Chicken Shop, Magdalene gave her mum A$40 for her pocket money to Fiji.

While Magdalene was 16 at high school, she was a member of the Sydney Chinese Youth club and took part in all types of Chinese Cultural dances.

After passing her Higher Leaving Certificate Exam (HSC), she studied at the University of Technology Sydney (UTS) and graduated with a Bachelor of Arts (Communications) degree.

In year 12 and during her studies at UTS, she helped as a volunteer on programmes and then later as a paid freelancer at 2 SER FM, the community radio station owned by UTS and Macquarie University. She enjoyed that.

After graduation, she worked as a paid Radio producer at 2 SER FM for about a year.

And then she returned to university to complete a Master of Technology (Information Systems Engineering) degree.

During her studies for her master's degree, she worked part-time at St George Bank as a Bank teller, and at the computer company COMPAC in Rhodes.

Later, she went on to work in full-time roles at IBM, Woolworths Limited, KPMG etc.

After a few years working in Sydney, she decided to travel overseas to gain more work experience.

She settled in London in the United Kingdom, working in digital consultant roles at Barclays, PwC, Johnson and Johnson etc.

In January 2019, she married Adrian Stefanczyk, a Web designer from Poland, at the Banjo Paterson Restaurant in Gladesville in Sydney.

Keeping the front lawn tidy when Magdalene was about 3 years old.

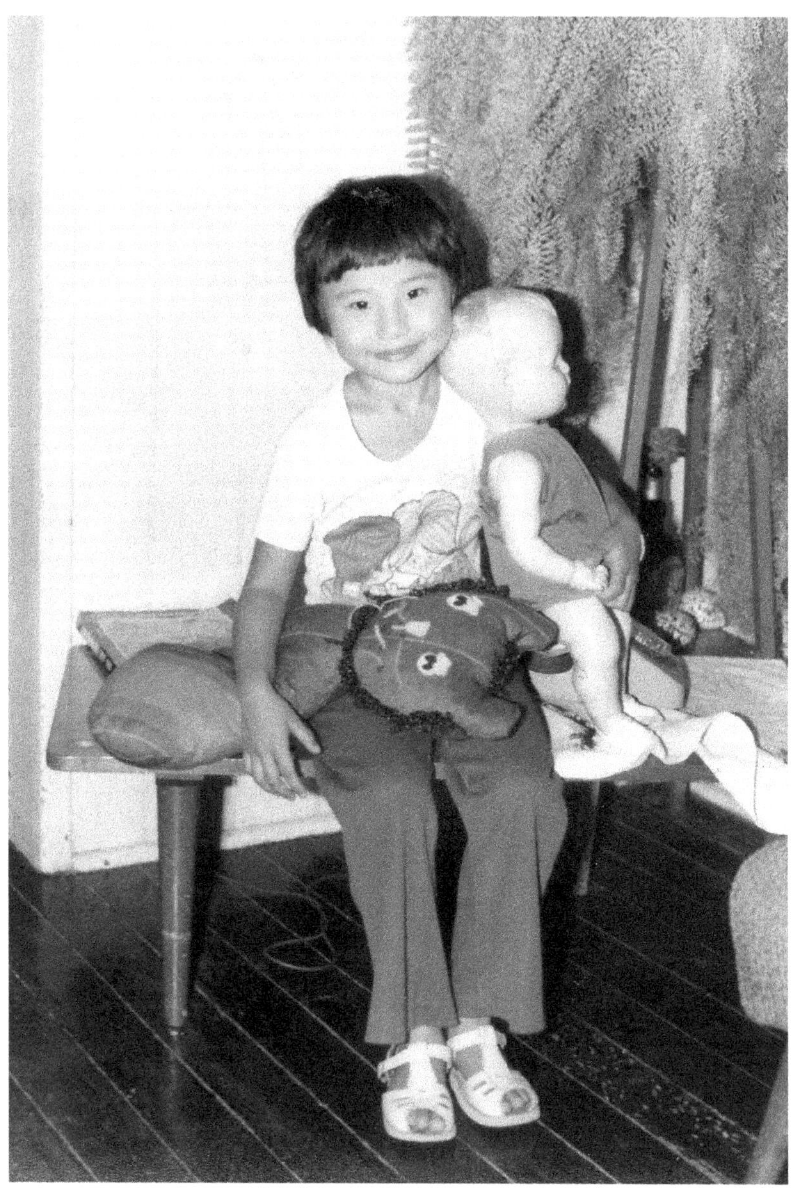

Magdalene with some of her favourite toys, about 5 years old.

Colette Fong and Magdalene performing a Chinese drum dance at a Double Tenth Celebration event at the China Club, Suva, 1984.

Magdalene's birthday, North Ryde, January 1987.

Photo taken on Magdalene's graduation day in May 2000.
She completed a Master of Technology (Information Systems Engineering) degree at the University of Technology, Sydney.

On Magdalene's wedding day, January 2019.
From left Tiana Yee, Frances Fong, Ian Fong, Magdalene Fong, Geralyne Fong Yee.
Our son Gerard's daughter Chloe Fong was a flower girl on the day.

CHAPTER 72

Robbery in front of my house in 18 Tanoa Street, Suva, Fiji

My family and I lived in a house at 18 Tanoa Street, Flagstaff, Suva, Fiji, 3 minutes walk to the Yat Sen Primary School. It was a cul-de-sac until a sub-division was made behind my house.

After I closed David's Restaurant the night before the robbery, my little daughter Geralyne, about 7 years old, wife Frances and I came back to our home. As we reached the top of the stairs, Geralyne told me she saw a "drunken" man meaning bad man, hiding on the left side of the house. Without fear, I gave chase but lost him. He took off through the back of the compound.

The next night, Frances and I returned home after a very busy day at the restaurant. It was payday, and as usual many policemen came to drink and dined at the restaurant. I had good takings that night, and the cash was placed inside the leather bag I always carried. One of my tax clients' books were also inside the same bag.

Frances went inside the house first, and into the kitchen. I was not far behind. As I approached the front porch, a shirtless Fijian man in heavy boots, rushed at me. I dropped my bag all of a sudden and didn't try to get it back, as at that moment I feared for my safety as well as for Frances who came out from the kitchen to the sitting room. She saw the robber, and was frightened, so she fell to the floor and sat there. She was heavily pregnant, expecting our third and youngest daughter Magdalene. Fortunately, Frances and the baby were not hurt.

After the shock I ran to the back of the compound where the sub-division was. I saw the watchman and asked him whether he had seen anybody running away with a bag. Your guess could be as good as mine. He said nobody came around. I was inclined to think that he was in league with the robber.

Losing hundreds of dollars and my client's books were not a big thing, but my life was more precious.

Later about my 33 years in Australia, I will write about the robberies in my mixed business corner shop in Croydon Park, NSW, Australia.

Photo taken at birthday party outside our house in Tanoa St, Suva, Fiji.

CHAPTER 73
Our youngest child Magdalene's 1-month-old party

Our eldest daughter Geralyne and second child Gerard, were full of excitement awaiting the birth of their baby sister Magdalene, and so were mum and me. Of course, wife Frances was no exception.

As the same with the two older children, I was present in the maternity room where Magdalene was born. She was an 8 lb 8 oz baby, the lightest of the three children.

Both our eldest daughter Geralyne and son Gerard, celebrated their 1-month-old parties at home. Invited guests were relatives and friends who came for ginger and pork sessions.

When Magdalene was born, David's Restaurant was in operation; so that provided us with facilities to put up a good party for little Bo, whose Chinese name is Fong Gar Bo.

I had the restaurant closed for the night, normally a busy Saturday night. Invited guests were relatives and friends, irrespective of whether they came for ginger and pork or not.

The restaurant was full, and a buffet dinner was provided. Some of the dishes served included Chinese Roast Pork, Cha Siu, Chicken Mushrooms, Chicken Cashew Nuts, Chicken Chow Mein and Prawn Stir-fry.

Besides seated guests, there were some standing, guess there could be more than 110 guests and staff. Everyone enjoyed the night especially our elderly guests who had been friends of my father.

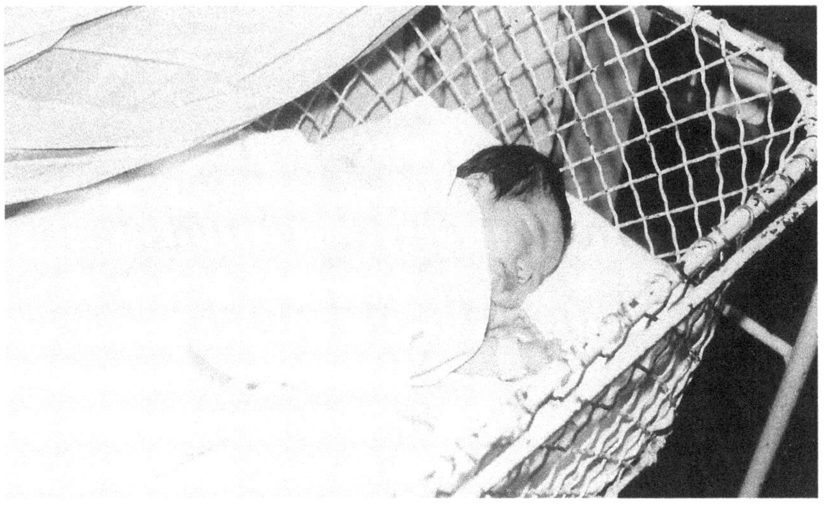

Magdalene 6 days old in hospital.

Magdalene 6 days old in hospital.
From left Frances Fong, Gerard Fong, Geralyne Fong checking out Magdalene who was fast asleep.

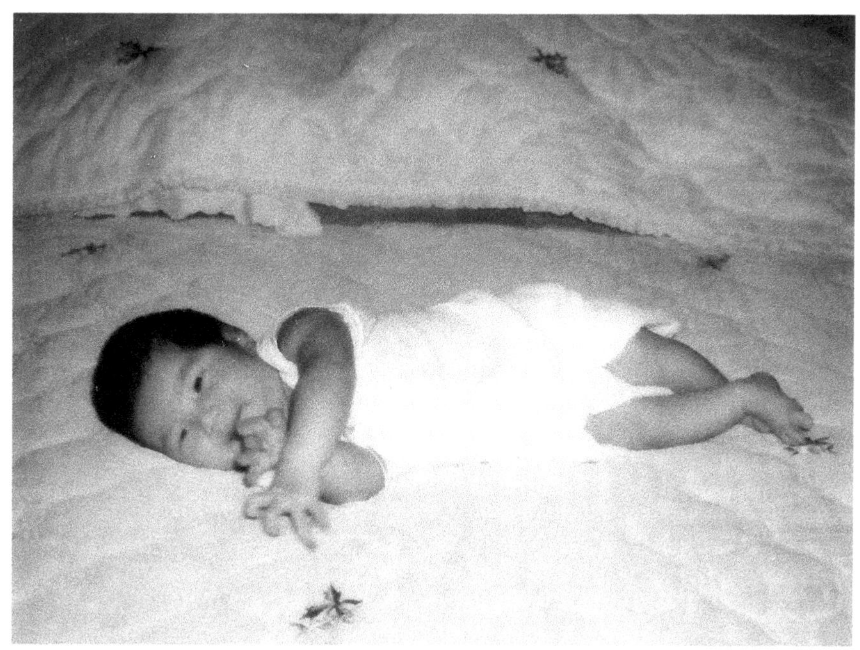

Magdalene, 2 weeks old.

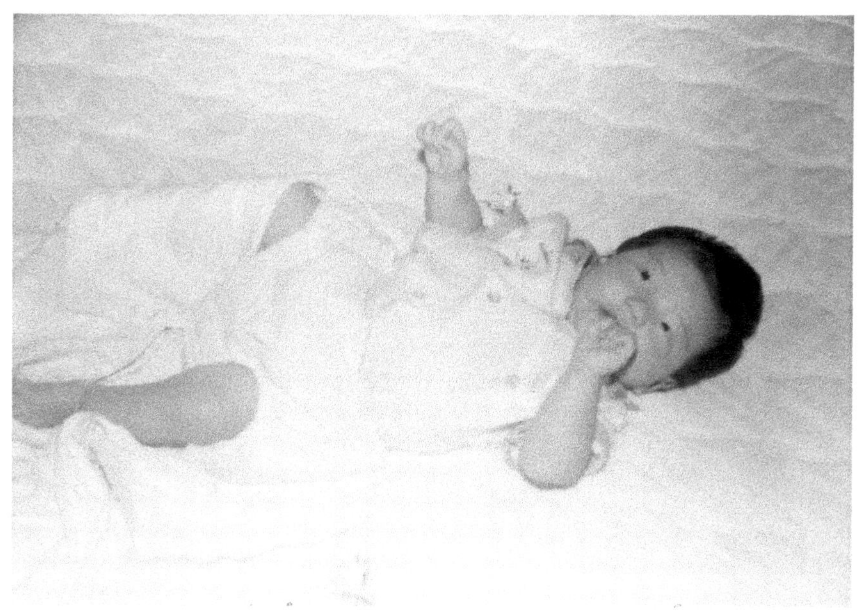

Magdalene, 1 month old.

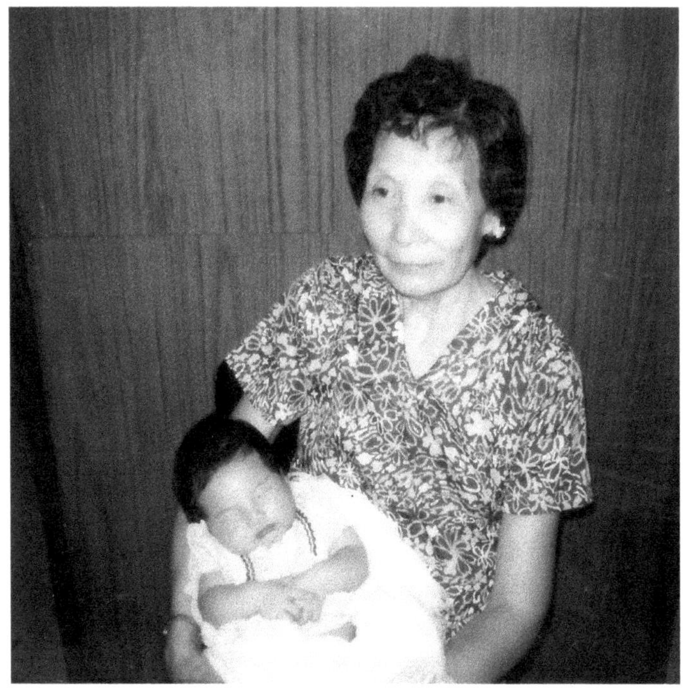

My mother Fong Lum Oy Wan with Magdalene at her 1-month old party.

At Magdalene's 1-month old party.

From left Frances Fong, Magdalene Fong, Monica Lum, Geralyne Fong.

At Magdalene's 1-month old party.
From left Frances Fong, Magdalene Fong, Gerard Fong, my mother Fong Lum Oy Wan, Geralyne Fong, Ian Fong.

CHAPTER 74
Frances Fong's trip to Taiwan

In early January 1984, Frances was fortunate to be given a free excursion trip to Taiwan for 8 days. Everything, flights, accommodation, meals, excursions, transport, etc were paid by the Taiwan Government.

In Taipei she was provided with a guide, who spoke English and a chauffeur-driven limousine.

Taipei, the capital of Taiwan, is a modern metropolis with Japanese colonial lanes, busy shopping streets and contemporary buildings. The skyline is crowned by the 509 metres tall, bamboo-shaped Taipei 101 skyscraper, with upscale shops at the base and a rapid elevator to an observatory near the top. Taipei is also known for its lively street-food scene and many night markets, including the expansive Shilin market.

She was driven to two private girls high schools, one of which had over 1,000 students. Each class averaged about 40 to 45 students. The discipline was perfect. The students continued with their written work while the class teacher, principal and Frances spoke for ten to fifteen minutes.

Before recess, the whole student body gathered in very straight lines in the quadrangle and performed certain exercises. Frances was amazed that no teacher was involved. A senior student directed the 1000 plus students from a high platform overlooking the body of students. There were no shouting or loud commands. Some music was played, and the leader performed certain actions and the whole student body followed her. Obedience and precision were exhibited fantastically.

That was impossible in the Fiji and Australian Schools.

Every day Frances was taken to various places and always to beautiful restaurants and hotels for lunch and dinner.

Frances and her guide were flown to Kaohshiung, a massive port city in southern Taiwan. It's home to many skyscrapers, such as the 248 metres tall Tuntex Sky Tower, and is known for its diversity of parks. Its focal point is the Love River, with walking paths and cafes along its banks, and cruise boats navigating its waters. Shopping options range from high-end malls to the Liuhe and Ruifeng night markets.

Again, they were provided with a limousine and chauffeur, hotel and meals.

All in all, Frances enjoyed her trip tremendously.

She was astonished by the cleanliness of the schools, the obedient students and the long hours the teachers worked, from 8 am to 5 pm.

No wonder, many students were high achievers.

Frances stayed at the San Polo Hotel, Taipei, January 1984.

From left the Education Officer, France Fong, her guide, the Principal of the Private Girls' Secondary School, Taipei, January 1984.

Frances Fong with her guide in Kaohsiung, January 1984.

With teachers in Kaohsiung, January 1984.

With guide in front of the Dragon and Tiger Pagodas in Kaohsiung, January 1984.

CHAPTER 75

Frances Fong's Mandarin study at The Beijing University of Languages

In September 1984, while Frances was the headteacher of the Yat Sen Primary School, she was given a 1-year fellowship by UNESCO to study Mandarin in Beijing.

She was accompanied by Judy Harm Nam, another student.

Both received air flights to Beijing, accommodation, meals, tuition and books.

They were given an allowance each month, and in addition, 500 yuans each to buy coats and boots, by the generous Chinese Government.

Frances was paid her usual salary by the Education Department of the Fiji Government.

She and Judy shared a bedroom up the 4th floor in the girls' dormitory. They were provided with 2 single beds, 2 wardrobes, 2 desks, and a large gas heater.

In the dormitory, girls from different countries such as Canada, United States, India, Sri Lanka, Japan, Australia, New Zealand, Korea, Indonesia and Fiji were housed. It was exciting getting to know girls from different countries.

Lectures were from 8 am to 12 noon. Lunch was served at noon.

Students were expected to practise their writing in the afternoon, and the next morning they were tested. It was indeed very difficult.

Frances found that her Chinese Cantonese dialect interfered with her Mandarin pronunciation. Despite that, she struggled on.

Some weekends, students were taken on excursions to the Great Wall, Fragrant Hills, Temple of Heaven, Tiananmen Square, Forbidden City, and the man-made lake where they enjoyed boating.

The foreign students enjoyed delicious meals in the evenings.

They were offered 8 varieties, and each variety was labelled by a number. Rice was the main staple food. There was always plenty of food for them.

Snacks and fruits were sold at the nearby market.

Little by little, Frances and other students learnt to speak some basic Mandarin words. They were thrilled to communicate with the lecturers and other people around them.

Frances had just about settled, and happy on her study routines in Beijing, but suddenly a phone call from her husband Ian Fong, had interrupted her from her stay in Beijing. He told her that the Australian High Commission Office in Suva, had informed the family to undertake medical examinations for migration to Australia, and she must come back to Fiji for this procedure.

On hearing the phone call, Frances immediately contacted the consular in charge of overseas students, to help her organise travel formalities to come back to Fiji. She was given a month's leave from the university. The consular took her to the airport in a limousine. He helped to check her in.

The Secretary for Immigration in the Australian High Commission in Suva advised Frances not to return to Beijing, as the family's migration papers had been approved. She was really disappointed for giving up her studies in Beijing.

Fortunately, Frances was not required to pay back any compensation to the Fiji Government.

She continued to be the headteacher of Yat Sen Primary School until the end of the 1985 school year and migrated with her family to Australia on 19 December 1985.

Frances and Judy Harm Nam joined the Fiji Chinese delegates at a banquet dinner for overseas Chinese, at the Hall of the Great People, October 1984. Frances told me that Lionel Yee who was the leader of the Fiji delegation, invited her and Judy to join the delegates to the banquet. He also told Frances about the fellowship and helped her with her application. Many thanks Lionel.

Frances, some of her classmates and their lecturer, 17 November 1984.

Frances and her classmates on excursion with their lecturers.

CHAPTER 76

Miscellaneous happenings in Suva, Fiji

I am now rounding up my time in Suva, Fiji, before my family and I migrated to Australia on 19 December 1985.

The first Chinese Ambassador to Fiji was Mr Mi Guojun, who came in May 1977, and left in 1980. He was from the district of Donguan, near Guangzhou, Guangdong, China. Mr Mi and his wife I believe, took part in the Long march in China. As they were from Dongguan where almost all the Suva market gardeners came from, they liaised closely with the market gardeners. The above paragraph may not be 100% accurate.

From Lionel Yee:

- The first Chinese official from PRC to arrive to set up office and stayed for 8 years was Jiang Cheng Chung 江承宗 as second secretary to be followed by counsellor Zhang ying and his wife li Nan 张英李南.
- He acted as charge de affairs ie. head in absence of ambassador. He was from Dongguan where many Fiji Chinese farmers came from. Then Mr Mi Guo Jun came as Ambassador 米国钧.
- From a hotel room in Travelodge to an apartment in Tropic Towers to a small house off Cakobau Rd.

I remember Fiji Times interviewed Mr Jiang on arrival asking him about himself. He replied, "It is not important". Wow, that was a different kind of talk!

In December 1980, the second Ambassador Mr Shen Zhiwei, came to take office in Fiji. He left in 1985.

In 1983, when my wife Frances became the headteacher of the Fiji Chinese Primary School (now Yat Sen), the Chinese Embassy generously invited my whole family, and Frances' relatives, to a fabulous dinner at the embassy in Nasese, Suva.

When my wife told Bill Yee, the Chairman of the Chinese Education Society which controls the running of the Yat Sen Primary School, that my family was contemplating migrating to Australia, for the children's future education. Mr Yee said he wished she could stay back and continue to be the headteacher. He also said that our children were bright and could gain scholarships.

Personally, I was reluctant to migrate, as my accountancy practice was getting along well. With the influx of market gardeners coming to Fiji, one existing tax client became three, as a result of a partnership and two individual tax returns.

I charged F$250 for three hours on each client. However, as urged by Frances and my mother to migrate, I gave in.

On 19 December 1985, my family and I migrated to Australia.

In 1986, I returned to Fiji and continued my accountancy practice for a year.

That was the end of my 33 years in Fiji.

Welcoming His Grace Bishop Pearce from American Samoa, who later became the first Archbishop of Fiji. From left John Paligaru, Emily Wong, Rosemary Paligaru, Anne Wong, His grace Bishop Pearce, Frances Fong, Ian Fong, and another parishioner in 1967.

With the chairman of the Overseas Chinese Association from Taiwan, China Club. From left Ivan Harm Nam, Mrs Harm Nam, Chairman, Frances Fong, Ian Fong.

Tebara Festival in Nausori.
Chinese Youths were requested to perform the Chinese Lion Dance.
Beating the drum was Bing Kin Fong, beside him was Ian Fong working on the chimes.
There were lots of excitement as the people in the crowd, had
only seen this type of lion dance for the first time.

Double Tenth Celebration, Suva Civic Centre, 1983.
My wife Frances Fong gave the keynote speech. She is third from the left.
I am standing on the furthest right.

Corpus Christi Teachers' Training College 30th Anniversary Dinner, Hotel Isa Lei, 1988.
Front left Henry Manueli.
Front right Bessie Kingdom.

Members of the Suva Chinese Youth Association farewelling the Fong Family, December 1985.

Farewell party for our family migrating to Australia in Nausori, put on by Bing King Fong, his nephew Chi Pui Fong, niece Siu Fong Lum, and their families. They provided an impressive spread of food.

CHAPTER 77
The day my family and I landed in Sydney

In memorial to Dixon Seeto (RIP), I dedicate this episode to a very kind man whose name was mentioned. Because of the difference in age etc, we had never had the opportunity to become friends, but my wife Frances taught all his younger brothers and sisters at the Fiji Chinese Primary school (now Yat Sen Primary and Secondary School).

On Thursday morning 19 December 1985, a very fine day, the family got up early, and full of excitement, had breakfast and awaiting to be picked up to go to Nadi Airport, as my family and I were migrating to Australia.

An elderly Indian man arrived with a van, loaded us and our luggage, and off we rode to Nadi Airport. Frances had arranged for the driver (doing part-time work off duty) who was the Catholic Bishop's chauffeur, as she knew him from the Corpus Christie Teachers' Training College days. We made a stop in Sigatoka, had a Chinese lunch there before we continued our journey to Nadi airport.

At the airport, Dixon Seeto of Air Pacific had kindly organised that we be allowed to check in extra luggage. That was a big help.

After a pleasant journey on the plane, we landed at the Sydney airport at approximately 9 pm. The weather was just beautiful.

We began life in a new country. What lies ahead will be told in my episodes on living in Sydney, Australia.

When we had gone through immigration and customs, we were greeted by my wife's younger sister Emily Wong who sponsored us. There were also our nephew Edmund Leong and our good friend Peter Chan of Belfield, who came to help with transporting the family and our luggage. Finally, we arrived at Emily's home in Linsley Street, Gladesville, where we stayed for 2 weeks, before we rented a house for 10 months in 30 Osgathorpe Road in Gladesville, close to Emily's home.

After we bought our house in North Ryde which we lived in for over 30 years.

At 10 am on Sunday Emily took our family to attend Mass at Our Lady of Peace Catholic Church in Gladesville. During Mass, we were happy singing similar hymns to those in Fiji.

7 Linsley Street, Gladesville, Sydney, NSW.
We migrated to Sydney on 19 December 1985 and stayed in a unit there for 2 weeks.

CHAPTER 78

Our rented house in 30 Osgathorpe Road, Gladesville

We stayed at my sister-in-law Emily Wong's place for 2 weeks, and during this time she took 2 weeks off from work to help us look for a car, furniture, beddings, washing machine, refrigerator, kitchen utensils, crockery, forks, and knives, etc.

After that my family rented a three-bedroom house in 30 Osgathorpe Road, Gladesville, close to her home, a distance of 1 km, 3 minutes by car, 950 metres, 13 minutes by foot.

Our neighbours on the left was an extremely friendly Australian couple, but the Australian one on the right whom we seldom saw was odd. He rammed his car engine at 6 o'clock every morning. Good alarm clock but a bit early.

There was a Supermarket called Flemings (part of Woolworths) up on Victoria Road and from the house a distance of 800 metres, 2 minutes by car, 350 metres, 5 minutes by foot.

We bought western groceries at the Flemings Supermarket and meat from the butchery in Victoria Road, Gladesville. For Chinese groceries, we went to buy them in Dixon Street in Chinatown.

The family was also keen on Chinese programmes on videotapes. We normally hired one in the weekends for $3 each, but it had to be returned the next day.

One day when Frances had stopped just outside Dixon street and we were loading a bag of rice and groceries from a trolley, when a truck came past and damaged our car's right rear. Frances drove the car and chased the truck across the Harbour Bridge until our children noted the company name, registration number and truck number. She then wanted to drive to a police station to report the incident. Being new to the country, we were not aware of a police station in West Ryde, and one in Gladesville, which were not far from home. She ended up at the Campsie police station far away in the south.

Frances, being the registered owner and driver of the vehicle, was informed to appear as a witness in court. She learned that the truck driver had a few convictions against him. The magistrate ordered compensation to be paid to Frances for the repair of the car. Well done Frances.

Priorities were focused on work. I chose to go back to Fiji to continue my accountancy practice. That was stupid of me.

Frances worked as a filing clerk at the Veteran Affairs' office in the city for two weeks, while she looked for a teaching position.

Soon she found a teaching job at the St Dominic Savio School in Rockdale, a private Catholic primary school that consisted of about 30 pupils from kindy to class 6. She taught classes 3 to 6, while another teacher, Cathy Malone, taught kindy, and classes 1 and 2. At the end of the third year, the school committee had to terminate her position, as 3 nuns from the St Dominic Savio Order had come from France to run the school.

Luckily, she immediately found work as a supervisor of the Eastwood Primary School Before and After School Care.

Soon after arriving in Sydney, she got herself registered with the NSW Education Dept, for a teaching position. The registrar said her qualifications were recognised by the Dept, and she could either teach in a primary or secondary school. As the salary scale was the same, she chose to teach at a primary school, which was easier.

It didn't take long before the Education Dept notified Frances that a teaching position was available at the Lidcombe Public School. She took it up and taught there for 17 years and 6 months before she retired in 2006, ending her teaching career of 44 years. The Principal and teachers farewelled her with a good afternoon tea party, which was attended by me, my children Geralyne and her son Jonathan, Gerard and his wife Clare. Our youngest daughter Magdalene couldn't attend as she had left earlier in the year to work in London. Frances' younger sister Emily Wong, her older brother Sai Sing Wong and his wife Yuk Kin Wong, and Frances' friend Jane Sing, also attended the farewell party.

The children's education was also a priority. Frances applied to the following schools:

- Marist Sisters College in Woolwich for eldest daughter Geralyne.
- Holy Cross College in Victoria Road, Ryde, for son Gerard.
- Our Lady Queen of Peace Primary School in Victoria Road, Gladesville, for youngest daughter Magdalene.

Geralyne walked up a little distance to Victoria Road to catch the school bus to school.

Gerard walked Magdalene and her classmate Margaret to their school, 500 metres from home, and 8 minutes on foot, then walked a further 7 minutes to his school.

Our family friend Alice Tam, who was operating a Chinese furniture and ornaments shop in the Birkenhead Point Shopping Centre, gave Geralyne a part-time job on weekends and school holidays. Later Alice opened a branch in the Queen Victoria Building in the city, and Geralyne was placed in charge of the shop whenever she was on duty there. She was given the responsibility of opening and closing the shop.

Frances' younger sister Emily Wong arranged a part-time job for Gerard at the Flemings Supermarket (part of Woolworths). In the beginning, he worked as a night filler, and later he was promoted to be in charge of the night fillers. While he was studying at Uni, he acted as relieving store manager during the weekends and school holidays.

He enjoyed working there, and he was popular with the staff.

The two older children earned more than enough for their pocket money.

Before I left for work in Fiji, Frances and I went to the manager of the ANZ Bank in Gladesville and applied for a housing loan. We were extremely fortunate to be given the loan to buy a house. The manager was an ex-army sergeant who opened his heart to our application. Even though I was working in Fiji he authorised the loan, as both Frances and I earned enough to meet mortgage payments.

While I was away from Australia, Frances and eldest daughter Geralyne spent long hours searching for a house within our budget. Finally, they found a suitable one in North Ryde, a four-bedroom house with a family room and a formal lounge. The house has a double garage and a double car port in front. It was our home from 1987 to 2019. With our children fully grown and living in their own houses, we decided to downsize to a 2 bedroom flat with a view of the Sydney City skyline above Top Ryde Shopping Centre in late 2019. There are lovely plants, trees and walking paths in the common area outside our building. It feels like a Fijian resort, especially at night time when lights illuminate the plants, trees and walking paths.

Our rented house at 30 Osgathorpe Road, Gladesville, January to October 1986.

Outside our rented house, 30 Osgathorpe Road, Gladesville, 1986.
Front Magdalene Fong.
Back Frances Fong, Geralyne Fong, my Mum Fong Lum Oy Wan, Sai Choy Wong.

At a function in Chinatown.
From left Frances Fong, youngest daughter Magdalene Fong, eldest daughter Geralyne Fong.

CHAPTER 79

Our home in 104 Twin Road, North Ryde

In October 1986, my family moved from our rented house in 30 Osgathorpe Road, Gladesville, to our new home in North Ryde.

Frances and I lived in this house for over 30 years until late 2019 when we downsized to a flat above Top Ryde Shopping Centre. Our three children are married and have their own homes.

Thank God, our house was free from mortgage for over 15 years. It was a four bedroom house with a family room and a formal lounge, and a double garage and a double car port in front, two verandas, one in the front and one in the back. There was also a large back yard. The front yard could accommodate about 15 cars for party time. The house had many windows right around, in fact too many windows to clean.

I was in Fiji, but Frances told me that with the help of her younger sister Emily Wong, nephews Edmund Leong, Christopher, and Stephen Wong, Clinton and Warwick Fong, the family hired a removalist, and loaded everything to be transported to the house we had just bought in North Ryde.

On arrival, our new Australian neighbour Brian Steele and his adult son David, came forward to render help. Frances thanked them for their good intentions and told them everything was under control, as the removalist had two helping hands besides our own helpers.

Brian and his family on the right side of our house continued to be our very good neighbours. Sadly, Brian passed away some years ago, leaving his widow Yvonne who is still living alone in her home. Brian was so good, for since we arrived, he mowed our lawn free of charge. He told me not to buy a lawnmower, as he was prepared to mow our lawn at any time. He said he got free petrol and oil from the golf club where he worked as a gamekeeper. I thought it wouldn't be fair for Brian to do so much for us, so I bought a lawnmower, and did my own thing. Guess what? He was furious: "I told you not to spend money to buy a lawnmower, as you are just settling in". It didn't take him long to understand, so the matter had been settled like that.

On the left of our house was an Australian couple with two young children, but we seldom saw one other, due to isolation. They were very cordial. After about three years they moved away. The new Australian neighbours had two young children. They were equally cordial. They had their old house demolished and a new two-story one built, and they and their grown-up children are still living next door.

Behind our house lived an old Australian couple who were very nice. Their house was separated by a low fence. Frances and my mother often communicated with them. Sadly, the old gentleman had passed away some years ago. His wife had since moved into a nursing home. Their house was sold to a Palestinian man and his Italian wife, with three young children. They renovated their house to a two-story building. They were friendly people.

It was close to shopping centres in Top Ryde, Rhodes, Homebush West, Eastwood, Macquarie centre, and the one in Cox's Road, North Ryde.

So many activities happened in this house during the years 1987 to 2019.

Our family home in North Ryde, October 1986 to November 2019.

Cars belonging to visitors, outside our home in North Ryde.

Ping pong table in the car port for our family home.
Our son-in-law Sen Yee and his children used to play when they visited.
Our little granddaughter Chloe Fong also played when she came
to visit, and I found myself picking up a lot of balls.

CHAPTER 80
My first job in Australia

During 1986 I was in Fiji rounding up my accountancy practice, and when I returned to Sydney in early December, I found that my family had moved into the house we bought in North Ryde. I was amazed that everyone in the family including my mother, seemed to have settled down well in the new country.

My mother and wife Frances were overjoyed to know that I wouldn't be going back to work in Fiji. And so was I, after spending almost a year alone working in Fiji.

First thing first, so I went straight away to the Australian Government Employment Agency and registered for a job application. Soon I received a phone call on 27 December 1986, from the Managing Director of two private companies, Undersea Pty Ltd and Dispensers Pty Ltd, asking me to go for an interview in Gladesville.

The man was Australian, very pleasant, and during the interview, he said he was satisfied with my qualifications and experiences and gave me a position as an accountant for the two companies. Undersea manufactured underwater spear guns, and Dispensers manufacturing paint dispensers. He offered me a salary of A$25,000 per annum with an annual increase of 5% on salary balance and I accepted. $25,000 in 1987 has the same "purchasing power" as $53,870.16 in 2017.

He also mentioned that he was a former senior electronics lecturer at the University of Wollongong. As the factories were closed for the Christmas period, he told me to report for duty on Monday, 9 January 1987. He also gave me a set of keys to the office and the factory. My responsibility was to open the office and factory at 8 o'clock in the morning.

I enjoyed my work but dreaded every Friday afternoon when I was preparing the payroll and hoping I would escape robbers. When preparing the wages, I had the computer clerk with me, and my office door closed.

I drove to work which was 4.3 kms, and 8 minutes by car from home. Frances was not so lucky, as she had to catch a bus from home to Gladesville in Victoria Road, changed bus to the city, then caught a train to Rockdale station, and finally got picked up by the Parish Brother to go to the St Dominic Savio Primary School. Every day after school Frances got a lift from the Brother to the Rockdale Train Station, then caught a train to the city, bus to Gladesville. She had to wait for me to finish work. and we drove home together.

Frances told me that after school, she often walked past the cake shops in the Town Hall station. There she saw many delicious cupcakes, slices, and pastries. Yummy she said. However, she wasn't tempted to buy any because of her strict budget. Thank God we are now making up for it.

After four and a half years my salary scale had reached $31,762.50. In other words, $31,762.50 in the year 1987 is equivalent in purchasing power to $68,442.04 in 2017.

I had a greedy idea that I could make more money by going into business, so I resigned from the Gladesville job, and bought a mixed business store in Croydon Park in the south.

Office and factory of Undersea Pty Ltd and Dispenses Pty Ltd where I once worked. My office was in the front upstairs. The building might have been sold. I took the photo on 26 January 2018. The footprint for the building is the same, but it's now used by a different company.

CHAPTER 81
Events in the year 1987 in Sydney

Many activities happened during the year 1987.

There were 2 picnics, 1 at the Auburn Japanese Garden and the other at the Lane Cove National Park.

During the year 1987, we had visitors to our home in North Ryde.

On 21 January, youngest daughter Magdalene celebrated her birthday.

On 31 January, my mother celebrated her birthday.

On 6 March, the eldest daughter Geralyne celebrated her birthday.

On 29 April, wife Frances celebrated her birthday.

On 3 June (Chinese Calendar), 28 July (English Calendar), I celebrated my birthday.

On 15 August son Gerard celebrated his birthday.

Our family hosted the 1987 Xmas Party for our immediate relatives.

Judy Wong visiting, 1987.
Front Geralyne Fong, Magdalene Fong.
Back Judy Wong, Frances Fong, Ian Fong, Gerard Fong.

Work friends from Yat Sen Primary and Secondary School in Fiji, visiting us in Sydney, 1987.

Tanoa Street, Suva neighbours visiting us in Sydney, 1987.

Sai Mar Chang visiting, 1987.

Family attending the wedding reception of Bernie Joe and
Michael Sue, outside the restaurant in Maroubra 1987.
From left Geralyne Fong (bridesmaid), Magdalene Fong, Gerard Fong,
my mother Fong Lum Oy Wan, Frances Fong, Ian Fong.

CHAPTER 82
My family activities in 1988

During the school holidays in January, my children Geralyne, Gerard and Magdalene spent a few days in a holiday house in Nowra owned by their friends' parents Geraldine and John Scimone.

Nowra

Nowra is a town in the South Coast region of New South Wales, Australia. It is located 160 kilometres south-southwest of the state capital of Sydney with its twin-town of Bomaderry, Nowra had an estimated population of 35,920 as at June 2015.

On the banks of beautiful Shoalhaven River, it is a delightful town on the NSW South Coast with intriguing museums, fascinating galleries, and enchanting river cruises. You'll enjoy delicious food and wine experiences and the Shoalhaven region's main town is close to gorgeous beaches too.

Rich soils support farmlands and vineyards, and the river estuary is part of Australia's Oyster Coast. Taste fresh regional produce at quality restaurants, such as award-winning Wharf Road, which overlooks the river. Visit cellar doors at Lyrebird Ridge Organic Winery and Cambewarra Estate Winery.

Accompanying them were the Scimones and their children Anna and Margaret, Uncle Sai Sing Wong and his son Christopher, and a friend Sen Yee.

Wife Frances and I stayed back. I had to go to work, and she looked after my mother.

By looking at the photos, the holidaymakers seemed to have enjoyed their trip.

During the year everyone in my family celebrated birthdays as they became due. It's rather strange that there are no photos available for these occasions.

The school year began with Frances teaching at a private Catholic primary school (St Dominic Savio) in Rockdale, eldest daughter and son Gerard started their first year at university, youngest daughter Magdalene continued her attendance at the Marist Sisters College in Woolwich.

We were all busy and enjoyed our doings, but my mother was left alone in the house.

At 78 years of age, mum, although she didn't know English, kept herself occupied while we were away from home. At noon she would watch the TV programme "Days of Our Lives", and "The Bold and The Beautiful" channel 10 between 4.30 to 5.00 pm, Monday to Friday. She often told us some stories of what she had seen.

World Expo 1988

World Expo 1988, also known as Expo 88, was a specialised Expo held in Brisbane, the state capital of Queensland, Australia, during a six-month period between Saturday, 30 April 1988 and Sunday, 30 October 1988, inclusive. Dates: 30 Apr. 1988 – 30 Oct. 1988 Visitors: 15,760,000.

It offered a glimpse of a wider world's possibilities, featuring technological novelties, cultural demonstrations, global cuisine and performances ranging from traditional dances of the South Pacific to water-ski acrobatics. Expo participants included 52 government agencies, 36 international governments, and 50 corporate organisations.

Upon entry, glowing humanoid robots greeted visitors in 32 languages. While awaiting entrance to main attractions, troupes of acrobats, clowns and comedians engaged visitors. Parades featuring computer-operated diorama floats, musicians and dancers snaked through the crowds twice daily.

When the World Expo was staged in Brisbane, Frances and the children travelled north by coach during the July school holidays. The two Scimone children Anna and

Margaret, and friend Sen Yee accompanied the family. It was an exciting experience staying in a 4-bedroom apartment, fully furnished. All of them got sick one by one because of the cold winter.

Our cousin Bill Fong and his daughter Michelle from Auckland spent a couple of days with the group. Bill took everyone to Yum Cha in Brisbane's Chinatown.

I stayed back in Sydney to look after my mother.

At the end of the school year, three St Dominic Savio nuns came from France to take over the school from 1989. Unfortunately, the order couldn't afford to keep and pay Frances, whose salary was on a government scale. She had to look elsewhere for a job for the following year 1989.

We went past the year 1988 peacefully and happily.

The Scimones' holiday house, Nowra, January 1988.

On the beach, Nowra, January 1988.

Welcome parade for World Expo, Brisbane, 1988.

CHAPTER 83
My family activities in 1989 in Sydney

It was a great shock for me, Frances and our children, to grieve over my mother's passing away on 2 January 1989.

Mum had been with us since January 1970. She had an excellent and loving association with my wife Frances. She and our house girls played a big part in looking after our children since they were born in Fiji.

The family loved her very much, and Frances and I are so ever grateful to her for teaching and talking to our children in the Chinese Zhongshan dialect.

She was in good health, but she died unexpectedly and peacefully, 29 days to reach her 80th birthday, and the family had been planning a big party for her.

As she was a converted Catholic, and a very good one too, so a Mass was arranged for her funeral at the Holy Spirit Catholic Church in Cox's Road, North Ryde. She was buried at the Rookwood Cemetery, Chinese Section.

Two weeks after my mother passed away, Frances was looking for a job. As all the teaching positions had been filled at that time, she was prepared to take on other jobs that were offered. Fortunately, she applied for and was accepted as the Co-ordinator for Before and After School Care, at the Eastwood Public School, where she worked from January to March.

While she was working in Eastwood, Frances went to check with the New South Wales Education Dept. In 1986 she had already registered as a teacher with the Dept. She was told that her qualifications were accepted by the Education Dept, and she could teach either in a primary or secondary school. At that time Salaries were the same, so she opted to teach in the primary.

Thankfully in March, the Education Dept informed Frances that there was a permanent position available at the Lidcombe Public School. She accepted the teaching position and became a Civil Servant, and commenced teaching in April, school term 2.

Lidcombe Public School is an innovative and dynamic school with a strong focus on quality learning and inclusive teaching programs.

The school serves a diverse multilingual community with the vast majority of its K to 6 students having a language background other than English. The school hosts special education facilities for students with mild and moderate intellectual disabilities.

She taught there until she retired in June 2006. The principal and the school staff gave her an afternoon tea retirement party. The Dept of Education presented her a silver medal for her service.

Life for the family went on normally during the year. No luxuries, but comfortable living, and above all, everyone enjoyed good health, as by then we had also got used to the Sydney winter.

Gathering around my Mum Fong Lum Oy Wan's grave, on burial day, January 1989.

Gathering at my Mum Fong Lum Oy Wan's grave, with tomb stone in place, January 1995.

Staff at Lidcombe Public School, 1989.
Front centre was the principal who agreed to take on Frances to teach at the school.

Frances making a speech at her afternoon tea party farewell, June 2006.

The principal making a speech at the afternoon tea party farewell, June 2006.

Teacher friend Joyce making a speech at the afternoon tea party farewell, June 2006.

Family photo at the afternoon tea party farewell.
From left eldest daughter Geralyne Yee Fong, Ian Fong, Frances Fong, son Gerard Fong, daughter-in-law Clare Kent.

CHAPTER 84
My family activities in 1990, 1991 in Sydney

Nothing exciting happened in the year 1990 except the 21st Birthday party of my eldest daughter Geralyne.

The year 1991 was brightened up with my eldest daughter Geralyne who got married on 2 February.

In September 1991, Frances, my eldest daughter and I, accompanied our youngest daughter Magdalene, for a trip to Griffith. She went along with her Chinese Youth Club members who had been invited by the Griffith Wine Festival committee, to perform cultural items.

Griffith is a major regional city in the Murrumbidgee Irrigation Area that is located in the north-western part of the Riverina region of New South Wales, known commonly as the food bowl of Australia.

From its earliest days, the area was populated by Italian workers, some of whom were initially employed by Australian farmers to run steamboats on the Murrumbidgee and Murray Rivers.

In the 1970's, Griffith was often associated with drug distribution (particularly marijuana) and organised crime, as depicted in 2009 in "Underbelly: A Tale of Two Cities", a popular TV show. However, Griffith is now associated with good wine and food, primarily as a result of its diverse population, with notable contributions by Italian Australians. Griffith's multi-ethnic population is now absorbing new national groups, including a significant Sikh Indian community. The city is a sister city with the Italian city of Treviso in the Veneto Region. Many Italians in Griffith are from the Veneto Region or the Calabria Region of Italy.

The Italian influence expanded the range of fruit and vegetables, and also significantly increased the number of wineries and the range of wines produced by the existing wineries in the region, such as McWilliam's. De Bortoli, Rosetto and other wineries were established by Italian immigrants, and today they are well known around Australia. In recent times they have been joined by one of the country's best-known wine labels, Yellow Tail, produced by Casella Family Brands. Casella, DeBortoli, McWilliam's, Warburn and Berton Vineyards are now among the top 20 wine producers in Australia.

On 15 October the same year 1991, I started operating a mixed business shop in Croydon Park, next to the suburb Campsie in the south.

Our daughter Geralyne and boyfriend Sen Yee at her 21st birthday in 1990.

Sen and Geralyne in their splendid wedding outfits at Sydney Harbour, 1991.

Family photo at the Chinese Garden of Friendship in Darling Harbour, Sydney, 1991.
From left Frances Fong, Sen Yee, Geralyne Fong Yee, Ian Fong.

Talking to a guy who migrated from China, Griffith, September 1991.
He was a former member of an acrobatic team.
He was the one who held up a long pole for the lion to perform up high.

CHAPTER 85

The 25th wedding anniversary of Frances and Ian Fong

On Saturday 4 May 1968, Frances and I were married at the Sacred Heart Cathedral, Suva, Fiji.

On Saturday 1 May 1993, we got the surprise of our lives when our three children secretly organised a party for our silver wedding anniversary. Early that evening, they told me to dress up in a suit and Frances to wear something nice. Then they took us to a Vietnamese restaurant in Marrickville, where relatives and friends had gathered to surprise us.

When we entered the restaurant, we saw our cousins from New Zealand, Bill and Janice Fong, Peter and Lois Chan, who were sitting inside. We thought we were dreaming. Our children had invited them to the party.

As we advanced a little further, we saw other guests who were made up of immediate relatives and friends in frequent contact.

A sumptuous dinner had been catered by the restaurant.

A beautiful cake was also provided.

In my speech on behalf of Frances and myself, I thanked our children for their kind thoughts and the most efficient way they had organised the surprise party. I even made a joke... More surprise parties are welcome.

Cutting the cake at the Vietnamese Restaurant, Marrickville, 1 May 1993.

25th wedding anniversary banner decorating the wall at the restaurant.

CHAPTER 86
Robberies at my Croydon Park shop, Croydon Park, NSW

From 15 October 1991 to 15 July 1996, I operated a mix business shop in 44 Wentworth Street, Croydon Park, next to the suburb of Campsie in the south.

After working for four-and-a-half years in an office in Gladesville, I decided to look for a small business to buy. Could it be a laundry, coffee shop or start a factory for mattresses but the last one would cost lots of capital which I couldn't afford. I had knowledge and experiences for all these types of businesses.

Finally, I arrived at buying a mixed business shop which was easier to run.

First of all, I got hold of the Australian Chinese Daily newspaper, and on the businesses for sale section. I found two mixed business shops for sale. One was owned by an Italian young man in Concord, and the other was owned by Lloyd Deb in Croydon Park.

Frances and I went to the Concord shop and found it unsuitable for me to operate as it had a huge slicer serving cold meats.

We then went to the shop in Croydon Park and found it was a suitable one. Besides general groceries it had a microwave heating up pie and sausage rolls. It was the first time I encountered a microwave. I heard that it contained radioactivity which was not safe for cooking food.

Before agreeing to buy the shop business I popped the question to the owner Lloyd: "Have you ever been robbed? He said yes, once by two Australian young men, one was brandishing a large blade knife. They forced him to back off and took his cash register away.

Robberies by sight is common among mixed business shops. It's so easy. A bloke just comes in with a knife and demands the till to be opened.

On the 13 October 1991, a professional stock taker was hired to have the stock-in-trade taken.

On 14 October 1991, Frances and I hired a removalist and moved into the shop to live in it.

On 15 October 1991, I opened the shop business. Apart from a little list of debtors taken over from the previous owner, a few customers came to ask for credit, but I managed to refuse their requests, except for one young lady in her late teens. She came with a note supposed to be written by her father, saying that her mother was hospitalised, and he vouched to be responsible for paying. I was stupid to let this young lady take goods on credit up to 300 dollars. I never saw her again.

During the first year of operation, a young Indian lad came to buy a packet of cigarettes. He put 3 one-dollar coins on my palm and quickly walked out of the shop. I started calling out to him to pay one more dollar, but he walked as fast as he could up Hampton Road to Georges River Road.

At about 10 in the morning, a group of 6 Lebanese young men came in two cars. Two remained outside while the rest came into the shop. Two fronting me in the serving counter, one walked to the left and another to the right. I became so scared and took a quick walk outside to see what was going on. The group probably sensed the shop was not a busy one, so they left. Afterwards I thought: could it be a robbery in disguise?

During the second year of operation, a big islander came from a local council truck, took a bottle of soft drinks from the fridge and walked off. I called out to him to pay, but he said to charge it down. What could I do under such circumstances?

During the third year of operation an Australian mother sent her two boys aged about 10 and 8 to the shop to buy ice cream. She told them to take the stuff and ask the shop keeper to book down. Before the boys opened the fridge, I told them it was not on. Their mother soon arrived and told me off for being racist.

One morning a lady in a car came before the shop was opened. She saw milk was inside the lane and took two bottles away.

The fourth year was a peaceful one. I had a large knife (similar to the grass cutting one in Fiji) which I had bought from a BBC Hardware Store, in case I needed it to protect myself.

Sometimes I took the knife outside the shop and pretended to cut grass that was not around. People saw the knife and knew I carried a weapon.

I survived four years from robberies.

During the fifth year, things happened.

About 10 on a Sunday morning, a Lebanese man in his early thirties, about 5 foot 6, came into the shop, gave me a one-dollar coin and asked for change to use the public phone. I obliged and opened my cash register. Before I took out the change, he quickly pressed his hands-on top of mine. In the presence of a few customers he grabbed a few notes and took off in a waiting car.

On the following Thursday about 6 in the evening, my wife Frances delivered some groceries to an old lady down the road near the Australian Rules Football Club. As soon as she left the shop, an olive skin man in his early thirties, slim build, came into the shop and asked to borrow a car jumper lead. I told him I didn't have one. He then ordered a packet of cigarettes, but instead of taking out his wallet from a pocket, he opened his shirt and took out a large blade knife and told me to open the till.

I was about to move back to grab a broomstick tied with a sharp blade, which could reach him before he could attack me. He quickly said: "Don't fight back, I got blokes outside". I got scared and opened my cash register and gave him 2 twenty-dollar notes. He took off hurriedly. I ran outside but couldn't see any car around.

On the same Saturday early in the afternoon, I was out shopping. The same robber came and said he was armed and demanded Frances to open the till. She refused. About the same time a young Australian boy came to buy bread. Frances told the boy that the man was trying to rob her. The boy looked at the man who was then holding a large knife. The boy froze and didn't know what to do. Luckily a well-built Italian customer came into the shop. Frances shouted to him to stop the robber. He said to her: "You must be joking Frances". The robber then ran away. The customer chased the robber, but he got away.

On the next Monday afternoon, Queens Birthday holiday, the same robber came into the shop and demanded more money from me.

I ran outside the shop yelling and swearing at the robber.

Frances heard me and knew that something was wrong. She ran out to the shop veranda and grabbed the iron plate Tip Top ice cream sign, to throw at the robber. I stopped her because she might be liable to pay compensation to the robber if he was hurt.

I asked Frances to ring the police. The robber ran away as fast as he could.

I ran into the bedroom and got hold of the car key and car lock, back to my car and gave chase. There was no police car patrolling at that time, otherwise the robber would be caught. I lost him when he took off along the concrete drains not far from the shop.

I was more than shaken after the Thursday night robbery, so I put an advertisement in the Australian Chinese Daily newspaper, to sell the business.

Our children and Frances' siblings all urged me to get rid of the shop business. They said I was three times lucky, but the fourth one might not be.

I sold it to an immigrant from China and agreed to help him and his wife to run the shop for one month, during the daytime 10 am to 5 pm Monday to Friday. It was free of charge.

Inside my shop at 44 Wentworth Street, Croydon Park, 15 October 1991.

Outside my shop.
From left is our niece Catherine Schurig holding daughter Julia, sister-in-law Yuk Kin Wong, Ian Fong, brother-in-law Sai Sing Wong holding grand nephew Roland Schurig. At the front is grand nephew Bernhard Schurig.

CHAPTER 87

My 60th birthday party

On Saturday 25 July 1998, which was 3 June 1998 Chinese Calendar, I celebrated my 60th birthday at home in North Ryde.

Telephone invitations were used to invite guests in Sydney and Wollongong. About 150 people attended, including my cousins Bill and Janice Fong from Auckland.

The lunch gathering was truly an enjoyable event. Plenty of chatting around, and plenty of food and drinks cold and hot had been provided.

At this stage of writing, I am thinking back of the occasion of how my family managed to stage this size of the party at home. It was amazing. Everyone in the family did a lot of work. My wife's siblings and their spouses came in full force to help.

Tables and chairs had been hired from party suppliers.

Our 3 children, Geralyne, Gerard and Magdalene decorated the garage and car port. Meanwhile, my son-in-law Sen looked after our grandson Jonathan, who was about 2 years old at the time.

My family did the bulk of the cooking of Crispy Roast Pork, Chicken Mushroom, Chicken Cashew Nuts, Curry Lamb, Stir-fry Prawns with Snow Peas. Frances deep-fried the wonton, brother-in-law Henry Leong deep-fried the breaded prawns and cooked sweet and sour pork, brother-in-law Sai Sing Wong and his wife Yuk Kin took care of the Chicken Chow Mein.

To think of it, the party was well organised, and it cost a lot cheaper than having it in a restaurant or a catered venue. It involved so many people and much work, and my family and I agreed, we wouldn't do it again, putting up a large party at home.

Overall, it was a great day to be remembered. Many thanks to everyone who helped to make it special.

In the front grandson Jonathan Yee full of laughs.
At the back from left son Gerard Fong, eldest daughter Geralyne Fong Yee, son-in-law Sen Yee, Ian Fong, Frances Fong, youngest daughter Magdalene Fong, Cousin Janice Fong from New Zealand.

In the front grandson Jonathan Yee clapping with joy.
At the back from left son Gerard Fong, eldest daughter Geralyne Fong Yee, son-in-law Sen Yee, Ian Fong, Frances Fong, youngest daughter Magdalene Fong, Cousin Janice Fong from New Zealand.

From left grandson Jonathan Yee, son-in-law Sen Yee, eldest daughter Geralyne Fong Yee.

CHAPTER 88

My wholesale business Ian D. Fong Wholesaler 1 July 1999 to 30 June 2004

After selling my shop at Croydon Park on 15 July 1996, I had been floating around for about two years.

All my three children had graduated from Uni. The eldest daughter Geralyne was married in February 1991. Son Gerard and youngest daughter Magdalene were both working and living at home.

From the proceeds of the sale of the shop, wife Frances' teaching salary, and the stay-at-home children's contributions, the family managed to live comfortably for the two years I was out of work.

By this time, it was impossible for me to find employment. Who would employ an old poke like me at the age of 60. I still had 5 more years before retirement age.

I wanted to earn some money, so I started to become a confectionery and soft drinks vendor. Got this idea from the vendors who used to come in their vans to sell drinks and confectionery to my shop in Croydon Park.

Frances and I went to a second-hand car yard in West Homebush and bought a good second-hand van for $11,000. A little later I found out that I could buy a fairly good one for $5,000.

In the beginning, I bought confectionery from Sweetcraft Pty Ltd, an established confectionery wholesaler in Lakemba, and a soft drinks supplier nearby.

My first trip on the sale run was to a takeaway shop in West Ryde. The owner from Europe was very pleasant, and after talking to me for some time, he told me he already had a supplier who was good and reliable. I got the message and said goodbye.

The following day, I went to a liquor shop in West Homebush. The Amanian owner was extremely friendly. I told him I had just started my vendor business. I saw chips, confectionery and soft drinks on display. Before asking him for an order I asked him for advice on how to get a new customer. He said, "Ask your intended customer at what price he bought the chips". There was luck for a sale to this liquor shop. The owner ordered a small number of drinks and told me to call again the following week. He might buy some sweets from me as well.

Next door was the Chinese cafe. I managed to obtain a little soft drinks order from the owner.

From there I went to a mixed business shop further up the road, around the corner. The owner was from Shanghai, China. After a while I convinced him that my prices were good. He bought a little quantity of sweets and soft drinks from me. After learning that I was from North Ryde, he recommended me to a customer in Buffalo Road in North Ryde.

Just imagine how satisfied and happy I was. Three new customers in a day.

From that day on, I became confident that I should be able to get more customers from other areas.

My next call was on this shop in Buffalo Road. A lady was serving in the shop, and her husband was a computer manager working for an Australian company. They were also from Shanghai, China. The lady bought some sweets and soft drinks from me. She recommended to me a customer in Leichardt. He was also from Shanghai, China.

I then called into a shop nearby in Quarry Road. The owner was an Italian, a very smooth-talking man. He said I came in the wrong time because he was negotiating to sell the business to a Maltese man, whose wife was looking after their shop in Putney. I was told to call in the next day.

The next day I called into the Quarry Road shop, and the new Maltese owner Charlie gave me an order which I delivered the following day. During delivery he told me to call on his other shop in Putney, and his wife would give me an order.

On the following day, I went along to the shop in Putney and got an order from the lady owner. From there I drove to a shop opposite West Ryde bus and train station. The owner was a Chinese lady from Singapore. She gave me an order and I supplied the following day.

Now I was prepared to call on the shop in Leichart. The owner was from Shanghai, China. He said his wife often went to Campbells Cash and Carry branch in Leichardt for specials. Anyway, as he was satisfied with my prices he bought some sweets from me.

I returned to Homebush West to the customers I had already been supplying. The shop owner around the corner asked me if I needed someone to help me, as he had a friend who was looking for a job. I told him to send the bloke to me for an interview.

The man called Wilson Wei, a Uni Statistics graduate from a Shanghai Uni, came to see me for an interview. His wife was an eye surgeon back in Shanghai, but her qualifications were not recognised in Australia, so she took a job working at a nursing home.

I told Wilson I could use him to do the deliveries, and I would go out and take orders from shops around Sydney. We agreed on simple terms, such as put down a deposit of $2,500, use his own van for deliveries and I pay him 5 % on the value of deliveries each day.

By this time, I had acquired many customers. I called regularly on the customers around North Ryde, West Ryde, Putney and Homebush West. Customers from far phoned or faxed in orders in the evenings. I would then invoiced by hand and summarised all the orders and faxed to my confectionery supplier. On the next morning Wilson would pick up from the confectionery supplier and the soft drinks from a supplier nearby.

Wilson and I had a very good working relationship for almost a year until he and his wife bought a fairly large mixed business in Canterbury.

Just a few days before Wilson was leaving, I had a car accident down Twin Road, about 200 metres from home. It was dark and little rain falling about 6.30 pm when I was driving home in my van. Instead of stopping and wiping the window screen I was driving forward slowly, and bumped a second hand Falcon car parked on the left side of the road. The car was a write-off, but insurance paid for damages. That side of the road was normally clear, but a man happened to be visiting that night, parked his car there.

Neighbours ran out to where I was. I was still conscious and stayed put inside the van. I told them not to move me at all, but to call my home and the ambulance.

My son-in-law Sen Yee and daughter Geralyne were visiting that night. They and my wife Frances rushed down the road to where I was. Shortly an ambulance arrived and took me to the Ryde Hospital where I stayed until midnight. After Xray's and check-up, I was released.

After the accident, I couldn't move my right arm at all, so I had to go for physio for a few sessions.

Wilson had just stopped working for me. An urgent delivery down the road was needed. Goods were picked up by me earlier. It happened that our sister-in-law Lina Wong from Levuka, Fiji, was visiting, so she and my wife Frances delivered the goods by using our car. The delivery included a few cartons of soft drinks, which were heavy for the ladies to handle.

Before Wilson left, and while he was doing the last few deliveries, he told customers I had a car accident and could no longer carry on my business.

When my right arm had been nursed back to normal, I started to carry on my vendor business around North Ryde, West Ryde, Putney and Homebush West.

One day when I was delivering goods to the shop opposite the West Ryde bus and train station, the Chinese lady owner recommended an Indonesian/Chinese man to work for me.

His name was Irvan to whom I later referred to as Uncle. He graduated with a mechanical engineering degree from the University of Jakarta, came to study in Australia, and graduated with an MBA degree at the Sydney University of Technology. He couldn't find suitable work as his first degree was not recognised in Australia. He was good with the computer. During the interview, I offered him a job and he accepted.

His job was to do all the invoicing in the morning, pick up goods from Lakemba, and deliver after lunch.

I registered a business name called Ian D Fong Wholesaler and started trading on 1 July 1999. The business sold mainly general groceries, confectionery, and soft drinks.

After three months, I had built up quite a clientele. I found out that the majority of the mixed business owners were from Shanghai, and they had bought shops from old European migrant owners. Some of these Shanghai customers talked on the phone every night, and they recommended me as an honest supplier.

Uncle and I couldn't cope with the volume of business, so I approached a Chinese Employment Agency in Chinatown for a Chinese delivery driver. Two came for an interview. One had a van, and that was handy. I hired him, and we agreed on 5 % on delivery of goods. I also hired the other applicant on an agreed wage payable daily. He could use my van.

By this time, I bought another second-hand van for $3,000 from a family friend, which was used mainly by uncle.

My double garage held goods bought on specials. For goods on deliveries each day, the driver who owned the van went to pick up confectionery and soft drinks from Lakemba, the other driver went to the nearest Campbells Cash and Carry store for groceries, soft drinks and sweets.

After 18 months the driver who owned the van resigned because his van was playing up.

My retired brother-in-law Sai Sing Wong was hanging around, so I requested him to help on an agreed wage to be paid daily.

So many activities for five years, but I ended up losing some money. My employees received their good shares of remunerations.

Since I had heart bypass surgery in June 2001, the family urged me to retire.

The business carried on until 30 June 2004, when I decided it was time to retire from all these activities.

Working on invoices, July 1999.

Irvan on the computer, 1999.

Goods such as potato chips, soft drinks, sweets etc, stocked up, ready for orders and deliveries.

Driver Paul and his van behind him.

CHAPTER 89

My first visit to China in the year 2000

During the first term school holidays in May 2000, my wife Frances, youngest daughter Magdalene and I visited China.

It was my first time going back to the village since I left for Fiji in September 1950. For Magdalene, it was her first time too.

It was in the early evening when we arrived in Hong Kong and stayed at a hotel in Nathan Road, Tsim Sha Tsui.

The next morning my cousin Fong Wing came to have breakfast at the hotel. Afterwards, he took us to lunch at his home in Wong Tsai Sin. The last time I saw him was when I was 8 years old back in the village in China.

I requested him to accompany us to go to my village, Dun Tou, Zhongshan, Guangdong, China. As he went back to the village occasionally, he was a big help to us, finding our way around the Zhongshan district.

We went by bus on a journey of distance 74.8 km and 3 hours, from Hong Kong to Zhongshan city, and stayed at the Zhongshan International Hotel.

On the night of our arrival, Frances' cousin Ung Kum Ling and her husband Lee Jeung Ming, came to visit us at our hotel. They invited us to dinner at an up-market restaurant in the city the following night. At dinner, we met their 4 sons and a daughter, together with their spouses and children. The dinner was absolutely sumptuous. After dinner, we were taken to meet Aunty Ung, Kum Ling's mother, wife of Frances' mother's older brother.

On the third day, and as soon as we arrived at my village, the first thing I wanted to do was to visit my former house. It had been given to a distant uncle, who had rented it to some people from the north of China. We had to ask a neighbour to get permission from the tenant (a young lady present), to go into the house. I got such a shock when I found a square concrete structure with a large cooking wok sitting on top in the sitting room. A bed with a mosquito net hanging down was placed on one side of the room. We went to the back of the house and found the roof in need of repairs.

From there we went to meet my 7th aunty, and her sons who were born after I left the village. They were sons of my 7th Uncle Fong War Mook and his second wife. My uncle was the head of the village, and after he passed away, his eldest son Fong Siu Kong took over the position. Uncle and his first wife had two sons. He divorced his first wife when she got crazy by claiming that the monkey god appeared to her in her dreams. She went to join her younger son Fong Siu Wai in Hong Kong, and the older son Fong Siu Yuen went to work in Zhuhai city, very close to Macau.

Cousin Fong Siu Yuen, his wife, daughter and son-in-law, and their son, came all the way from Zhuhai city to meet us in the village. One of uncle War Mook's sons working in Zhuhai also came to meet us.

Cousins Wing and Siu Kong booked the village restaurant for our party for about 50 relatives and neighbours. The food was banquet style, very tasty. I paid for the party and gave red packets to some children. It was wonderful meeting up with all these people although the only ones I knew before were 2 neighbours (men) who were older than me.

Immediately after the party, cousin Wing ordered a taxi to take us back to the hotel in the city. He said we were overseas visitors, and it might not be safe for us to hang around too long.

The next day cousin Wing and the three of us went by taxi to the Ho To village, which was about 10 kilometres from our hotel. There we visited my mother's older brother's daughter Lum Fung Yee, a year younger than me. Her husband was a caterer for parties and equipment hire. We also visited an old widower, husband of my cousin Wong Say Chow.

Cousin Sai Chow Wong, my mother's older sister's daughter, was adopted by my parents when her parents went to find work in Hong Kong. After the China/Japan war her parents returned from Hong Kong to live in their village. Sai Chow went back to join them. When she was living with my mum and me, she attended our village school, and was well-liked by her school mates. She was a beautiful girl, very intelligent, very kind, and very obedient to my mother. She was loved by mum and me.

On another day, my brother-in-law Sai Sing Wong's wife's brother came to visit us at the hotel. He received a letter from his son John Wu in Sydney, who wrote to him and asked him to meet up with us. One of his sons brought him on a motorbike, from his Sha Kai Hee village about 20 kilometres away. He invited us to go to his home. We all took a taxi to his home and met his wife there. John Wu's younger brother took us to a cafe to have some Won Ton soup. The won tons were wrapped very small but plentiful and tasty.

The next morning, Uncle Wu, Frances, Magdalene and I, went by taxi to visit the houses of Frances' father and mother. First, we went to her father's village in Cheung Jou, and through the help of a couple of old residents we found the house. From there we went to her mother's village in Fu Choong, and we were also lucky to see an elderly lady who guided us to the house. Mission completed.

In the afternoon I went to a travel agency to book a trip to Guangzhou (Formerly Canton City).

The next day a driver with a 9-seater van and a lady tour guide, took the 5 of us to Guangzhou where we visited a few places popular with tourists, and an up-market store in a trade centre. It was quite surprising for us to find that the prices of shoes and clothing, were almost the same in Sydney's Myers stores.

For a few days in Zhongshan we managed to visit the people and places as previously planned.

Back in Hong Kong, and with the help of cousin Wing, his wife and son Johnny Fong, we went to offer worship at my father's grave in the Zhongshan Section Cemetery,

Sandy Ridge, New Territories in the China side. After my father passed away, he was buried in the Hong Kong government cemetery, but after 7 years by law, his bones had to be exhumed and taken away to an appropriate place to keep.

The six of us went by train from Hung Hom station on a long journey to Lo Fu, caught a taxi to Sandy Ridge police post, applied for a permit to enter the China side, caught a taxi with permit to enter the cemetery. We waited for at least 3 hours for the permit to be approved.

In 1974 my mother and son Gerard 4 and ½ years old then, went to Hong Kong and paid people to take my father's bones to be buried in a new grave in Sandy Ridge.

During the few days left, we met up with my cousin lam Fung Kwan and her husband Jeung Kin Kong for breakfast at a French De La France restaurant. It was the first time that we met them. Kwan was my mother's older brother's daughter, who lived with my mother in Hong Kong before she was married. She and her husband were a fantastic couple.

We went to pay homage to the Wong Tai Sin Temple, and there my daughter Magdalene and I consulted a lady fortune-teller to read our palms.

I will elaborate on this when I come to write about my fortune tellers.

An important and must-visit Aunty Wong (my mother's eldest sister) in a hospital in Hong Kong. She was in her 90's. She and mum looked very much alike.

On another afternoon, we met up with my eighth Uncle Fong War Kit's daughter, Fong Shuk Ching. She and her husband lived in Mei Foo Suen Cheun (Broadway). The last time we met was when we were kids in our village. In the evening, they and their family hosted a fabulous seafood dinner in an up-market restaurant in Broadway. That was a dinner we often talk about.

We were invited by Frances' cousin Wong Sai Chong's children and families for dinner at an up-market restaurant in Mongkok. The dinner was delicious, and it was good to meet our Wong cousins.

We also invited Cousin Fong Wing's family for dinner at an up-market restaurant in Tsim Sha Tsui.

On our last day in Hong Kong, we visited Victoria Peak which housed properties with the most expensive prices in the world.

Finally, we arrived back home in Sydney, where we have been living since 19 December 1985. Nothing like home as they say.

During my two weeks' absence my employee Irvan did well, and together with my already retired brother-in-law Sai Sing Wong who voluntarily helped, carried on my business.

On my return and after checking the stock-in-trade (Inventory) and the bank balance, I found a little profit was made. I was satisfied.

Offerings at my father's grave, Zhongshan Section Cemetery,
Sandy Ridge, New Territories, China, May 2000.

Worshipping at my father's grave.

Lunch with my cousin Shuk Ching, at a restaurant in Mei Foo Sun Cheun (Broadway), Kowloon, Hong Kong.
Front sitting Shuk Ching Fong Tsui, Tsui Chee, Ian Fong, Magdalene Fong.
Back standing Wayne Fong and his girlfriend, Frances Fong, Wendy Tsui.
Shuk Ching is my eighth uncle War Kit's daughter. My father War Sut was the sixth brother in the family of 8 boys and an eldest sister.
Shuk Ching and I were kids in our village until she and her mother left for Hong Kong in the late 1940's.

CHAPTER 90
Our homestay students

A homestay is a cultural exchange between an international student or visitor and a local individual or family in the host country. The "host" provides accommodation and support for an agreed-upon period of time and rate.

I don't know where my wife Frances got the idea from in regard to having overseas students staying at our home.

From 1 July 2000 to 30 June 2006, Frances and I had been homestay parents for 31 students from Singapore, Indonesia, Hong Kong, China, Russia and Taiwan.

We had 3 students at a time, and each was provided with a furnished bedroom, breakfast, and dinner. For the initial stay of 4 weeks, the homestay agency paid their board to us, and for those who continued to stay on, they paid us directly for a minimum of 4 weeks.

Students over 18, stayed for the minimum duration of 4 weeks, and they could move on to places of their choice. Those under 18 were required to be under guardianship, and on reaching 18 years of age, they too had a choice to remain or sought accommodation elsewhere.

On the whole, all those students who lived with us were well behaved. While they were with us, they helped with the dishwashing which was the minimum required duty.

They normally stayed quietly in their own bedrooms while they were at home, and they seldom came out to the common room to watch TV programmes.

Frances and I had enjoyed having the students, but we ceased taking anyone on from 1 July 2006, as we decided it was time to travel and visit countries overseas.

CHAPTER 91
The reunion of Wong War Sik's descendants in Sydney, December 2000

Grandpa Wong War Sik is my father-in-law.

Early in the year 2000, my nephew Patrick Wong and my eldest daughter Geralyne Fong Yee, contacted their parents, uncles and aunties in Sydney. The purpose was to arrange for a reunion for all the descendants of Wong War Sik.

For better facilities, Sydney was chosen for the gathering.

Generous Patrick paid airfares, passport and visa application expenses, for some in Fiji who couldn't afford to do so.

A banquet had been organised for everyone at the Fook Yuen Seafood Restaurant in Chatswood. This involved a fair bit of money, and who would stand for it. So, my wife Frances suggested all her siblings and their children who were working, each to fork out A$500 to help defray expenses.

The descendants, children and grandchildren's in-laws attended the joyous occasion. Family friend Alice Tam and her son Patrick were also invited, and to which they attended. Apologies came from grandsons Gary Wong of Tokyo, Timothy Wong of Melbourne, who couldn't attend because of family and work commitments.

Among them were business owners and including children who are now grown-ups, 2 high-tech technicians, 6 commerce graduates, 2 lawyers, 4 masters graduates, 2 teachers, 1 public accountant, 1 PhD (Dr of psychology), 2 engineering graduates. Not bad coming from an old overseas Chinese who like most contemporaries, had never had/ or little Chinese education before they left China.

My father-in-law could read Chinese newspapers, and these were often mailed by his grandnephews David and Alan Wong in Hong Kong; they are now living in Toronto, Canada.

People from Fiji stayed with relatives who could accommodate them. Paul Wong, his wife Patricia together with their 6 children, were comfortably accommodated in a 4-bedroom furnished house in Chiswick, freely provided by our family friend Alice Tam.

During their time (Christmas and New Year period) in Sydney, relatives from Fiji, Paris and Seattle, were entertained, separate small parties galore. They all had an enjoyable stay in Sydney.

After a memorable banquet at the Fook Yuen Seafood Restaurant in Chatswood, the relatives from Fiji, granddaughters Catherine Wong Schurig from Paris, Jean Wong Baever from Seattle, returned to their homelands.

Reunion photo for Wong War Sik descendants, December 2000.

CHAPTER 92

Frances Fong's 60th birthday

On 29 April 2001, my wife Frances celebrated her 60th birthday with relatives and friends at the Dragon Restaurant in Parramatta.

My eldest daughter Geralyne Fong Yee's friend owned the above restaurant. She and her husband Sen Yee who often went to dinner at this restaurant recommended Frances to have her party there. It was popular and well known to diners for just good food.

All the guests came happily to the party, and they indeed enjoyed delicious Chinese dishes provided.

Frances and I at her birthday party.

Front grandson Jonathan Yee.

Back from left younger sister Emily Wong, Frances Fong, younger sister Anne Fong.

From left Nada Cheung, Frances Fong, Merryn Kent, Margaret Harrison, Jane Sing.

Family photo.
From left Ian Fong, Magdalene Fong, Frances Fong, Geralyne Fong Yee, Gerard Fong, daughter-in-law Clare Kent.

Front from left youngest daughter Magdalene Fong, Frances Fong, grandson Jonathan Yee. Back from left son Gerard Fong, daughter-in-law Clare Kent, son-in-law Sen Yee, eldest daughter Geralyne Fong Yee, Ian Fong.

From left Frances Fong, Yuk Kin Wong, Sai Sing Wong.

Beautiful and tasty chocolate birthday cake.

CHAPTER 93

My heart surgery in June 2001

Open-heart surgery is any type of surgery where the chest is cut open and surgery is performed on the muscles, valves, or arteries of the heart. According to the National Heart, Lung, and Blood Institute (NHLBI), coronary artery bypass grafting (CABG) is the most common type of heart surgery done on adults.

Heart bypass surgery, or coronary artery bypass surgery, is used to replace damaged arteries that supply blood to your heart muscle. A surgeon uses blood vessels taken from another area of your body to repair the damaged arteries.

About 2.30 am in the middle of May 2001, I felt itchiness on my chest. This was not the first time, as it happened quite often before this.

After breakfast later in the morning, I went straight to see a doctor in the Top Ryde Surgery where I always consulted. The GP who attended me was a Sri Lankan lady, Dr De Silva. She ordered an ECG test, and it showed that my heart had a problem. She told me I must be admitted to the Ryde Hospital for further tests, and I had to be transported by an ambulance or a relative. I rang my brother-in-law Sai Sing Wong, who was retired, and always ready to help any relative in need, whenever there was a problem. I also rang my wife who was at school, and she was immediately released by the principal to see me at the Ryde Hospital.

Sai Sing came straight away to the surgery to take me to the hospital, but I asked him to come to my home and have some lunch first. At my home, we had a meat pie each and then he took me to the Ryde Hospital. With Dr De Silva's referral, I was immediately admitted by the Emergency Dept. Soon I was taken to a room for tests to be conducted.

Within half an hour, a young Aboriginal lady doctor came to see me, and inserted a peripheral venous catheter on my hand, and extracted blood from me for testing.

I had a packet of cigarettes and a cigarette lighter with me and wanted to have a smoke in my room. I found that all the windows were locked, so the smoking idea was out of the question. Since then I gave up my smoking habit of 50 years. I had my lungs checked in 2016, and they were cleared of cancer signs. Almighty God, thank you.

The next day Dr Edward Barin, a cardiologist consultant at the hospital, came to check me out. The resident doctor related to him that my blood tests showed that I had a minor heart attack.

On the third day in thc hospital, I was taken by ambulance to the Royal North Shore Private Hospital for an angiogram test. There the doctors found two of my arteries were blocked. I was then taken back to the Ryde Hospital.

On the fourth day in the Ryde hospital, Dr Barin came to tell me that I needed bypass surgery to repair the two blocked arteries.

On the fifth day I was taken by ambulance to Royal North Shore Private, and I was admitted.

After going through Xray's and a series of tests the following day, I had been informed surgery will take place on Monday, two days later.

Dr Donald Ross and his assistant, a Chinese Surgeon I can't remember his name, operated on me for about 3 hours. My chest was cut open. After the surgery was done, I was transferred to the emergency unit for two nights, monitored by a doctor and nurse on duty. When I became conscious the first night, I was shocked to find a pipe inside my chest leading to my nose.

My good nephew Patrick Wong came to visit me on the first night, and knowing that I always love crispy roast pork, he brought a serve of Chinese Roast Pork and Rice to cheer me up. I had to give this a miss as I was not strong enough to eat solid food at that time.

When I went to Dr Ross' surgery for a follow-up check, he told me I was lucky to have two spare arteries in my chest, so he used them instead of transferring from other parts of my body. He also told me that he was a consultant to the Zhongshan hospital in my district in China where I came from. Not long after that I heard he retired from practice as a surgeon. He was only in his late forties, might be in the early fifties.

I spent a week in Royal North Shore Private, and during this time I suffered great pains whenever I coughed. I was given a little morphine and strong pain killers to ease my pains.

North Shore Private didn't allow me to stay for more than a week and recommended the Hirondelle Private Hospital in Chatswood for me to rehabilitate.

An ambulance transported me to this private hospital. I stayed there for two weeks and returned to my home.

From then on, I felt reasonably good and could drive my car and van, but I took it easy.

During the time I was in hospital, my employee Irvan and the drivers continued working on my wholesale business. It was very hard on Frances after school and in the evenings. She had to balance the cash brought back by the drivers, as well as taking phone orders. Faxed in orders and invoices were taken care of by Irvan.

Thank God, at this stage of writing, I am feeling better than before my bypass surgery in June 2001.

Thanks to my cardiologist Dr Barin, who checks me up once in a year, as he finds that I am getting along fine after each ECG and ultrasound tests. Prior to this he was checking on me twice a year.

With my two daughters at the cafe, Royal North Shore Private Hospital, 18 June 2001.

CHAPTER 94

My fortune tellers

When I was in Fiji, my mother sent me a large piece of paper containing black and red writings written by a fortune teller. For information to him my mother supplied my age, time and date of birth. With this little information the fortune teller wrote about my life.

The paper which I am keeping has so many complicated technical words, some in a circle.

However, I can understand the passage on my character, favourable careers either military or business, marriage and so on.

The fortune-teller wrote that he could see me live till 63 years of age, longer it would be due to my good luck. Three children will be farewelling me at my funeral. He said that if I had a fourth child, it would bring about tears of grief.

Some people believe in fortune-telling while many don't but criticise this practice as well as feng shui.

Well as for me I do believe in fortune-telling but not feng shui which has many silly interpretations.

My fortune-teller told I would live till 63 years of age, longer it would be due to my good luck.

When I was 64 years of age, I had 2 heart by-passes meaning two arteries were repaired, and my life was saved.

Three children will be farewelling me at my funeral.

True, at present I have three children, anymore would bring sorrow to the family.

He also told me one day I would marry a maiden from the south seas. I had never dreamed of marrying her, but she had an interest in me as her future husband.

In China I only knew my father was working in Fiji, but I didn't know where Fiji was.

You know what happened, I married Frances Wong, born in Levuka, Fiji.

At Wong Tai Sin Temple, Hong Kong, 2000, a female fortune-teller said I would live till 107, but a knock in the centre of my forehead would reduce 30 years, and surely, I did receive a knock accidentally in Sydney.

At the age of 77 I dreaded the whole year thinking that I would die on any day of that year. However, I survived and on the first day on reaching 78 years of age I was overjoyed to be still alive.

My Cardiologist says if I don't smoke, I would live till 85.

Computer Survey tells 85.

First Fortune-teller in China said 63.

I turned 80 years old on 15 July 2018 (Chinese calendar).

What to believe? Hahaha.

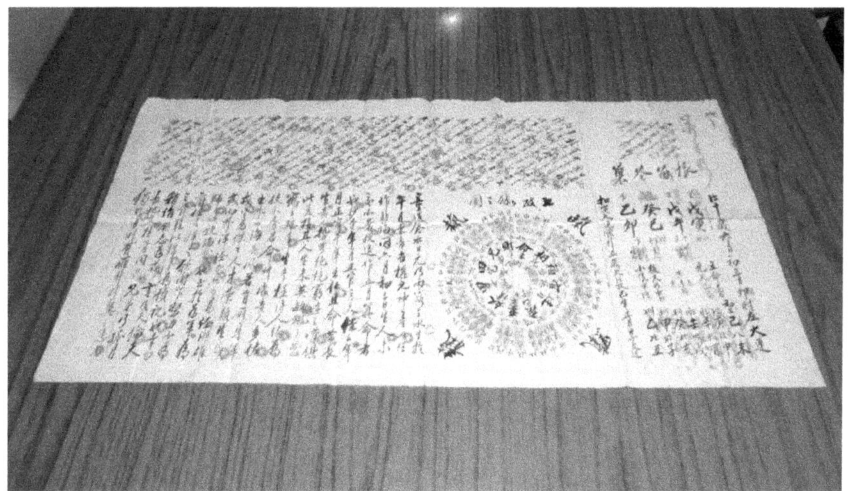

My first fortune teller in China wrote about my life on this piece of paper in 1951.

At Wong Tai Sin Temple, Hong Kong, 2000.
A female fortune-teller said I would live till 107, but a knock in the centre of my forehead will reduce 30 years, and surely, I did receive a knock accidentally back in Sydney.
At the age of 77 I dreaded the whole year thinking that I would die in any day of that year. However, I survived and on the first day on reaching 78 years of age I was very happy to be still alive.

CHAPTER 95
Trafalgar Europe Tour 2005

This was the first trip my wife Frances and I had done since we ceased having homestay students from overseas.

We teamed up with Frances' younger sister Emily Wong, our friends Queenie Wong, Margaret Harrison and Patsy Mar, and booked for a European Tour with the travel agent, Trafalgar Tours. It is a travel company that provides guided holidays to over 200 destinations worldwide. The company is owned by The Travel Corporation which has been in business since 1947.

From Sydney, Frances, Emily and I flew through Singapore, and stayed there for two days before flying to London. We stayed at the IBIS hotel in Islington for 2 days. Queenie, Margaret and Patsy had already booked into the hotel.

On the third day at 7.30 am in the morning, a Trafalgar Tour coach with a driver from Portugal, and an Australian lady tour guide, came to pick us up from the hotel. From there the coach continued picking up passengers from other hotels.

The coach dropped the tourists at the Trafalgar office to use the toilet facilities. I was the last one to leave while Frances and our troupe had already gone back to the coach, leaving me behind. When I came out of the toilet facilities, I went to the spot where the coach had left us, but it wasn't there. It had moved to another spot. I went back to the office and waited for someone to get me. I had no mobile phone with me as it was held by Frances. At last, the coach came back to pick me up from the place where I was waiting.

Lesson one: When travelling on a tour, always stay together.

At Dover in England, the coach with us tourists in it boarded a ferry to Parris. During the journey, we got off the coach and had lunch on board.

After landing in Calais, France, the coach continued its journey to Amsterdam and many places. By the end of the coach tour, we had visited 11 countries and 23 cities in Europe.

The coach tour ended in Paris, so Frances, Emily and I, took the opportunity to visit our niece Cathy Wong Schurig, her husband Fritz and their family. We stayed at their home for 5 days.

Fritz took us to visit St Michael the Archangel Church in Normandy, and Cathy took us to visit the Art Gallery and the Palace of Versailles in Paris.

From Paris, we flew to London, and Queenie, Margaret and Patsy joined us for the trip to Hong Kong, where we met up with our relatives. Margaret and Patsy were on their separate ways. All of our troupe met at the Hong Kong airport before returning to Sydney.

Our tour took 23 days to complete. The coach went through countless tunnels through different countries. I remember the coach went as far as Barcelona and Madrid in Spain, visited Lourdes, the Basilica of the Sacred Heart and the Eiffel Tower in Paris, and the coliseum in Rome.

The coach trip from Barcelona to Madrid in Spain, a distance of more than 800 kilometres, took almost 8 hours. The only driver made 2 stops for refreshments and toilet facilities.

It is with regret that I can't remember all the places of countries and cities we had visited.

Here are some photos which indicate places we had visited.

Frances and I in Monaco.

Front row from left Margaret Harrison, Julia Schurig, Cathy Schurig, Roland Schurig. Back row from left Emily Wong, Fritz Schurig, Bernhard Schurig, Frances Fong and Patsy Mar.

After the Trafalgar Tour of Europe, our group met up in the Hong Kong airport before returning to Sydney, 2005. From left Emily Wong, Queenie Wong, Patsy Mar, Margaret Harrison, Frances Fong, Ian Fong.

CHAPTER 96

Our family's 20th anniversary in Australia

Two weeks before the 19 December 2005, our youngest daughter Magdalene reminded us to celebrate our anniversary of 20 years in Sydney, after migrating from Fiji. Thanks to Frances' younger sister Emily, who boldly went out to sponsor our family including my mother, to settle in Australia.

Our family is forever indebted to Emily. Gratefully appreciated.

It was an occasion not to be missed, as the new country which we had settled in, had given us more satisfaction than as expected; such as a comfortable home, suitable employment, children's education, medical benefits, affordable food and clothing prices, and importantly cordial neighbours.

Frances and I bought a 4-bedroom house with a formal lounge and a family room, two verandas in the front and the back of the house, a large double garage, double carport, on a large piece of land.

Initially Frances found a teaching position at St Dominic Savio, a Catholic private school in Rockdale. Later, she became a civil servant and taught at Lidcombe Public School for 17 years and retired from there. She was presented with a silver medal by the Dept of Education.

I worked as an accountant for an Australian owner of two private companies: Undersee Pty Ltd and Dispensers Pty Ltd., for 4 and ½ years when I decided to run my own business. I bought a mixed business shop in Croydon Park, and operated it for 5 years. After that I operated a wholesale business on general groceries, soft drinks, confectionery, and chips etc until I retired in 2005.

Our eldest daughter Geralyne and youngest daughter Magdalene attended the Marist Sisters College in Woolwich. Magdalene also attended Our Lady Queen of Peace Primary School in Gladesville. Our son Gerard attended Holy Cross College in Ryde. All of them attended universities. Geralyne graduated with a Bachelor of Economics. Gerard graduated with a Bachelor of Business. Magdalene graduated with a Bachelor of Communications and also a Master of Technology degree. They are now employed by reputable firms and hold positions of responsibility. They also own their own homes and cars.

Medically, we have been looked after by good GP's and specialists. Good hospitals are close by.

In Sydney we are blessed with many varieties of food: Australian, Chinese, Italian, Greek, Vietnamese, Korean, Indian, Thailand, other Continental cuisine and many more.

Our neighbours on all sides of our house are very good Australian families.

Overall, life for us in Sydney has been very good so far, apart from the insults I had personally encountered.

Inside the Campsie Trade Centre one afternoon, an Indian driver (might be from Fiji) inside his van, came close to where I was turning in the corner and shouted "Chin miy wa".

While driving on the road in Georges River Road in Croydon Park, a tough-looking Australian guy inside his truck in front of me, put out his right fist and kept on waving till he reached the traffic light in Ashfield.

On one occasion, I stopped at a traffic light in Lakemba before turning right into Georges River Road, a Lebanese truck driver turning right into Lakemba Road, swore at me.

Outside my shop in Croydon Park, a driver inside a van drove past and shouted abuse at me.

One day outside my house when I was picking up letters from the mailbox, a driver in his truck drove past and shouted foul words at me.

Most shockingly, the driver of an NRMA van shouted abuse to me when he drove past me in Wicks Road, near my house. It was about 6 pm at that time while I was going for a walk.

I was driving on the middle lane down Wicks Road, and I waved a friendly gesture to an Australian driver inside his truck, driving alongside on the left. He shouted back with abuses.

Inside the Coles Supermarket in Ashfield, I was in an aisle when a couple walked past me. The man said he could smell a stench.

All the above greats might have not encountered any Vietnamese youths. Otherwise, there could be serious consequences for them. One night in the city, a gang of Vietnamese youths in a car, drove closely past a Tongan man and his lady companion. He shouted at them to stop. Some youths came out of the car and confronted the big fellow. One of the youths stabbed him fatally, and he died afterwards.

Summing up the above, the former Chinese lady ombudsman of Australia, a Harvard scholar once told of an insult. She said she was in a restaurant in Brisbane and an Australian while walking past her table commented "I can smell a stench".

To celebrate the occasion, our family put on a little dinner party for our immediate relatives and a few friends. A whole sucking pig of 3 and ½ kilos graced the table of Chinese dishes.

Family's 20th anniversary in Sydney, 19 December 2005.
We presented Frances' sister, Emily Wong, who sponsored us to immigrate to Australia with flowers.

Immediate family members with Emily Wong.
From left Magdalene Fong, Emily Wong, Ian Fong, Frances Fong, Geralyne Fong Yee with her husband Sen Yee, Sen holding their daughter Tiana Yee, their son Jonathan Yee is in front of Sen, Gerard Fong and his wife Clare Kent.

Food, glorious food on the day.
It included a baby suckling pig, a Chinese delicacy.

CHAPTER 97

Visits to Canada and USA 2006

We have relatives and friends in Vancouver, relatives in Toronto, London (Ontario, Canada) and Boston in the USA.

Frances and I planned a trip to visit them living in the above cities. We set out on our own without joining any tour group.

The Canadian Airline plane took 9 hours 50 minutes to fly us to Honolulu, Hawaii, made a stop for 3 hours, and then continued its flight of 5 hours 55 minutes to Vancouver.

In the Vancouver airport, we had to wait for 3 hours before boarding a plane to fly to Toronto, and the journey took 4 hours.

Frances' first cousin's son David Wong and his wife May were waiting to greet us on arrival. From there they took us to their home in London, a city not far from Toronto, a distance of 193.4 km. The car journey took 2 hours 9 minutes.

We spent a few comfortable nights at David's beautiful home in London, Ontario.

On the first night we were treated to a wonderful dinner with his family at home, half a lobster on special fried rice for each person. Tea and dessert followed afterwards.

On the second day, David and his wife May took us to visit Niagara Falls, a distance of 200.7 kms and 1 hour 59 minutes by car. We had lunch at the Falls, but we didn't dare to take a boat ride down in the water which was often rough and dangerous. We also visited a tourist resort not far from Niagara Falls.

On the third day David and his wife May, took us to London, a city in Ontario, and had lunch at one of the trade centres. lunch at one of the trade centres.

On the fourth day, our youngest daughter Magdalene and her friend Eunice Tjabadi, came from London, United Kingdom, to join us. They stayed at the Marriot Hotel in Toronto.

On the fifth day, Magdalene and her friends Eunice and Phuong Truong, came in a rental car and picked us up for a trip to Montreal and Quebec. After visiting Montreal, Phuong had to return to Toronto, to take her mother to see a specialist. The trip to Quebec was abandoned.

On the sixth day, Frances and I returned to stay with David and May.

On the seventh day, David and his wife May, took us (Frances, Magdalene, Eunice and I), to Toronto. The journey by car, and a distance of 112 km, took 1 hour and 41 minutes. The roads were mostly very good and straight.

The four of us, David and his wife May, Frances and I, stayed at his younger brother Allan's flat, while Magdalene and Eunice stayed at David's younger sister Betty Wong Jean's house. We met David's mother (Frances' first cousin's wife).

In Toronto the next day, Betty took us to the city of Toronto, and we visited the CN tower and the autumn festival of lights donated by China and erected by artists from China. For the remaining of the day, Frances and I, treated the gang for lunch in a Chinese restaurant in the city.

On the night before we left Toronto for Boston by bus, Frances and I invited Frances' cousins and their mother Cheung Gar So, for a dinner in an up-market Chinese Seafood restaurant in Toronto. That was the last time we saw Cheung Gar So alive. She was a great lady, very kind and loving. I remember when she found out that I like Cantonese Operas, she wanted to give me some of her cassettes, but I declined her offer and told her that I could watch the operas on YouTube.

The following evening, David took the four of us (Frances, Magdalene, Eunice and I), to the bus terminal in Toronto.

We caught a Greyhound bus to Boston, USA. The bus could only go as far as Buffalo, USA, and another driver with the USA driving licence will take over. The journey took 2 hours and 10 minutes and a distance of 94.6 km. The bus left Toronto at 11.55 pm.

By the time we arrived at Buffalo, it was about 2.15 am. After going through customs, it was about 4 am.

The bus driver on the Canadian side had gone off duty, and the one from the USA side would start at 6 am. By bus from Buffalo to Boston would take 10 hours 36 minutes.

By waiting for 2 hours for the driver to arrive, and another 10 hours 36 minutes by bus, it seemed that the whole day would be gone. In view of this situation, Magdalene and her friend Eunice suggested for us to catch a plane to Boston. The flight would take 1 hour 20 minutes.

We all agreed, so we went by plane from Buffalo to Boston, although it cost much more.

From Boston airport we took a taxi to Quincy, Boston, where cousin Norena Wu Fong and her family lived. We stayed there for three days.

The next day, as Norena and her husband Charlie, were both occupied in their hairdressing salons, we took their four children out to the city of Boston, went for a land bus/river cruise around the Charles River. We had lunch afterwards.

In the evening, the Fong family treated us to a sumptuous seafood buffet dinner at a restaurant.

The next morning, Magdalene and Eunice went by train to tour Harvard University.

Frances and I stayed back. We missed that opportunity, but on our second trip to Boston, Frances and I went for a tour around the Harvard campus.

After 3 days in Boston, the four of us travelled by a Greyhound bus from Boston to New York. The bus driver was a Chinese man in his early forties, and he took 4 hours 15 minutes and a distance of 346 km to get us there. On the way we could see the sign leading to Yale University. In New York we stayed 3 days at a 4-star hotel. During our stay, Frances, Magdalene and I, took a coach tour of the city, visited the Empire State Building, Statute of Liberty, and had enjoyed a good evening meal in Time Squares, a popular tourist street. Magdalene's friend Eunice spent her time with her boyfriend who was working in New York.

From New York we flew to the Vancouver airport, where our host and good friend Ming Ko, was there to greet us.

We stayed at Ming's beautiful home for 1 week. He and his wife Helena took us (Frances, Magdalene and I) out to the Taiwanese Cultural Festival, Chinese Gardens in the city, and the famous Stanley Park, Night Market in Richmond, and also to the Peach Arch Park in the border dividing Canada and USA. Magdalene's friend Eunice, before she returned to London, United Kingdom, she and Ming's daughter Theresa, spent a day mountain hiking.

Our cousin Joan Wong Chan and her husband Watson Chan, invited Frances, Magdalene and me, to their home for dinner. They put on special Indian dishes for us. The next day, they took us to the Canadian border near Seattle, USA, for shopping, and we had lunch in a cafe afterwards.

For the first time we met Frances's first Cousin Wong Sai Cheong's eighth son Victor and his wife Lilian. They took us out for a Western lunch.

Our friend John Francis Fong made arrangements with his friends, entertained us with Dim Sum (Yum Cha) lunch, and with another group of friends in the evening, took us to dinner at another restaurant in the same suburb in Vancouver.

We also met up with Mr and Mrs Joe Wun Hong, their son David and wife May and their children. They invited Frances, me and Ming ko, for dinner at an up-market Chinese Restaurant in Richmond. Unfortunately, I have misplaced the photo taken at the restaurant.

Having thoroughly enjoyed our visits, Magdalene returned to London, United Kingdom, and Frances and I spent a week in Honolulu, Hawaii, before we returned to Sydney.

In Honolulu, Frances and I met up with her first cousins, John and Benny Ung, their spouses and families, on her mother's side. They took us for Yum Cha lunch, and dinner at an up-market restaurant. John drove us around Honolulu and took us to visit his parents' graves.

It was wonderful to meet up with them for the first time.

Frances and I visited the Honolulu Chinatown, which is smaller than the Sydney Chinatown. We also went by bus to Pearl Harbour, and visited the battleship museum, toured around, and had lunch there.

Frances was excited to take her first swim at the famous Waikiki Beach.

Visit to Vancouver.
We stayed with our friends Ming Ko and Helena Ko.
Sitting from left Helena Ko, our daughter Magdalene's friend
Eunice Tjabadi, Magdalene Fong, Frances Fong.
Standing from left Ming Ko, his daughter Theresa Ko.

Out at yum cha lunch.
Sitting from left Eunice Tjabadi, Ming Ko, Helena Ko, Frances Fong.
Standing from left Ian Fong, Magdalene Fong.

Lunch with Frances' cousin Betty Wong Jean in Toronto.
Betty is wearing glasses, sitting closest to the camera.
Her daughter Maureen Jean is sitted second from the left.

CHAPTER 98

China Tour 2007

Our friend, Robina Fong joined Frances and me, for a tour of a few large cities, in China, conducted by China Best Tours.

We flew direct to Beijing and stayed in a 5-star hotel for three days.

Our youngest daughter Magdalene who was working in London, came to Beijing to join us on the third day.

During the first two days in Beijing, the three of us, Robina, Frances and I, visited the Beijing University of Languages where Frances (on a UNESCO scholarship) once attended, and a huge Walmart supermarket within walking distance of the hotel. We also went to an acrobatic performance, and that was fantastic.

We also caught a bus near the hotel where we were staying. A young lady conductor asked me where we wanted to go. I knew a little Mandarin then and told her we wanted to go for a ride. I used Cantonese grammar.

"You Che Ho" meaning going for a ride. "Ho" meaning river.

She asked, "What river".

Then I said in Cantonese grammar "Dou Fung" literally meaning going around the wind.

She asked, "What wind".

The conductor was confused.

Fortunately, an old man sitting near us told us the bus was not travelling around, and it would stop at the end of its destination. I could buy a one-way ticket and get off the bus and catch another bus which would come back to where we first caught. That gentleman spoke to me in English and said he studied in Paris, but he knew some elementary English.

Since that time I was determined to pursue the study of Mandarin.

In the evening of the third day, our friend Dr Kam Young's son Rafael who was working as a lawyer in Beijing, came for a courtesy visit, and had coffee with us.

On the fourth day, our tour guide who is fluent in English, came to the hotel to pick us up to go to the airport. Our tour had officially begun.

Our tour group of 16 and the guide, flew to Yichang city. A coach picked us up from the airport and took us to a location in the Yangtze River where the cruise boat was berthed. Labourers with carrying poles took our luggage to the boat, and we were allocated our respective cabins.

The boat set sail downstream through the Yangtze River for 3 days and 3 nights to Chongqing city. (Cantonese Chungking).

Accommodation and food on board were first class.

During the three days on board the cruise boat, day excursions were arranged for tourists who wished to visit areas such as temples etc. There were entertainments at night such as folk dancing, and tourists were asked to stage their own talent contests. Most surprisingly, the young ladies who normally worked as waitresses, performed a spectacular French Can Can dance.

At night while the boat cruises along the Yangtze River, we could view beautiful sceneries on both sides of the river, full of buildings and fancy lighting.

After three days and nights the boat reached Chongqing city. We got off and were taken by coach, a small size one which was very comfortable for the 17 of us, to an up-market hotel restaurant. We were surprised the lunch dishes were cooked with Cantonese style flavour, and soup and dishes were very tasty, much to our liking.

By this time, a local guide was engaged to take us around the city. We went for a body and foot massage at a parlour where all customers were treated in a large room.

We visited the residence of the former president of China Chiang Kai Sek, which was situated on top of a hill, and fancy it had no windows. The coach also took us to several places popular with tourists.

From Chongqing we flew to the ancient city of Xian and stayed at a 4-star hotel for 1 day and 2 nights.

During the day we visited the City Wall and the Terracotta Army Museum. At night we were entertained at a dumpling dinner inside a theatre, where a troupe of dancers with very colourful costumes, performed various folklore dances.

From Xian we flew to the beautiful city of Hangzhou. While in Hangzhou we were taken for a cruise around the famous West Lake, a tea tasting centre, and a fabulous lunch at a restaurant.

Marco Polo was supposed to have served as governor of Hangzhou for 3 years during his 17 year stay in China.

From Hangzhou, the coach took us 4 hours 10 minutes and a distance of 311 km to Suzhou, a city located in southeastern Jiangsu Province of East China, about 100 km (62 miles) northwest of Shanghai.

In Suzhou, we visited a tourist area up on a hill, where lots of souvenirs were sold. At the bottom of the hill, a young man with one leg came to me begging, so I gave him some money. When I got to the top of the hill, he was already up there, and wanted to beg from me again. I refused him as I had already given him some money before. It was disappointing that we didn't take a boat cruise around the many canals in Suzhou. At that time, we just didn't think of taking the boat cruise (might be short of time). The tour didn't arrange one for us.

From Suzhou the coach continued its journey of 1 and ½ hours and a distance about 100 km to Shanghai.

In Shanghai, we stayed at a 4-star hotel as always arranged and provided by the tour operator, for 2 days and 2 nights.

The coach and tour guide took us to some places popular with tourists, such as the Yu Garden or Yuyuan Garden, or Shanghainese "Yuyu" lit, Garden of Happiness. It is close to the Yuyuan Tourist Mart, a clothing and fancy goods shopping centre.

We also visited the Shanghai Science and Technology Museum.

Lastly, we visited at night, the Oriental Pearl Radio & TV Tower.

The next morning, we said goodbye to the city of Shanghai and caught the Shanghai Maglev (Magnetic Levitation) train, the world's fastest commercially operating train, with a top operating speed of 431 kph (268 mph), which exceeded 500 kph in testing. It did the 19 mile journey to Pudong airport in 7 minutes.

From Shanghai, Robina Fong, Frances and I flew to Singapore. Our daughter Magdalene returned to work in London. We stayed at a 4-star hotel for 2 days and 2 nights. There we went on an excursion to Sentosa Island and had a beautiful lunch there. Robina and Frances took a cable car ride, but I remained on the island (frightened of heights).

We booked an overnight coach tour to Penang Island, a state in northwest Malaysia.

In Penang Island we stayed at a hotel for one day and one night. There we visited the Penang Snake Temple, and up a hill, a famous temple in the area.

From Penang Island, a coach took us to Kuala Lumpur, the capital of Malaysia. We stayed at a hotel for one day and one night. There we visited the Kuala Lumpur Tower, Eye on Malaysia, and from the distance, we saw the Petronas Twin Towers.

For dinner in a cafe near our hotel in Kuala Lumpur, we tasted a sumptuous Chinese dish called stir-fry duck eggs with bitter melon. I have never forgotten this dish. I have tried cooking it at home a few times, but the taste wasn't the same.

After our stay in Kuala Lumpur, the coach which had aeroplane seats, so comfortable, took us back to Singapore. We were served with breakfast and a light lunch, coffee included.

Our trip had ended the same night, and we said goodbye to Singapore the last port of call.

We finally arrived safely at Sydney airport, and Robina's future son-in-law Paul and his father picked us up and took us home.

Our Bestours tour group in Tiananmen Square, Beijing.
Frances is helping to hold the Bestours flag in the middle. I'm standing behind her. Magdalene is standing on the furthest right.

Picture taken in the lobby for cruise ship that we were on during the tour.
It sailed down the Yangtze River.
From left Robina Fong, Frances Fong, Ian Fong, Magdalene Fong.

On a boat trip.
From left Ian Fong, Magdalene Fong, Frances Fong.

On a boat trip.
From left Ian Fong, Frances Fong, driver for boat, Magdalene Fong, Robina Fong.

Dinner out in restaurant.

Magdalene Fong and Frances Fong outside an ancient temple.

Ian Fong with terracotta warriors (reproduction).

The terracotta museum in Xian.

With our tour guides in Shanghai.

CHAPTER 99

My 70th birthday party

On 5 July 2008, I celebrated my 70th birthday at the Emperor Garden Restaurant in the city. I was born on 3 June 1938 (Chinese Calendar). My birthday falls on a different day in July every year, and that's confusing to my family.

In early July every year, Frances and my eldest daughter Geralyne, would ask me when my birthday is. I have to look up the calendar which has both English and Chinese dates in them and let them know.

Many thanks to Frances and my 3 children Geralyne, Gerard and Magdalene, who had generously contributed to the party expenses, namely the banquet at the restaurant and the large beautiful cake.

Eldest daughter Geralyne, organised the invitations to guests and table sittings. My 3 children also helped in decorating the restaurant as well as receiving the incoming guests. Son-in-law Sen Yee arranged the sound system and the music for the evening. Daughter-in-law Clare and her father Jon Kent, compiled the photos in a video that was screened at the restaurant.

Thanks a lot to all the above people.

It was a surprise to me that in the morning on 5 July 2008, when Frances organised a tea ceremony at home where the children, daughter-in-law Clare, grandson Jonathan, and granddaughter Tiana, served tea to me.

Geralyne took a photo of me, and had it mounted on a large board, for the guests to sign.

The MC, Ron Ah Tong, did a terrific job. His ukulele performance was just fantastic.

Many thanks go to Benson Wong my MBHS classmate, who proposed the toast of the evening to me.

A lot of thanks too, go to Dr Kam Young, Peter Chan and Charlie Chow, who volunteered to say a few kind words about me.

In my reply to Benson's toast, I thanked him and all the guests, especially the friends and relatives from Brisbane, Melbourne, and those who travelled from London, Boston USA, Fiji and New Zealand to attend my party. I asked my children, son-in-law, daughter-in-law, and grandson Jonathan and granddaughter Tiana to stand up to show themselves, and they did so. I also requested all the MBHS old boys to stand up and show themselves. There were about 24 of them present, but only a handful of younger ones stood up to show themselves. The older ones were rather shy to do so. Those old boys from my immediate family were myself, my son Gerard, my son-in-law Sen Yee, my nephews Chris and Stephen Wong. I almost forgot another one Colin Whippy, who is my niece Annette Wong's husband.

By looking back at the 300 photos taken at the party, it was a very jovial occasion for everyone present. I am glad that all the wonderful guests enjoyed the party.

Chinese tea ceremony at home in North Ryde.
From left Frances Fong, Ian Fong.

From left Geralyne Fong Yee, Ian Fong.

From left Gerard Fong, Frances Fong, Ian Fong.

From left Frances Fong, Clare Kent, Ian Fong.

From left Frances Fong, Magdalene Fong, Ian Fong.

From left Jonathan Yee, Frances Fong, Ian Fong.

From left Frances Fong, Tiana Yee, Ian Fong.

Cutting my birthday cake.
From left Ian Fong, Frances Fong.

Family photo.
From left Frances Fong, Jonathan Yee, Ian Fong, Magdalene Fong, Adrian Stefanczyk, Geralyne Fong Yee, Tiana Yee, Sen Yee, Gerard Fong, Clare Kent.

Family photo with my relatives from Australia and New Zealand.

My lovely wife Frances Fong beaming at the camera.

Sitting from left Magdalene Chan, Margaret Harrison, Patricia Johnson, Jane Sing, Emily Wong and Wanita Russell. Standing from left Angela Yee, Yuk Ching Wong, Chi Lem Tsom, Frances Fong, Ian Fong, Peggy Lee Shoy and Dick Lee Shoy.

CHAPTER 100
China Trip 2010

In early May 2010 my eldest daughter Geralyne informed Frances and me that she and her family were taking a trip to visit her husband Sen Yee's siblings in Taishan, China. When I was very young, I heard of the 4 Szeyup districts Kaiping, Taishan, Xinhui and Enping. My father worked for Kwong Tiy & Co Ltd in Suva, Fiji, for many years. This company was owned by people from Kaiping.

My father's friend Wong Chun from Xinhui, proprietor of War Hing Laundry, Amy Street, Suva, Fiji, looked after me for three years 1952 to 1954. Uncle Wong Chun was a very kind man, and he treated me like a son, giving me free board, free pocket money for ironing the soldiers' thick khaki shirts and short trousers. I helped with the cooking and the washing of dishes.

When I told Frances, I wanted to join Geralyne and her family for the trip, she immediately agreed for us to go along, as she knew that I always wanted to visit the Szeyup districts.

Kaiping is a city in southern China, in the Pearl River Delta. It's known for the diaolou (fortified towers) that dot the nearby rural villages. Many of these well-preserved towers, including Kaiping Diaolou and Jingjiangli Village, are a fusion of Chinese and Western architectural styles. Outside of the city, Liyuan Garden features sculpted gardens, canals, grand archways and Italian-inspired pavilions.

Kaiping (開平), formerly romanised in Cantonese as Hoiping, is a county-level city in Guangdong Province, China. It is located west of the Pearl River Delta and administered as part of the prefecture-level city of Jiangmen. The surrounding area, especially Sze Yup (Cantonese romanization: 四邑), is the ancestral homeland.

Taishan, formerly romanised in Cantonese as Toishan, in local dialect as Hoisan, and formerly known as Xinning or Sunning, is a county-level city in southwestern Guangdong, China. It is administered as part of the prefecture-level city of Jiangmen. During the 2010 census, there were 941,095 inhabitants, of which approximately 394,855 live overseas.

Xinhui, formerly romanised as Sunwui and also known as Kuixiang, is an urban district of Jiangmen in Guangdong, China. It grew from a separate city founded at the confluence of the Tan and West Rivers. It has a population of about 735,500, 98% of whom are Han Chinese but many of whom speak a dialect of Cantonese.

Enping, formerly romanised as Yanping, is a county-level city in Guangdong, China, administered as part of the prefecture-level city of Jiangmen. Enping administers an area of 1,698 km2 (656 sq. mi) and had an estimated population of 460,000 in 2005. Its diaspora accounts for around 420,000 overseas Chinese.

On 5 December 2010, our troupe consisted of Frances, me, Geralyne, her husband Sen, and their children Jonathan and Tiana, embarked on our journey to China via Hong Kong. From there we caught a Dragon Airplane to Guangzhou (Canton City).

On arrival, Sen's siblings (2 older sisters, 2 older brothers, and a younger sister) were waiting to greet us. They came in a fifteen-seater van to accommodate us all and our suitcases. The road trip from Guangzhou to Taishan was approximately 2 hours.

Frances and I stayed in Taishan for a week, attending the feasts which were put up by Sen's siblings and families. It was a memorable trip and they took very good care of us all.

In the following week, Frances's nephew Zhenghe Li from Zhongshan City, came by car to pick up Frances and me, and we travelled to Macau.

Geralyne and her family remained in Taishan, and they spent their time with Sen's siblings and families.

Frances became sick during our 3 days in Macau, so we couldn't do any sightseeing. She consulted a young lady doctor near our hotel and was given antibiotics. She was told that if her illness persisted after 3 days, she would be admitted to a hospital. Luckily, Frances felt better after 3 days.

It was time for us to go to the Zhongshan City (Shiqi City), where we met up with Frances' cousin and families. Nephew Zhenghe picked us up and whilst we were on our way to Zhongshan City we passed Zhuhai City, and a beautiful bay. We felt tranquillity and a breath of fresh air.

In Zhongshan City, we stayed at a 4-star hotel called the Zhongshan International. The hotel had 2 restaurants, one for Yum Cha lunch and dinner, and the other was for seafood buffet lunch and dinner.

We invited Frances' cousin Ung Kum Ling (her father is Frances' mother's older brother), her husband Chong Ming Li, their children and families, for a seafood buffet dinner.

Soon Geralyne and her family also joined us in Zhongshan City. Kum Ling's son Zhenghe and his wife and daughter took us out for dinners. The first night was to a food court with many stalls offering colourful and varieties of food. The second night was at a restaurant where a-la-cart menu was served.

Zhenghe and his family, his parents, his siblings and families, treated us to a fabulous dinner at an up-market and very renowned restaurant. The dinner served up some mouth-watering dishes with memorable experiences for us all.

Zhenghe took Frances and me, Geralyne and family, to visit my village, and then her parents' villages. Photos will show where they are situated.

It was now time to go to Hong Kong. Early in the morning, Zhenghe brought a van, and fitted all of us in it. He drove us to the Guangzhou City airport via a route bypassing the city in order to avoid the traffic.

The Dragon Airplane flew us from the Guangzhou airport to the Hong Kong airport.

Frances and I stayed at a hotel about 200 metres from the hotel where Geralyne and her family stayed.

In Hong Kong, our priority was to visit my father's grave in Sandy Ridge, New Territories, China. I contacted my cousin Fong Wing and his family to help take us there. Wing had a problem walking, but his wife and son Johnny, went along with us. Wing's wife brought along tea, whisky, and all the essential utensils for worship. We bought roast pork, whole boiled white chicken with head, fruits, paper clothes and paper money and incense sticks etc.

We journeyed by MTR (Local Train) from Hung Hum in Kowloon, to Lo Fu, then applied for a permit to enter the Chinese New Territories Section from the local police post. We were told to pick up the permit in a couple of hours later, although Geralyne had previously organised our permits from Sydney, and the sergeant in charge assured Geralyne that there was no problem.

What a big fuss it was!

In the meantime, we went to a nearby shopping centre and had Yum Cha lunch. After lunch, we went to the police post to pick up the permits, then we caught 2 taxis registered with permits to enter the cemetery area, and the drivers waited until we finished our worshipping formalities.

In Kowloon, we contacted some of our relatives and invited them for dinners.

On Christmas Eve, Geralyne's family treated Frances and me to a fabulous seafood buffet at the Inter-Continental Hotel, facing the Hong Kong harbour. It was an amazing buffet and we all had a great evening.

On Christmas Day, Geralyne and her family, took us to Ocean Park. We all enjoyed the day out.

In the morning of 30 December 2010, we commenced the last leg of our journey arriving safely at Sydney Airport.

Outside the Helen Bergh Hotel, Kaiping, December 2010.
From left Sen Yee, Geralyne Fong Yee, Tiana Yee, Jonathan Yee, Frances Fong, Ian Fong.

With eldest daughter Geralyne and her family.

With Frances' cousins/nephews and their families inside a Chinese restaurant in Zhongshan City.

With son-in-law Sen Yee's siblings and families, inside hotel in Taishan.

CHAPTER 101
My sleep apnea problems

What is sleep apnea? "Apnea" literally means "no breath" or "stopping breathing". Many people have sleep apnea, (also known as sleep apnoea) but may not even know it. In fact, sleep apnea affects more than three in 10 men and nearly two in 10 women, so it's more common than you might think. If you think you might have sleep apnea, it's important to recognise some of the common symptoms and what you can do about it.

Common symptoms of sleep apnea are:

- Snoring, gasping or choking sounds while you're asleep
- Fatigue / excessive daytime sleepiness
- Heavy snoring
- Poor concentration
- Poor memory
- Low Energy
- Waking up unrefreshed
- Gasping / interrupted breathing while asleep

Early in 2010, my wife Frances told me she could hear me snoring badly while sleeping at night.

Since then, I became aware of the things happening.

If I didn't get up right away after lunch, I could be just sitting down and started dosing off to sleep by the table. The same happened after dinner.

After a short while on the computer, I would fall asleep.

One day when I was driving from Strathfield to Homebush West, I was on the left lane not far from the corner turn to go to West Homebush, I suddenly fell asleep. The front left tyre got punctured with a 3-inch hole, and the car stopped. Luckily, I was on the left side of the road, and if I were in the middle lane I could have died from a fatal crash in a pile-up of cars. When I woke up, I drove the car with the punctured tyre to the service station opposite the corner.

Very shortly after that accident, I was driving to the city and stopped at the red traffic light in Lyons Road. I fell off asleep, and as soon as the green light came, I woke up and continued driving.

Having gone through all the above happenings, I began to reason out something was wrong with me and sought medical help from specialists. At that time, I had never heard of sleep apnea problems.

I consulted my cardiologist Professor Edward Barin, who told me I had sleep apnea symptoms, so he sent me to see a sleep apnea specialist Dr Andrew Chan.

Dr Chan arranged for me to go into the North Shore Public Hospital, to spend a night there, undergoing a test. The nurse on duty put many electrodes on my chest and monitored me for eight hours through the night.

An appointment was made to see Dr Chan. He confirmed that the overnight test in the hospital reported that I had been diagnosed with Obstructive Sleep Apnea, a sleep breathing disorder, and require treatment with a Nasal Continuous Positive Airways Pressure (CPAP) machine worn during sleep.

Dr Chan said I needed therapy to combat these symptoms. Very simple really, he said. Go along to any supplier and choose an appropriate machine, and wear the mask connected to it every night when you go to sleep.

With that advice, I went to the sleep apnea machine suppliers and found a suitable one. It's a Respironics machine from Philips Respironics Australia in Chatswood.

I started using the machine since 7 April 2010. It gives me a complete sleep overnight. On occasions, I tried to go without it, but I couldn't fall off to sleep.

I consult my specialist Dr Andrew Chan once a year, and he is satisfied that the therapy is working.

Now I don't fall asleep as often as I used to.

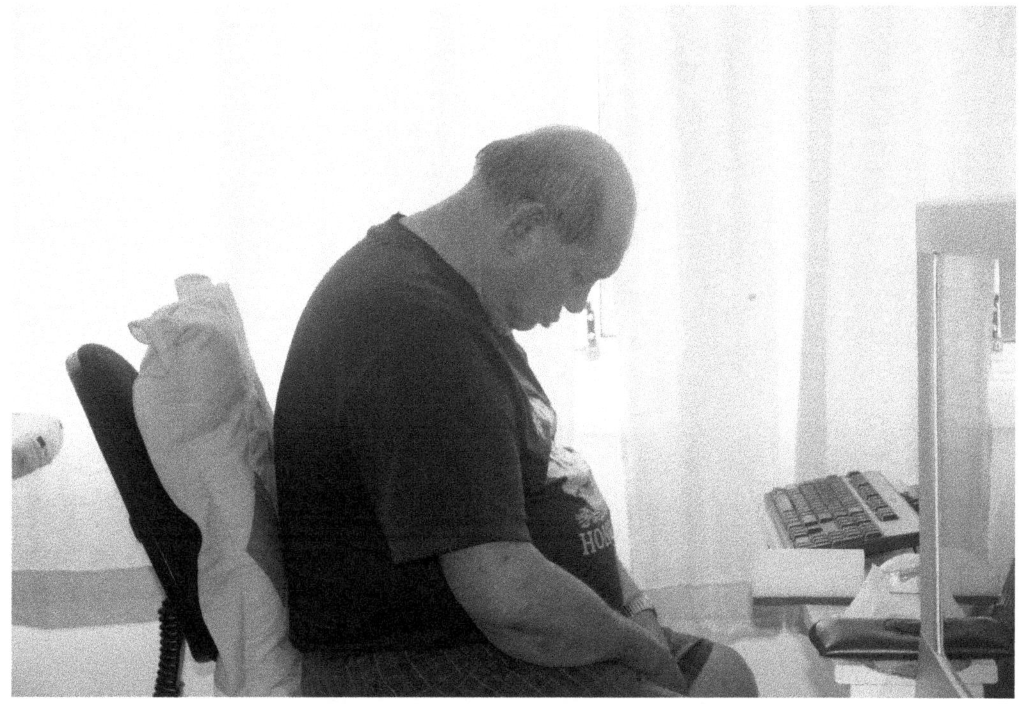

My granddaughter Tiana took this photo in the evening of 22 January 2012.
This was the result of not using the machine for 4 hours the previous night.

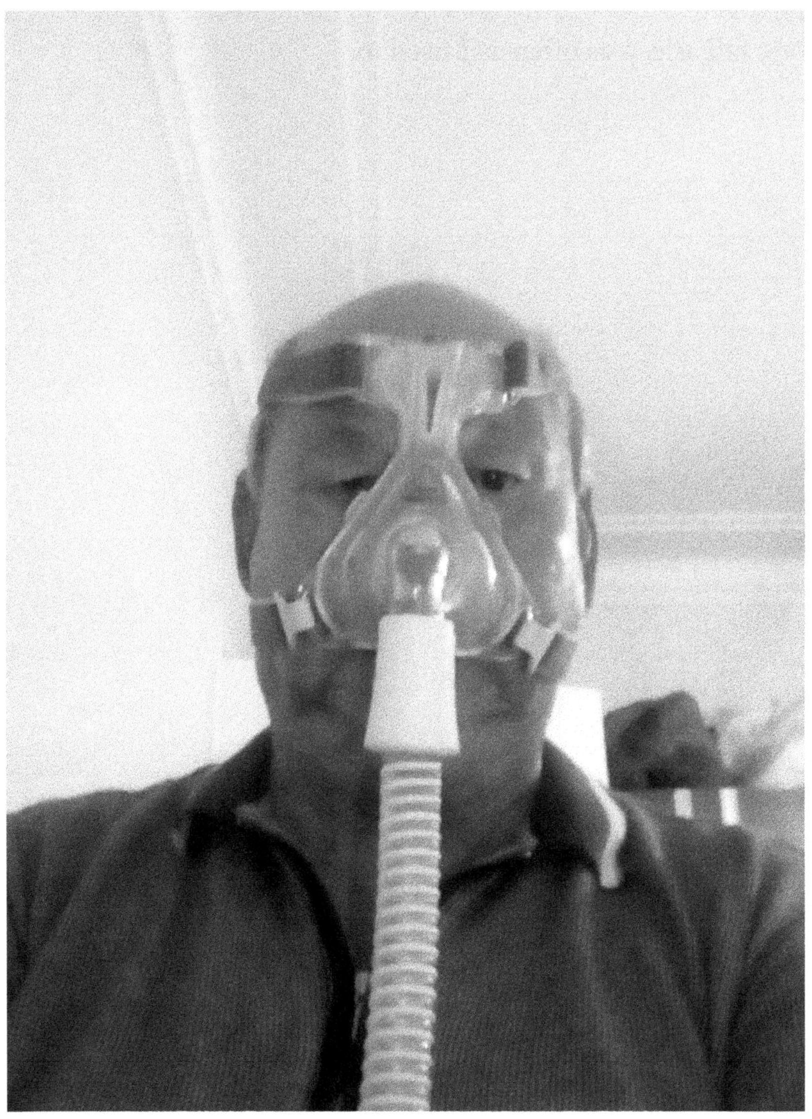

The mask I wear when going to sleep at night.

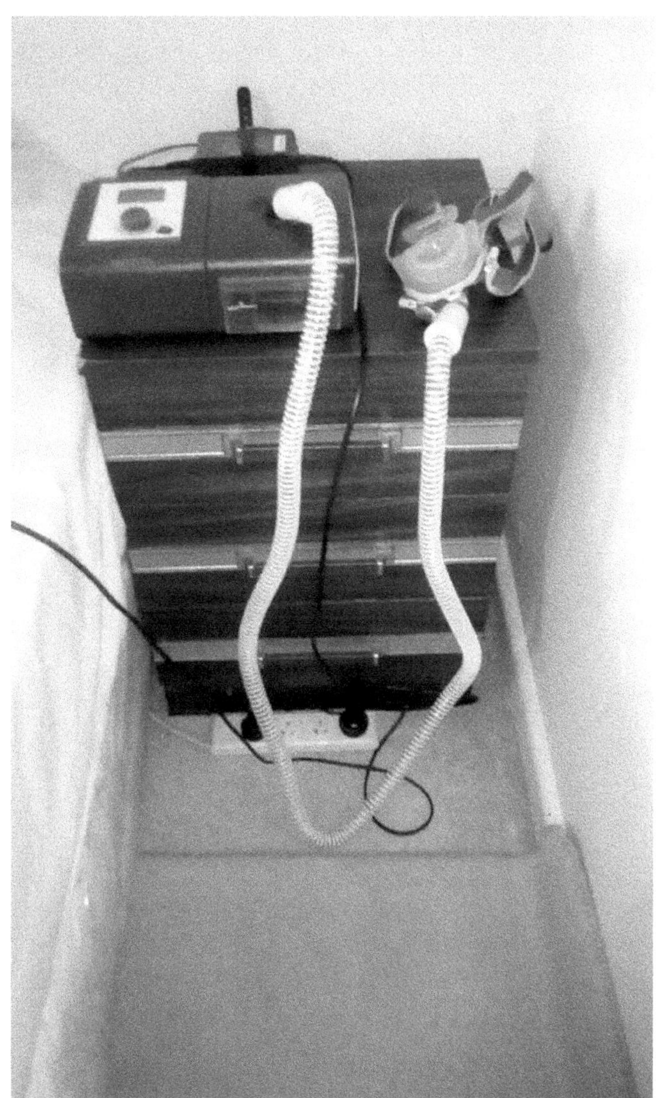

The Sleep apnea machine and mask I use to go to sleep at night.

CHAPTER 102

Frances Fong's 70th birthday party

My wife Frances celebrated her 70th birthday at the Stanford Hotel in North Ryde, on Friday, 29 April 2011. Prince William and Kate Middleton got married that evening, and we were able to see them on TV.

Frances invited all the immediate relatives and a few friends in Sydney. She was very happy to see her Loreto High School mate Margaret Harrison, and her ex-Fiji friends Queenie and Benson Wong from Auckland, and Robina Fong from Suva, Fiji.

It was an enjoyable gathering for all present, the atmosphere was jovial, and the seafood buffet dinner provided by the hotel was superb.

Many thanks to our eldest daughter Geralyne, for organising the party and the gorgeous birthday cake, and daughter-in-law Clare, for preparing the beautiful take-away party bags.

Party favourite for Frances Fong's birthday at the Stanford Hotel, North Ryde, 29 April 2011.

The lovely hand piped birthday cake.

With grandchildren Tiana and Jonathan Yee.

With granddaughter Tiana Yee.

With family members.
From left Gerard Fong, Clare Kent, Ian Fong, Jonathan Yee,
Sen Yee, Frances Fong, Geralyne Fong Yee.
Standing at the front is our granddaughter Tiana Yee.

CHAPTER 103
Volendam Cruise 2012

In May 2012, my brother-in-law Sai Sing Wong, his wife Yuk Kin Wong, Frances and I, boarded the cruise boat Volendam at the Sydney Harbour wharf.

I was 72 years of age then, and I thought I might be the oldest to board a boat cruise. It was quite a surprise and relief to me when I saw quite a number of older men and women, some with walking sticks and some were on wheelchairs.

The first port of call was Noumea. The boat berthed early in the morning and left at 6 pm the same day. It was not as big as Suva, and hygienically it was not as clean as Suva.

After Noumea the boat called in at the Mystery Island. Passengers who wished to visit the island were transported by the boat's tenders.

Next the boat arrived in Suva, Fiji, where it berthed early in the morning and left at 6 pm the same day. I had lived in Suva for 33 years, and apart from being away in New Zealand for 3 years. That was my first-time setting foot in Suva after my family and I migrated to Australia. I found the only people I knew were the owners of the Yon Tong Chinese grocery store in Marks Street. Since I left on 19 December 1985, Suva had been flooded with new immigrants from China.

The next call of port was the Manning Island in the Gilberts. Passengers were transported by tenders (lifeboats) to visit the island.

From there the boat sailed to Honolulu, Hawaii. As usual the boat berthed early in the morning and left at 6 pm in the evening. During the day, the 4 of us contacted our cousins John and Ben Ung and their families who took us for Yum Cha lunch in the city. It was good to meet up with them.

From Honolulu, the boat crossed the International Date Line, sailed for 6 days direct to Vancouver. After a journey of 23 days from Sydney, the boat finally arrived at the Vancouver wharf.

Our friend Ming Ko and Cousin Joan Wong Chan's husband Watson Chan were at the wharf to greet us and took us to our respective places. Sai Sing and his wife went to stay at Watson's home. Frances and I stayed at Ming's home.

The same afternoon after our arrival, Ming's daughter Theresa invited us to stay for a couple of nights at her holiday house in Whistler. The troupe included Theresa, her parents Ming and Helena, Frances and me, Sai Sing and his wife, Watson and his wife Joan, travelled by 2 cars to Whistler. Theresa's holiday house was beautifully constructed with strong Canadian wood, and the pillars were gigantic. There were 7 bedrooms with built-in bathrooms and toilets.

After one night the 4 of them, Watson and Joan, Sai Sing and Yuk Kin returned to Vancouver. Frances and I stayed an extra day in Whistler.

On our way back to Vancouver, Theresa took us to visit an old copper mine.

For the remainder of the week in Vancouver, relatives and friends took us out for Dim Sum (We say Yum Cha in Sydney), lunches and dinners.

Our niece Jean Baever, her husband Bruce and their children, drove up from Seattle to join us in Vancouver.

Together with Sai Sing and his wife, we visited Kwan Jack War (from Levuka) at a nursing home. He was very happy to see us.

A gathering was held at Cousin Joan Wong Chan and her husband Watson's home.

Friends Agnes Wong and her sisters-in-law Marianne and Betty Wong, and Mavis Chang Leong brought some dishes with them. Talking about the spread of good food, yummy is the word.

Time to leave Vancouver, so we flew to Boston, where Sai Sing wanted to meet up with his niece Norena Fong and family. Sai Sing and his wife stayed at Norena's home. Frances and I stayed at a hotel.

The next day after arrival, Norena and her husband Charlie Fong, took us to Yum Cha in the city. While Sai Sing and his wife did their own things, Frances and I visited Harvard University.

I remember Norena's daughter Theresa Fong was on uni holidays, so she was free to drive the 4 of us, Sai Sing and his wife, Frances and me, to visit a Trade Centre, where we also had lunch there.

After 4 days in Boston, we flew to San Francisco.

The 4 of us visited the Chinatown, Fisherman's Wharf, the Golden Gate Bridge, and the Alcatraz Federal Penitentiary or United States Penitentiary. Alcatraz Island was a maximum high-security federal prison, 1.25 miles (2.01 km) off the coast of San Francisco, California, which operated from August 11, 1934, until March 21, 1963.

After 3 days in San Francisco, we flew to Auckland, New Zealand, where we spent 3 days visiting our relatives and friends.

Sai Sing and his wife stayed with their cousins Queenie and Benson Wong, and Frances and I stayed at a hotel in Parnell, a short walking distance to my cousin Bill Fong's home.

While we were in Auckland, we visited our cousin Patrick Wong and his families, who put on a very good spread of curry dishes.

Johnson Chong, his wife Kwai, Children Jonathon and Selma, invited us for dinner at their home in Mangere. They put on such a spread of good food that we lost count of the number of dishes.

One afternoon, we visited our long-time friend Willie Fong and his wife Amy. They surprised us with afternoon specialties.

We also met up with another long-time friend Keith Yee Joy and his wife Shirley, who took us to Yum Cha at a huge restaurant in Howick.

Before we left Auckland, we invited Cousin Bill Fong and his wife Janice for breakfast at our hotel.

Bill and his family treated Frances and me, Sai Sing and his wife, to a great dinner at a restaurant in Remuera.

From Auckland we flew back to Sydney, arriving safely.

We visited Alcatraz Island during our Volendam Cruise in 2012. 1.25 miles off the coast of San Francisco, California, it operated from August 1934 to March 1963.

At Whistler, Vancouver.
From left Joan Chan, Ian Fong, Frances Fong, Yuk Kin Wong, Sai Sing Wong, Watson Chan, Helena Ko, Ming Ko.

Breakfast at Theresa's holiday house in Whistler, Vancouver.
Front sitting Frances Fong, Ming Ko, Theresa Ko.
Back standing Joan Chan, Helena Ko, Yuk Kin Wong, Sai Sing Wong, Watson Chan.

Entertained by cousins in Honolulu, Yum Cha at a restaurant, Honolulu, Hawaii.

Posing on a snowmobile at Whistler, Vancouver.

CHAPTER 104
Diamond Princess Cruise 2013

To start our cruise, Frances and I, brother-in-law Sai Sing Wong, his wife Yuk Kin Wong, friends Yuen Kwai Sang and his wife Winnie, flew from Sydney to Bangkok. We stayed at the Novotel Hotel for 3 days before embarking the cruise ship Diamond Princess for Tianjin, China.

On the first night we were experiencing the Thai people, with their buckets of water, water guns and hose pipes, wetting people in the streets. We were told it was their New Year celebrations, and that was customary for throwing water on people.

We were walking to have dinner at the MBK Shopping Mall, which was not far from the hotel. About quarter way we came across some Thai youths using buckets of water, water guns, and hose pipes, wanting to wet us.

Songkran is an annual festival which takes place over three days during the traditional Thai New Year, April 13th-15th (in almost all provinces). The official Songkran festival lasts three days but in reality, the whole week is taken over by a mass celebration as the whole country shuts down for a momentous water fight. Wild scenes of exuberance can be seen throughout the Kingdom with music, dancing, drinking and people drenched from head to toe. Water guns, hose pipes, buckets, in fact, anything you can get your hands on can be used to splash people, and one thing is for certain: you will get wet!

We quickly moved away from them and returned to the hotel. We had no choice but to stay and eat dinner in the hotel that night.

The buffet dinner at the hotel was very tasty and satisfying, but very expensive.

On the first day, Frances and I met up with friends from Auckland, Benson and Queenie Wong, Augustine and Gabrielle Fong, and their children Kevin and Colette and Alex Chang. Joe and Caroline Chang from Fiji also joined us.

We all (except Sai Sing and his wife, Kwai Sang and his wife who stayed back), went to a huge restaurant where it supplied raw meat, seafood, crabs, fruits and vegetables. We just chose what we wanted, and arranged for the cooks inside the large kitchen, to cook for us, just tell them what flavours we wanted, and they did the job. Apart from the delightful steamed fish, the curry crab with eggs dish was really good.

On the second day all of us visited the Grand Palace and the Emerald Buddha Temple in the morning. In the afternoon, we visited the floating market. In the evening we all went to a fantastic show/concert performed by famous Thai artists. Before the show, a buffet dinner had been provided for us. It was alright, and there were lots of cakes and fruits and soft drinks.

On the third day, Frances and I, Sai Sing and his wife, Kwai Sang and his wife, walked to the MBK Shopping Mall, where we had lunch and dinner.

On 17 April 2013, all of us embarked the cruise ship Diamond Princess, at the Laem Chabang cruise terminal. The larger ships dock at Laem Chabang International Terminal. It is situated 30 minutes away from Pattaya, direction North, and an hour and a half away from Bangkok, direction Southeast.

The Diamond Princess Sailed from 17 April to 3 May 2013 to Singapore, Phu My, Na Trang, Hong Kong, Shanghai, Nagasaki, Busan, Tianjin.

On each port of call, we all went ashore.

When the ship berthed in Hong Kong, Frances and I, Sai Sing and his wife, had Yum Cha at the Fook Lam Moon restaurant in Tsim Sha Tsui, Kowloon. Each table was served by a waitress, and the costs were high.

Fook Lam Moon 福臨門 is known to be a popular Chinese restaurant for the rich and famous, with a status of being the "Cafeteria for the Wealthy". We wouldn't have gone there if we had known about this.

Kwai Sang and his wife went to meet up with his wife's brother in the New Territories.

During the journey on board the ship, we went to formal dinners, used the gym and played ping pong. Frances and I did a little swimming.

After arriving in Tianjin, we boarded an arranged bus to Beijing. The non-stop journey took 2 and ½ hours.

After arriving in Beijing, our friends from Auckland and Fiji went on their separate ways.

Frances and I, Sai Sing and wife, Kwai Sang and wife, had booked for a 7-day tour of Beijing. The cost for each person was A$99 which included 5-star hotel accommodation, free breakfast, lunches and dinners, and free bus tours to selected places.

It was too good to be true, and eventually we found out that the Chinese government provides half the costs, travel agents provide 25 % and the hotels and shops 25 %. The providers' aim was to promote tourism. We were taken to shops, but we were not obliged to buy anything.

We were surprised to see Vincent Yee, his wife Margaret and his sister Rosie O'Connor, at the hotel foyer. They happened to be on the 7-day tour with us.

On the first day in Beijing, the tour guide who could speak Cantonese, came with a coach and took us to Tianjin for a non-stop return trip. There were no toilet facilities between Beijing and Tianjin, and some lady tourists complained madly to the driver who, of course couldn't oblige a stop.

Some Chinese passengers rode with us in the coach came from Vancouver.

In Tianjin we visited a shop that sold dried sweets and dried food items. Some bought a little bit. We had lunch at a very big restaurant there. The food was delicious.

On the second day the same tourists were taken to see the Great Wall, the Forbidden City, and the Temple of Heaven.

On the third day, the tour bus took us to visit an up-market Trade Centre, very fashionable indeed and expensive items were sold there. It was the Wangfujing Street

Shopping Centre. Wangfujing (Chinese: 王府井; pinyin: Wángfǔjǐng; literally: "Prince's Mansion Well") is one of the most famous shopping streets of Beijing, China, located in Dongcheng District. The majority of the main area is pedestrianised and very popular shopping place for both tourists and residents of the capital. Since the middle of the Ming Dynasty there have been commercial activities in this place. In the Qing Dynasty, ten aristocratic estates and princess residence were built here, soon after when a well full of sweet water was discovered, thereby giving the street its name "Wang Fu" (princely residence), "Jing" (well). Many exotic foods are served on Wangfujing snack street.

We also visited the Beijing Olympic Park.

On the fourth day, were taken to the Chende Mountain Resort, a return journey of 6 hours.

The Mountain Resort in Chengde (Chinese: 避暑山莊; pinyin: Bìshǔ Shānzhuāng; literally: "Mountain Villa for Avoiding the Heat"; (Chinese: 離宮; pinyin: Lígōng), is a large complex of imperial palaces and gardens situated in the city of Chengde in Hebei, China. Because of its vast and rich collection of Chinese landscapes and architecture, the Mountain Resort in many ways is a culmination of all the variety of gardens, pagodas, temples and palaces from various regions of China.

We had lunch at a very good restaurant in Chende. On our return to Beijing we had dinner at a very good restaurant also.

On the fifth day, we were taken to see the Ming Tombs.

On the sixth day, we visited a People's store, which sold expensive jewellery items, ornaments, and furniture, etc. Prices quoted for jewellery were exorbitant. A Jade bracelet was quoted as US$30,000, but after bargaining, it was sold for A$3,000.

On the seventh day, we were taken to a Tibetan Hospital. Except for me, the others were treated to foot washing and drying. All of us were referred to a few doctors for advice of treatments. I consulted one of the doctors there, about the tiny moulds on my face. He said I had a lot of toxic in my body and needed treatment. He brought out 2 boxes of tablets which would last 6 months; and the costs US$6,000. Immediately I told him I couldn't afford that sort of money, and besides I could get treatment in Australia, which wouldn't cost much.

After the 7-day guided tour, we spent 2 more days in Beijing, visiting the Beijing World Park.

Beijing World Park is a theme park that attempts to give visitors the chance to see the world without having to leave Beijing. The park covers 46.7 hectares and is located in the southwestern Fengtai District of Beijing. It is about 17 km from Tiananmen, the City centre, and 40 km from the Capital International Airport.

On the next day, we visited another up-market shopping mall, which sold expensive clothes and fancy lines. Inside the mall Frances and I had Crispy Roast Pork for lunch at a restaurant owned by a Hong Kong Chinese. Sai Sing, his wife, Kwai Sang and his wife, went for lunch at another restaurant.

From Beijing we flew to Hong Kong, and stayed at the Kimberly Hotel in Tsim Sha Tsui, Kowloon, for 3 days.

On the first night, we met up with Sai Sing's son Stephen and his family. In a combined effort, we invited all the Wong cousins living in Hong Kong for a banquet dinner.

The following day, I invited my older cousin Fong Wing for Yum Cha. His wife had something to do, and his children were all at work, so they couldn't come.

On the third day, cousins on my mother's side took Frances and me to Yum Cha. From there we visited my 90-year-old cousin Say Ying Wong (lady) who had dementia, at a home in Kwun Tong, Kowloon.

On the fourth day, we left Hong Kong and arrived safely in Sydney, home sweet home.

Buffet at the Novotel Hotel, Bangkok.
Front from left Winnie Yuen, Yuk Kin Wong, Sai Sing Wong.
Back from left Kwai Sang Yuen, Ian Fong, Frances Fong.

Christian martyrs on the wall, Nagasaki, Japan.
From left Benson Wong, Queenie Wong, Frances Fong, Ian Fong.

At the Nagasaki Peace Park located in Nagasaki, Japan, commemorating the atomic bombing of the city on 9 August 1945 during World War II. It is next to the Atomic Bomb Museum and near the Peace Memorial Hall. Established in 1955, and near to the hypocentre of the explosion, remnants of a concrete wall of Urakami Cathedral can still be seen.

At the Nagasaki wharf.
From left Benson Wong, Winnie Yuen, Sai Sing Wong, Yuk Kin Wong, Frances Fong, Ian Fong, Queenie Wong, Brian Wong.

At a huge restaurant in Bangkok.
Sitting from left Frances Fong, Caroline Chang, Gabrielle Fong, Queenie Wong, Colette Fong.
Standing from left Benson Wong, Kevin Fong, Ian Fong, Brian Wong, Joe Chang, Augustine Fong, Alex Chang.

CHAPTER 105
Dubai and Europe visits 2015

In June 2015, our youngest daughter Magdalene who was working in London, enticed Frances and me, to take a trip to London and also visit some other cities in Europe. She said she could take time off from her work, and accompany us on some short trips We were quite motivated, so we decided to take on Magdalene's offers.

On 28 August 2015, we flew by an Emirate Airlines plane to Dubai, and spent 2 days there. Our travel agent in Sydney had booked a walking tour for us. The taxi driver dropped us 2 stops short of the meeting place with our tour guide. We had to take the train for two more stations. On arrival we met the tour guide and another young male tourist from New Zealand. Our walking tour commenced at a hot temperature of 40 degree centigrade, and after half an hour Frances and I withdrew from the walk, because it was too hot. The young man from New Zealand continued with the guide. The guide said we would miss a terrific Arabian dinner afterwards. We took a taxi back to our hotel.

On 31 August we flew by an Emirate Airlines plane to the Heathrow airport in London, where Magdalene met us on arrival.

Frances and I stayed at her flat while we were based in London.

London

Magdalene, her boyfriend Adrian and his sister, took us to dine at a very good Japanese restaurant in Soho, and we enjoyed the Sushi and Sashimi there.

Frances and I went to Yum Cha and lunches at the Wan Chai Corner Restaurant, and other restaurants in Gerrard Street in Chinatown. Sometimes Magdalene joined us for Yum Chas and dinners.

One night we invited Magdalene's friend Jessica Tsang for a seafood dinner at the Wan Chai, to celebrate the moon festival.

Magdalene, her friend Elodie, Frances and I, went to the Ping Pong Restaurant, a Chinese chain restaurant for dim sum, fruity cocktails and flowering teas. It was near the London Eye, Southbank in London.

Magdalene treated us to The Ritz Hotel for a High Tea afternoon. It was an experience, but very expensive.

Frances and I experienced the exotic prices at Harrods, a luxury department store located on Brompton Road in Knightsbridge, London. A simple lunch cost us 50 English pounds. A brand name short pants cost 95 English pounds.

Trafalgar Square was not a place to be missed. It is visited daily by tourists all over the world. Frances and I witnessed a Japanese Festival there.

Magdalene took us to the Hay's Galleria, a mixed-use building in the London Borough of Southwark situated on the south bank of the River Thames featuring offices, restaurants, shops, and flats. Originally a warehouse and associated wharf (Hay's Wharf) for the port of London, it was redeveloped in the 1980's. It is a Grade II listed structure.

Magdalene and us, met up with our nephew Martin Shew from New Zealand and his friend David, and went to a dinner at the Canteen Restaurant in the South Bank. After dinner, we walked through the Embankment Bridge, and saw beautiful lights in the distance.

Magdalene took us to an Indian Tandoori Restaurant in the Strand. Man, the roti's were so good, and the curry dishes were very delicious too.

During the moon festival we bought moon cakes from a shop in Chinatown, and a large one contained 6 duck yokes. You can guess what the taste was like.

Magdalene and we visited the Cambridge and Oxford universities, which we heard so much about.

She also took us to the Kensington Palace grounds, we had lunch at the restaurant there, and spent an hour or so around the palace grounds, saw swans swimming in the lake.

Frances and I wanted to tour Buckingham Palace. We were there on 1 October 2015, and were very disappointed, when we found out that the Palace Tour had ceased on 26 September and would re-open the next summer.

Our next visit was to the British Museum, located in the Bloomsbury area of London, United Kingdom. It is a public institution dedicated to human history, art and culture. It houses a vast collection of world art and artefacts and is free to all visitors.

Magdalene suggested the Somerset House was one to pay a visit. It is a large Neoclassical building situated on the south side of the Strand in central London, overlooking the River Thames, just east of Waterloo Bridge. It is a new kind of arts centre in the heart of London, designed for today's audiences and creatives, offering a diverse and dynamic public programme of contemporary arts and culture. We spent a couple of hours looking around the place and had lunch there.

Our leisure trip with Magdalene to Brighton was quite enjoyable. It was Yum Cha first at a Chinese Restaurant, then a long walk along the beach to the amusement centre.

Prague

Magdalene and our first visit out of London was to Prague. We had our first lunch at the Mustek Restaurant, and a buffet dinner at a Chinese Restaurant.

The next day we visited the Prague astronomical clock, or Prague orloj, a medieval astronomical clock located in Prague, the capital of the Czech Republic. The Orloj is mounted on the southern wall of the Old Town Hall in the Old Town Square. The clock mechanism itself has three main components: the astronomical dial, representing the position of the Sun and Moon in the sky and displaying various astronomical details, statues of various Catholic saints stand on either side of the clock; "The Walk of the Apostles", a clock clangs hourly, and shows figures of the Apostles and other moving sculptures-notably a figure of Death (represented by a skeleton) striking the time; and a calendar dial with medallions representing the months. According to local legend, the city will suffer if the clock is neglected and its good operation is placed in jeopardy; a ghost, mounted on the clock, was supposed to nod its head in confirmation. According to the legend, the only hope was represented by a boy born on New Year's night.

We then continued to the famous Charles bridge. It is a historic bridge that crosses the Vltava river in Prague, Czech Republic. Its construction started in 1357 under the auspices of King Charles IV and finished in the beginning of the 15th century. The bridge replaced the old Judith Bridge built 1158–1172 that had been badly damaged by a flood in 1342. This new bridge was originally called Stone Bridge or Prague Bridge (Pražský most) but has been known as "Charles Bridge" since 1870. As the only means of crossing the river Vltava (Moldau) until 1841, Charles Bridge was the most important connection between Prague Castle and the city's Old Town and adjacent areas. This "solid-land" connection made Prague important as a trade route between Eastern and Western Europe.

The bridge is 621 metres (2,037 ft) long and nearly 10 metres (33 ft) wide. It is decorated by a continuous alley of 30 statues and statuaries, most of them baroque style, originally erected around 1700 but now all replaced by replicas.

After lunch in the afternoon, we hired a 1920 Ford Replica which took us across the bridge, and back to the city proper.

On the third day of our stay, we visited the Prague Castle, a castle complex in Prague, the Czech Republic, dating from the 9th century. It is the official office of the President of the Czech Republic. The castle was a seat of power for kings of Bohemia, Holy Roman emperors, and presidents of Czechoslovakia. The Bohemian Crown Jewels are kept within a hidden room inside it.

According to the Guinness Book of Records, Prague Castle is the largest ancient castle in the world, occupying an area of almost 70,000 square metres (750,000 square feet), at about 570 metres (1,870 feet) in length and an average of about 130 metres (430 feet) wide. The castle is among the most visited tourist attractions in Prague attracting over 1.8 million visitors a year.

In the evening we went on a cruise around the city river coast. We were told dinner on board was first class, but we were very disappointed as cheap food like fish and chips were served.

Fatima and Lisbon

Our second trip out of London was to Fatima. We flew to Lisbon and stayed at a hotel for 2 days. On the first day, a booked tour guide and his private van came to pick us up to go to Fatima. We had lunch at the Dom Duarto Restaurant nearby.

On the second day in Lisbon, we went to Yum Cha lunch at the Hong Palace Restaurant, and we were surprised to find customers consisted of about 90% of white people. We caught a taxi up to the highest point of the city of Lisbon for sightseeing. On our return to the hotel, we hired a tutut car which took us around the harbour.

Paris

From Lisbon we flew to Paris, where we stayed at the home of our niece Cathy Wong and her husband Fritz Schurig. We were there for 4 days. One suitcase with my medication inside was lost, and Cathy took us to a nearby pharmacist to buy some required medicine for me. The pharmacist obliged by supplying on condition that I produce a prescription the next day. The next morning, Cathy took us to see a GP doctor for a prescription, and the consultation fee was about 120 Euros. We spent the rest of the day at her home.

On the second day, Cathy took us to visit the Palace of Versailles. In the evening at about 9 pm, the airline found the lost suitcase and delivered it to Cathay's home.

On our third day, her husband Fritz took us to the city of Amiens, and we had lunch at a Chinese Restaurant. Amiens is a city and commune in northern France, 120 km (75 mi) north of Paris and 100 km (62 mi) south-west of Lille. It is the capital of the Somme department in Hauts-de-France. The city had a population of 136,105 according to the 2006 census. It has one of the biggest university hospitals in France. Amiens is a city in northern France, divided by the Somme river. It's known for the Gothic Amiens Cathedral and nearby medieval belfry. Shops and cafes line the Quartier St.-Leu's narrow streets. Floating market gardens ("hortillonnages") dot the city's canals. The Musée de Picardie shows art and antiquities spanning centuries. Nearby, the Maison de Jules Verne is a museum where the science fiction author once lived.

Krakow

On the fourth day at lunchtime, we flew from Paris to Krakow, Poland, and spent three days in an apartment there.

On the first day, we had breakfast at a hamburger joint next door and went by coach on a tour to the Auschwitz Concentration Camps. The tour was very distressing as we were shown where the people, mainly Jews, lived in very crampy conditions. We also saw old clothes, shoes, wigs, hair, and hats that belonged to the people who were gassed to death. The gas chambers were horrible.

On the second day, we had breakfast at the Chopin Open Restaurant in the square and visited the Gallerias Shopping Centre; we had lunch at a Chinese cafe there. In the evening we dined at the Europijska Restaurant.

On the third day, we took a horse-drawn carriage ride around the old and new city of Krakow, and on our way, we passed the Jewish centre.

Back in London the three of us applied to the Russian Embassy for visas to visit Moscow and St Petersburg. After a week our visas were granted. We had already paid for our return air tickets, and were preparing for a flight to Moscow, and intended to leave London on 12 October 2015.

Emergency trip to Fiji

On 4 October 1915, sad news came from Levuka, Fiji, informing us that Frances' eldest brother Len had passed away. In view of that, we had to abandon our trip to Russia.

Our return tickets from London with Emirate Airlines were not helpful, as there was no flight available right away. We had no alternative but to resort to changes to airline tickets to Hong Kong via Mumbai, then by Fiji Airways from Hong Kong to Nadi, Fiji. Flights and waiting time took 34 hours London to Nadi.

There was a big queue in front of us at the Nadi airport customs, and we were worried we might miss the bus from Suva to Natovi. Fortunately, I spotted a customs officer, who told us he was from India, working in Nadi. I requested him to help by letting us through the customs. He quickly led us to bypass the queue and asked a customs officer to check and let us through.

From the airport we immediately caught a taxi to Tamavua, Suva, where Frances' older brother Sai Sing Wong and his wife, older brother Michael Oey Wong, two younger sisters Anne and Emily were waiting. Some refreshments had been provided for Frances and me. Soon after, we all went by 2 taxis to the bus station and boarded a bus to the Natovi Jetty. From there we caught a ferry to Levuka, Ovalau Island.

We arrived in Levuka in the evening before the funeral took place the next day.

After the funeral, Frances stayed back in Levuka for 2 days. I went with my eldest daughter Geralyne and her family to Suva, where she paid for my accommodation at the Grand Pacific Hotel for 1 night. The GPH is a 5-star hotel and world-famous.

Return to Sydney

The next day we were off to Nadi airport, and flew to Sydney, arriving safely. Our son Gerard, his wife Clare and daughter Chloe, picked me up from the airport, and took me to dinner at the Lan Yuan Seafood Restaurant in the Top Ryde Shopping Centre.

All you can eat sushi and sashimi made to order in Soho, London, 15 August 2015.
From left Frances Fong, Ian Fong, Magdalene Fong,
Adrian Stefanczyk, Agnieszka Stefanczyk.

Afternoon Tea at The Ritz Hotel, London, 16 August 2015.
From left Ian Fong, Frances Fong, Magdalene Fong.

Dinner at the Canteen Restaurant, Southbank, London, 23 August 2015.
On the left Magdalene Fong, Martin Shew, David Cook-Doulton.
On the right Ian Fong, Frances Fong.

CHAPTER 106
My friendship with David King

Their family name is Liu (Mandarin), Lau or Low (Cantonese), and they are descendants of Liu Bang. Chinese 刘邦.

A great emperor of China. Emperor Gaozu of Han (Chinese: 漢高祖; 256 BCE – 1 June 195 BCE), born Liu Bang (劉邦), was the founder and first emperor of the Han dynasty, reigning from 202 – 195 BCE. He was one of the few dynasty founders in Chinese history who was born in a peasant family. For more interesting reading go to google Wikipedia, the free encyclopaedia.

David used his father's last name "King". Narsley used his father's last name "Lau".

One day in 1991, a red two-door Mercedes- Benz parked outside my corner shop in Croydon Park. A good looking and healthy Chinese guy from the car, came into the shop and gave me a surprise visit.

"David King", I shouted. What a surprise! "Hello, my friend", he said calmly; such as his usual quiet nature. I asked him how he knew I was operating this store business, and he said Peter Chan (Insurance man of Belfield) told him. David also said he lived nearby, about a kilometre away from my shop.

We last saw each other at the end of the school year at the Marist Brothers' High School in 1955. We were classmates in Forms 3 and 4. After Form 4, I went to study at the Sacred Heart College, Auckland, New Zealand.

David spent some time in my shop, and we talked and talked. He mentioned that he owned properties and had a news agency in Paddington, near the city. During our conversation, he related to me that when he and his family arrived in Sydney, he rented a flat in Campsie, and the landlord gave him notice to vacate due to the noisy disturbances his very young children had caused. He and his family then moved to another unit in Enfield owned by an Indian from Fiji. The landlord was good, but he never missed his time to collect rent every week. After the unhappy disrespect in Campsie, David was determined to use his brains and hard work to build up his wealth. He and his younger brother Leslie started operating a Commercial Cleaning business and prospered. When their partnership had ceased, David bought the news agency in Paddington, and Leslie bought one in the Circular Quay area. Leslie also bought a Clancy Franchise store in the same area.

Since that meeting, we came into contact but not often.

I will now go back to the day in October 1950 after I came from China. My father took me to visit his friend uncle Lau Mack King and his family in Wailoku, Tamavua. There I was acquainted with David, Narsley and Leslie. Their two brothers between David and Leslie were sent for education in China. Uncle and Aunty had a market garden, did dalo and vegetable planting, and besides reared some chickens. For lunch, Aunty cooked chicken curry and rice, which I enjoyed very much. That was the first time I tasted a curry dish.

From then on, David and Leslie attended St Felix College, and his brother Narsley and I were in class one at St Columba's Primary School. Since then we had lost contact.

In form 3 at the Marist Brothers' High School, David and I became classmates, but we didn't communicate with each other at all. The same as in form 4.

In form 4, I was in the school's athletic team and first fifteen squad, but no sign of David.

In forms 5, David started playing rugby and took part in field events in athletics. When he got to form 6, he was captain of the school's first fifteen in rugby. He was also a prefect and house captain of Alphonsus House.

While at form 6 David was selected in the Fiji Secondary School rugby team to tour Tonga. He also played for the MBHS old boys rugby team Albions which won the Suva European rugby competition for 1957. He played hooker in the front row.

If he was playing in the Fijian rugby union competition, he would have been chosen to represent Fiji.

In 1958 David was invited by the Imperial rugby team on its tour to New Zealand.

Our contact came back when David invited my wife and me to his 60th birthday party held at his new home in Maroubra. On that night the Bledsloe Cup match between Australia and New Zealand was played. There was no tv in the sitting room, and as fanatic fans like Dr Kam Young, me and a few others, were eager to watch the match, so we went to the storehouse where there was a tv set. We were disappointed when the tv didn't work. David then said we could go upstairs to watch the game, but we declined his offer.

The next time David and I met was at his wife Violet's funeral service in church. He told me the shocking news that he was suffering from Parkinson's disease.

Son Brendan, his wife Anne and family, were looking after their mother Violet and Father David when Violet had cancer until she died on 20th March 2012. Then they looked after David until he passed away.

Whenever our MBHS classmate Benson Wong and his wife Queenie came over from New Zealand, I would arrange a visit to David's house in Maroubra. His daughter-in-law Anne put on fantastic lunches.

On 27 August 2016 last year, David celebrated his 80th birthday at his home in Maroubra. It was full of wonderful atmosphere. His son Eugene and family came from America for the celebrations. A terrific spread of Island food was served. There was also Island entertainment.

Sadly, David passed away on 25th May 2017. He is survived by his children Donna, Brendan, Eugene and their wives, and 9 grandchildren.

We miss you David. Rest in peace.

At David King's home in Maroubra.
Marist Brother's High School classmates from left Gordon Rounds, David King, Ian Fong, Benson Wong, Ken Janson.

Marist Brother's High school classmates taken at David King's 80th Birthday, Maroubra, 27 August 2016.
From left Justin Lee, Chris Grant, Arthur Lee, Ian Fong, David King, Ken Janson, Craig Grey, Leslie King.

Lunch at David King's home in Maroubra.
From left Lesley King, Frances Fong, Ian Fong, David King,
Sarah King and daughter, Anne King, Maria King.

At David King's home in Maroubra, celebrating his 80th birthday, 27 August 2016.
Crowd gathered to watch the Island Entertainment.

CHAPTER 107

The 50th wedding anniversary of Frances and Ian Fong

For better or for worse, for richer or for poorer, in sickness and in health, we have stayed together.

We have not disappointed Frances' parents Wong War Sik and Wong Ung Sau, and my parents Willie War Sut Fong and Fong Lum Oy wan.

On Saturday 5 May 2018, Frances and I celebrated our 50th wedding anniversary at the Golden Hawk Chinese Restaurant, 117 Ryedale Road, West Ryde.

We were married on 4 May 1968, but we chose Saturday 5 May 2018 for the celebrations, as the date was convenient for our guests to attend.

Initially, we had sent out invitations to 192 people, including relatives and friends who had in the past, invited us to christening, birthday and wedding parties.

Apologies to those whom we missed out.

As a result of circumstances, only 130 guests attended the Chinese banquet party. Those who couldn't come were due to 3 deaths, some who didn't travel now, some had prior function arrangements, a few older ones were over 90 years of age, some older ones had no transport, some in their 80's who didn't drive at night, some people had surgery bookings on their list and so on.

Of those guests who attended our celebrations, they provided fun and laughter, and by looking at them in the party, we found smiling faces. Photos will show the true spirits of the party.

To us, the highlight of the night was the presence of ex-students educated by the Catholic Schools.

Present at the party were 24 Marist Brothers' High School old boys, 6 Loreto High School old girls and 18 St Joseph's Secondary School old girls.

Our youngest daughter Magdalene and her fiance Adrian Stefanczyk, came from London to attend our party.

Our friend, Watson Chan came from Vancouver, Canada.

Our friends Queenie and Benson Wong, Alex Chang, Rosemary and Victor Giborees came from Auckland, New Zealand.

Our friends Patricia Johnson, Rosemary and John Paligaru, our Godson Clement Paligaru, our nephew Martin Shew and friend David Cook-Doulton, our niece Cathy Wong and her daughter Hanaelina, came from Melbourne.

Our friends Lilian and Philip Wong, Willie Mar, Doris and Roderick Lee, Angela and Anthony Delvin, came from Brisbane. Philip was our best man.

The rest of our guests lived in Sydney.

The lovely presents the guests had brought with them included many red packets.

Our eldest daughter Geralyne, was almost in everything in organising our party. First, it was the invitation cards she helped us to choose and decide on. Secondly, she prepared the table lists for our guests. Thirdly, on the party day, she herself, her younger brother Gerard and his wife Clare, and younger sister Magdalene, helped in receiving the guests.

Our niece Stefanie Whippy Broadbridge baked and decorated a beautiful cake for the occasion.

Our son-in-law Sen Yee was responsible for preparing and showing the photos on three screens. He had constructed three stands for the screens.

Our photographers Alex Chang and Adrian Stefanczyk did their job professionally.

MC Christopher Yee Joy was very articulate and did a fantastic job for the evening.

Our darling granddaughter Chloe Fong was the first to congratulate us on this happy occasion, making a speech in front of everyone.

Benson Wong who said many kind words about us, proposed the toast of the evening to us.

Leslie King honoured us by saying Grace first and complimented Frances and me afterwards.

Ken Janson serenaded during the night with some beautiful songs, while Henry Foon with his keyboard, provided wonderful music. They did it voluntarily. Just as well, otherwise we couldn't afford to hire them to perform, as they are well-known musicians.

It was a night to remember!

Making my speech.

Benson Wong making a speech.

Lesley King making a speech.

Family photo.
From left Geralyne Fong Yee, Sen Yee, Frances Fong, Ian Fong, Magdalene Fong, Adrian Stefanczyk, Clare Kent, Gerard Fong.

Family from Australia and New Zealand.
From left Geralyne Fong Yee, Frances Fong, Gerard Fong, Ian Fong, David Cook-Doulton, Martin Shew, Janice Fong, Magdalene Fong, Michelle Fong.

Loreto High School old girls.
From left Anne Fong, Frances Fong, Rosemary Giborees, Emily Wong, Jane Sing, Margaret Harrison.

Ken Janson serenading and Henry Foon on the keyboard.
Front is Christopher Yee Joy, our MC for the night.

Our granddaughters, Chloe Fong (facing camera) and Tiana Yee (side on to camera).

CHAPTER 108
My 80th birthday party

On the night of 3 June 1938 (Chinese Calendar), I was born in the Dun Tou Village, now grouped as part of the Sha Kai district, Zhongshan, Guangdong, China. The day falls on a different day in July (English calendar) each year.

My passport date of birth is in November 1938. I can't remember how this date was recorded.

At that time, my father was in Fiji, thus the male responsibility fell upon my grandfather's hands.

Before I came out into this world that night, grandpa was more than excited, while waiting for my arrival. I was told he paced nervously around our house compound until the village midwife delivered me safely.

On Sunday morning 15 July 2018, my dear wife Frances prepared a sumptuous breakfast for us (Frances, my youngest daughter Magdalene and me). We attended the church Mass at 10 am.

Magdalene went back to work in London after attending our 50th wedding anniversary party on 5 May 2018 but came back to be with us for a little while.

In the evening, my immediate family including our 4 lovable grandchildren Jonathan, Tiana, Chloe and Rachel, celebrated my 80th birthday at the Crystal Seafood Restaurant in the Carlingford Court Shopping Centre.

I opted for a small party as already I had a big one on my 70th birthday at the Emperor Garden Restaurant in the Sydney Chinatown, and also a fabulous 50th wedding anniversary party with my dear wife Frances, at the Golden Hawk Chinese Restaurant, West Ryde, on 5 May 2018.

We had a wonderful dinner, which was enjoyed by all of us.

My 80th birthday dinner at the Crystal Seafood Restaurant, Carlingford Court Shopping Centre, 15 July 2018. Posing with the beautiful birthday cake.

Getting ready to blow the candles.

Blowing the candles.

Family photo.
Sitting from left Frances Fong, Ian Fong, daughter-in-law Clare Kent holding granddaughter Chloe Fong, daughter Magdalene Fong.
Standing from left grandson Jonathan Yee, Geralyne Fong Yee, son-in-law Sen Yee, granddaughter Tiana Yee, son Gerard Fong holding granddaughter Rachel Fong.

Printed in Australia
AUHW020932100221
340981AU00004B/9

9 781504 321785